Simulation for the Social Scientist

Second Edition

Simulation for the Social Scientist

Second Edition

Nigel Gilbert and Klaus G. Troitzsch

Open University Press

Open University Press
McGraw-Hill Education
McGraw-Hill House
Shoppenhangers Road
Maidenhead
Berkshire
England
SL6 2QL

email: enquiries@openup.co.uk
World Wide Web: www.openup.co.uk

and Two Penn Plaza, New York, NY 10121-2289, USA

First published 2005
Reprinted 2010, 2011

A catalogue record of this book is available from the British Library.
CIP data applied for.

ISBN-13 978 0335 21600 0 (pb)   978 0335 21201 7 (hb)
ISBN-10 0 335 21600 5 (pb)   0 335 21601 3 (hb)

Typeset by the authors with LaTeX 2_ε

Printed in Great Britain by CPI Antony Rowe, Chippenham and Eastbourne

Contents

Preface

This book is a practical guide to the exploration and understanding of social and economic issues through simulation. It explains why one might use simulation in the social sciences and outlines a number of approaches to social simulation at a level of detail that should enable readers to understand the literature and to develop their own simulations.

Interest in social simulation has been growing rapidly world-wide, mainly as a result of the increasing availability of powerful personal computers. The field has also been much influenced by developments in the theory of cellular automata (from physics and mathematics) and in computer science (distributed artificial intelligence and agent technology). These have provided tools readily applicable to social simulation. Although the book is aimed primarily at scholars and postgraduates in the social sciences, it may also be of interest to computer scientists and to hobbyists with an interest in the topic. We assume an elementary knowledge of programming (for example, experience of writing simple programs in Basic) and some knowledge of the social and economic sciences.

The impetus for the book stems from our own research and the world-wide interest in simulation demonstrated by, for instance, the series of conferences on Simulating Societies held since 1992. The proceedings of the first two of these have been published as *Simulating Societies* (Gilbert and Doran 1994) and *Artificial Societies* (Gilbert and Conte 1995) and subsequent papers have appeared in the *Journal of Artificial Societies and Social Simulation*.

Since we wrote the first edition of this book in 1997–8, interest in social simulation has been growing even more rapidly, and a number of friends and colleagues encouraged us to update the text. Hints about what could be improved came from participants of annual summer workshops that we have been organizing since September 2000 and from participants of advanced simulation workshops which we have been organizing since April 2003, both of which we plan to continue. The Simulating Societies conference series became part of the annual conferences of the newly founded European Social Simulation Association.

The book starts with an introduction describing the opportunities for using simulation to understand and explain social phenomena. We emphasize that simulation needs to be a theory-guided enterprise and that the results of simulation will often be the development of explanations, rather than the prediction of specific outcomes. Chapter 2 sets out a general methodology for simulation, outlining the typical stages through which simulation models pass. The remainder of the book considers seven approaches to simulation. Most of the chapters follow the same format: a summary of the approach, including an introduction to its historical development; a description of a representative software package supporting the approach; an explanation of the process of model specification, coding, running a simulation and interpretation of the results; and descriptions of examples of the approach to be found in the research literature. Each chapter concludes with an annotated bibliography. The approaches considered are: system dynamics and world models; microanalytical simulation models; queuing models; multi-level simulation; cellular automata; multi-agent modelling; and learning and evolutionary models. This second edition includes a new chapter (Chapter 9), which offers additional advice on how to design and build multi-agent models.

This book would not have been started and, even less, revised, without the encouragement of a world-wide network of friends and colleagues who find the field of social simulation as fascinating as we do and who regularly provide excuses for us to sample antiquities in Italy, cuisine in Paris, tapas in Catalonia, the architecture of ancient German university towns, the culinary specialties of Dnipropetrovs'k in the Ukraine, and the rolling countryside of England, not forgetting the adobe houses of Santa Fe, New Mexico and the castle of Kazimierz Dolny on the Vistula River in Poland. This book is dedicated to this virtual community – and to our wives, who are now used to seeing us hunched over computers, day in and day out.

We thank Edmund Chattoe, Georg Müller, Silke Reimer, Claudio Cioffi-Revilla, Sean Luke, Wander Jager, Michael Möhring and a number of students of our universities, including Alan Roach, Matthijs den Besten, Anna

Katharina Weber and Lu Yang for their comments, and Sue Hadden, Justin Vaughan, Mark Barratt and Jennifer Harvey of the Open University Press for their help with the preparation of the manuscript.

Nigel Gilbert

September 2004   *Klaus G. Troitzsch*

Chapter 1

Simulation and social science

Using computer simulation in the social sciences is a rather new idea – although the first examples date from the 1960s, simulation only began to be used widely in the 1990s – but one that has enormous potential. This is because simulation is an excellent way of modelling and understanding social processes.

This book has been written for social scientists interested in building simulations. All research should be theoretically informed, methodologically sophisticated and creative. These qualities are especially necessary when doing simulations because the field is only about 20 years old, so there are no well-established traditions to rely on, and there are a wide variety of approaches to simulation from which to choose. One additional skill needed by the researcher wanting to use simulation is some facility in using computers (all simulations nowadays are run on computers). It helps to know how to write simple programs, although the first half of this book does not demand any programming knowledge at all, and the second half needs only a beginner's level of skill.

Simulation introduces the possibility of a new way of thinking about social and economic processes, based on ideas about the emergence of complex behaviour from relatively simple activities (Simon 1996). These ideas, which are gaining currency not only in the social sciences but also in physics and biology, go under the name of complexity theory (see, by way of introduction, Waldrop 1992). However, we do not consider the theoretical implications of simulation in any depth in this book although there are frequent references to the theoretical foundations. Instead, the book focuses on the practical and methodological issues of how to do simulation, covering matters such as the approach to adopt, the stages one should expect to go through and the traps and difficulties to avoid. In this first chapter, we discuss the types of problem and purposes for which simulation is best suited, present a few examples of simulation as it is used in social science and develop a classification of the types of simulation that will be described later in the book.

What is simulation?

Simulation is a particular type of modelling. Building a model is a well-recognized way of understanding the world: something we do all the time, but which science and social science has refined and formalized. A model is a simplification – smaller, less detailed, less complex, or all of these together – of some other structure or system. A model aeroplane is recognizably an aeroplane, even if it is much smaller than a real aeroplane and has none of its complex control systems. More relevant to social science are statistical models which are used to predict the values of dependent variables. Chapter 2 describes the idea of modelling and the differences between statistical models and simulation models in detail.

Like statistical models, simulations have 'inputs' entered by the re-searcher and 'outputs' which are observed as the simulation runs. Often, the inputs are the attributes needed to make the model match up with some spe-cific social setting and the outputs are the behaviours of the model through time. An example – based loosely on the work of Todd (1997) – may make this clearer. Suppose that we are interested in how people choose a marriage partner. Do you (perhaps, did you?) keep looking and dating until you found someone who meets all your romantic ideals, or do you stop as soon as you find someone 'good enough'? Do people use a sufficiently rigorous search procedure or, as Frey and Eichenberger (1996) suggest, should they search longer, possibly reducing the divorce rate as a result?

Asking people about their searching behaviour is unlikely to be very helpful: they may not be following any conscious strategy and may not reveal it even if they do have one. Instead, we might set up a model (in this case, a computer program) which embodies some plausible assumptions and see what happens, comparing the behaviour of the program with the observed patterns of searching for a partner.

This example is typical in several ways of how simulations can be used.

- When we have a theory of how people choose mates, we can express it in the form of a procedure and ultimately in the form of a computer program. The program will be much more precise than the textual form of the procedure and is therefore helpful in refining one's theory. Simulation can thus be used as a *method of theory development*.

- Once the theory is formalized into a program and we have made some assumptions, the program can be run and the behaviour of the simulation observed. Let us assume that we have a population of simulated potential suitors, each with a 'suitability' score chosen at random. Suppose further that the simulated person looking for a partner (the 'agent') can date potential suitors, selected at random, one after the other. At the end of every date, the agent has to choose whether to settle down with that person or break up and go on to date another suitor. This decision has to be made without knowing about the suitability of others whom the agent has not yet met and without the possibility of ever going back to a rejected suitor.

Figure 1.1: The mate searching game

55	116	149	217	117	81	308	193	78	239
85	15	294	110	219	275	151	310	191	75
110	21	23	132	259	264	194	59	273	239
166	254	136	100	172	30	172	288	128	276
94	169	38	208	145	73	147	13	256	280
312	187	158	124	203	264	142	241	192	54
27	216	316	301	0	183	250	112	30	19
189	273	29	111	259	97	256	249	130	13
53	253	15	273	148	6	97	295	22	238
98	141	88	60	279	211	35	160	304	10

Instructions: Cover up the rows of numbers with a piece of paper and gradually reveal them, starting from the top left corner, working downwards row by row. Wait for a couple of seconds between revealing each new number (this represents the time you spend dating your potential partner!). Decide for yourself when you want to stop. The last number you revealed is the suitability score of the person you would 'marry'. What is the best strategy to maximize the score, while minimizing the number of partners you have to date? (Try not to cheat by looking before you start either at the overall distribution of numbers or how many numbers there are in all.)

- To get the feel for this, cover up the array of numbers in Figure 1.1

with a piece of paper and then, moving the paper from left to right, row by row, gradually reveal more and more numbers. These numbers represent the suitability of successive dates. Stop whenever you feel that you have seen enough scores, remembering that if you spend too long dating you will have missed many years of married bliss!

- The suitability score of the selected partner is the 'output' for one run of the simulation. We can repeat the simulation many times. Since in the simulation the suitors are given random scores and the agent picks them in random order, the result may be different for each run, but the average score over a large number of runs will be useful. We can thus see that simulation allows the researcher to conduct experiments in a way that is normally impossible in social science.

Todd (1997) explores a number of possible strategies, including those that have been proved analytically to be optimal in terms of finding the best partner, but which require unrealistic amounts of search, and some other strategies that are much simpler and have better results when one takes into account that search is expensive in time and effort. He also begins to investigate the implications for search strategies when there is a possibility that you might want to settle down with a partner but the partner may still be wanting to continue to search for someone else. Even in this much more complex situation, simple strategies seem to suffice.

The uses of simulation

The example of strategies for searching for a partner illustrates one purpose of simulation: to obtain a better *understanding* of some features of the social world. We can observe dating behaviour going on all the time but the underlying strategies that people use are hard to discover directly, so simulation can be useful. However, this is not the only value of simulation (Axelrod 1997a).

Another classic use of simulation is for *prediction*. If we can develop a model that faithfully reproduces the dynamics of some behaviour, we can then simulate the passing of time and thus use the model to 'look into the future'. A relatively well-known example is the use of simulation in demographic research, where one wants to know how the size and age structure of a country's population will change over the next few years or decades. A model incorporating age-specific fertility and mortality rates can be used to predict population changes a decade into the future with fair accuracy.

Another example is the use of simulations for business forecasting.

A third use of simulation is to develop new tools to *substitute* for human capabilities. For example, expert systems (Hayes-Roth *et al.* 1983) have been constructed to simulate the expertise of professionals such as geologists, chemists and doctors. These systems can be used by non-experts to carry out diagnoses which would otherwise require human experts.

These and other simulations have been used for *training*. For example, an expert system that classifies rocks according to the likelihood that valuable minerals will be found in them can be used to train novice geologists. Flight simulators can be used to train pilots. And simulations of national economies can be used to train economists (see, for example, the simulation of the British economy available on the World Wide Web at http://www.bized.ac.uk/virtual/economy/).

A related use of simulation is for *entertainment*. Flight simulators are used not only for training pilots, but also for fun on home personal computers. Some simulations sold as games are very close to being social simulations of the type described in this book. For example, in Maxis' SimCity, the user plays the part of a city mayor and can alter property tax rates and other parameters to build a simulated city.

The major reason for social scientists becoming increasingly interested in computer simulation, however, is its potential to assist in *discovery* and *formalization*. Social scientists can build very simple models that focus on some small aspect of the social world and discover the consequences of their theories in the 'artificial society' that they have built. In order to do this, they need to take theories that have conventionally been expressed in textual form and formalize them into a specification which can be programmed into a computer. The process of formalization, which involves being precise about what the theory means and making sure that it is complete and coherent, is a very valuable discipline in its own right. In this respect, computer simulation has a similar role in the social sciences to that of mathematics in the physical sciences.

Mathematics has sometimes been used as a means of formalization in the social sciences, but has never become widespread except, perhaps, in some parts of econometrics. There are several reasons why simulation is more appropriate for formalizing social science theories than mathematics (Taber and Timpone 1996). First, programming languages are more expressive and less abstract than most mathematical techniques, at least those accessible to non-specialists. Second, programs deal more easily with parallel processes and processes without a well-defined order of actions than systems of mathematical equations. Third, programs are (or can easily be made to be) modular, so that major changes can be made in one part without the need to change other parts of the program. Mathematical systems often lack this modularity. Finally, it is easy to build simulation systems that include heterogeneous agents – for example, to simulate people with different perspectives on their social worlds, different stocks of knowledge, different capabilities and so on – while this is usually relatively difficult using mathematics. Examples in which we compare mathematical and simulation treatments of a problem can be found in Chapters 3 and 6.

It is the use of simulation for experiment, proof and discovery in the social sciences which is the major concern of this book.

The history of social science simulation

Computer simulation in the social sciences had a difficult birth (Troitzsch 1997). Although there are isolated earlier examples, the first developments in computer simulation in the social sciences coincided with the first use of computers in university research in the early 1960s (Figure 1.2). They mainly consisted of discrete event simulations or simulations based on system dynamics. The former approach, described in Chapter 5, models the passage of units through queues and processes in order to predict typical throughput – for example, the waiting time of customers in a queue or the time a city's police cars take to reach an emergency (Kolesar and Walker 1975). The system dynamics approach makes use of large systems of difference equations to plot the trajectories of variables over time – for example, the Club of Rome studies of the future of the world economy (Meadows *et al.* 1974; 1992). System dynamics and world models are described further in Chapter 3. The Club of Rome simulations that predicted global environmental catastrophe made a major impact but also gave simulation an undeservedly poor reputation as it became clear that the results depended very heavily on the specific quantitative assumptions made about the model's parameters. Many of these assumptions were backed by rather little evidence.

This early work also suffered in another respect: it was focused on prediction, while social scientists tend to be more concerned with understanding and explanation. This is due to scepticism about the possibility of making social predictions, based on both the inherent difficulty of doing so and also the possibility, peculiar to social and economic forecasting, that the forecast itself will affect the outcome.

One approach that did blossom for some years became known as 'Simulmatics' (Sola Pool and Abelson 1962). The Simulmatics project was

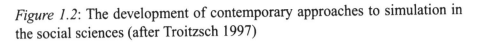

Figure 1.2: The development of contemporary approaches to simulation in the social sciences (after Troitzsch 1997)

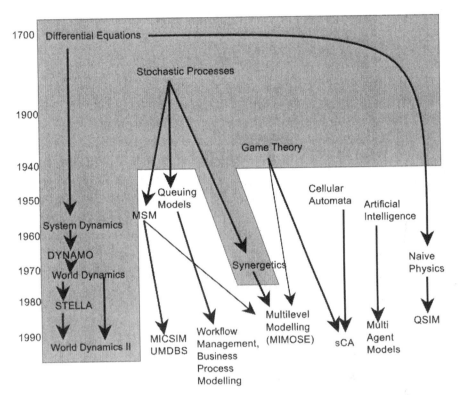

Legend: grey shaded area: equation based models; white area: object, event or agent based models; 'sCA' means cellular automata used for social science simulation; the other names of tools are explained in the respective chapters

originally designed to advise John F. Kennedy's presidential campaign. It tried to predict the reactions of voters to the measures taken by Kennedy and his campaign team, and was also used to understand voters' behaviours in the referendum campaigns about the fluoridation of drinking water, which were frequent in the United States in the early 1960s (Abelson and Bernstein 1963). The latter project was very similar to present-day multi-agent simulation (the term was only coined some 20 years later). Fifty simulated individuals were exposed to information about the topic of the referendum from several different channels and additionally exchanged information among themselves. How much information they absorbed and how much of this led to attitude change depended on their simulated communication habits, but above all on their current attitudes (for example, the more extreme their current attitude was, the less susceptible they were to new information). The whole model included 51 rules of this kind, of which 22 refer to communication channels and other sources of information and 27 concern information exchange among the simulated individuals (the remaining two determine the ballot cast at the end of the simulated campaign).

Another approach that has thrived for more than two decades, impelled by policy concerns, is rather misleadingly called 'microsimulation' (Orcutt *et al.* 1986; Harding 1990). This is a very specific technique, yet until recently was the only form of simulation that had widespread recognition within the social sciences. Microsimulation, described in Chapter 4, is based on a large random sample of a population of individuals, households or firms. Each unit is 'aged' using a set of transition probabilities, which determine the chance that the unit will undergo some change during the passage of a year (for example, the probability that a woman within a certain age range will give birth to a child). After every unit has been aged by one year, the process is repeated for the next year, thus advancing the sample through simulated time. Aggregate statistics can be calculated and used as estimates of the future characteristics of the population. Microsimulation has become well established in some parts of the world (particularly in Germany, Australia and Canada) where its results have been influential in devising policies for state pensions, graduate taxes and so on.

Microsimulation has some characteristics that are instructive when compared with other approaches to simulation. First, it has no pretensions to explanation: it is simply a means of predicting future fiscal distributions. Second, it treats each unit (person, household or firm) individually: there is no attempt to model interactions between units. Third, the motivations or intentions of the units are disregarded: each unit develops from year to year only in response to the throw of the dice represented by a random number generator.

Apart from microsimulation, little was heard about simulation during the 1980s, in marked contrast to the situation in the natural sciences where simulation is now a basic methodological tool. However, in the early 1990s the situation changed radically, mainly as a result of the development of multi-agent models which offered the promise of simulating autonomous individuals and the interactions between them. These opportunities came from techniques imported from the study of nonlinear dynamics and from artificial intelligence research.

Physicists and mathematicians had been trying to understand the properties of large aggregates of matter and had devised models called cellular automata to do so. These models have been applied to explain the properties of magnetic materials, turbulent flow in liquids, crystal growth, soil erosion and in many other areas of science (Toffoli and Margolus 1987). In all these cases, the properties of the material as a whole can be modelled by simulating the interactions between the component units (molecules, soil particles or whatever). Cellular automata consist of a large grid of cells in a regular arrangement. Each cell can be in one of a small number of states and changes between these states occur according to rules which depend only on the states of the cell's immediate neighbours. Cellular automata form a useful framework for some models of social interaction, for example the spread of gossip between people and the formation of ethnically segregated neighbourhoods. They are described in more detail in Chapter 7.

Another approach that has been influenced by ideas from physics is multilevel modelling (Chapter 6) which has taken its inspiration from the theory of synergetics, originally developed for application to condensed matter physics.

Artificial intelligence is an area of computer science concerned with the development of simulations of human intelligence and with building tools which exhibit some of the characteristics of intelligent behaviour. Until recently, artificial intelligence had only been involved with modelling individual cognition, but in the 1980s there was increasing interest in distributed artificial intelligence, a field which examines the properties of interacting artificial intelligence programs. With the growth of the Internet and the World Wide Web, many artificial intelligence researchers became interested in software 'agents', programs that can receive or collect information from other computers, assess it in the light of their past experience and decide what action to take (Doran 1997a). Both distributed artificial intelligence and the agent technology strands of research developed models which, because they involved interacting autonomous agents, could be applied to the simulation of human societies. Distributed artificial intelligence and multi-agent systems are discussed in Chapter 8. Chapter 9 considers strategies and techniques for designing multi-agent models.

Artificial intelligence researchers have also devoted a great deal of attention over the last decade to techniques of 'machine learning' (Michalski *et al.* 1983), which allow computer programs to increase their knowledge and their procedural skills by learning from experience. Models with the ability to learn are very useful both for simulating the cognitive processes of individuals and for modelling whole societies which adapt over time to new circumstances. Chapter 10 discusses some approaches to modelling learning and their application to social simulation.

Simulating human societies

This brief history of social science simulation research indicates that several of the approaches used in contemporary social simulation were originally developed in fields such as physics and artificial intelligence. Although the subject matter of the social sciences differs from that of the natural sciences and different issues are important in modelling societies compared with modelling, for example, aggregates of physical particles, these science and engineering techniques are proving to be very useful. On the other hand, some issues are specific to the social sciences and the relevance of computer simulation to understanding human societies therefore needs to be considered carefully.

One of the themes of social simulation research is that even when agents are programmed with very simple rules, the behaviour of the agents considered together can turn out to be extremely complex. Conventional statistical methods for analyzing social systems are almost all based on the assumption of a linear relationship between variables. That is, the effect on the dependent variable is proportional to a sum of a set of independent variables. But this is a very restrictive assumption. A new interdisciplinary field called complexity theory (Waldrop 1992; Kauffman 1995; Sole and Goodwin 2002) is developing general results about nonlinear systems. An example: consider pouring a steady stream of sand out of a pipe so that it mounts up into a pyramid. As you pour on more sand, there will be little landslides down the side of the pile. While the pyramidal shape of the pile and, in particular, the angle of the side are predictable, depending on the properties of the average sand grain, the timing, location and scale of the landslides are unpredictable because the slippage is nonlinear. Once a grain of sand starts sliding, it pulls others along with it and there is positive feedback leading to a mass of sand slipping (Bak 1996). Similar nonlinearities are thought to cause stock market crashes.

From the point of view of the scientist or mathematician, nonlinear systems are difficult to study because most cannot be understood analytically. There is often no set of equations that can be solved to predict the characteristics of the system. The only generally effective way of exploring nonlinear behaviour is to simulate it by building a model and then running the simulation (see Chapter 6). Even when one can get some understanding of how nonlinear systems work, they remain unpredictable. However much one studies stock markets or the properties of sand, it will still be impossible (in principle) to predict the timing of a crash or a landslide.

This does have some lessons for explanation in the social sciences. For instance, conventional philosophy of social science has often made too ready a connection between explanation and prediction. It tends to assume that the test of a theory is that it will predict successfully. This is not a criterion that is appropriate for nonlinear theories, at least at the micro scale. Complexity theory shows that even if we were to have a complete understanding of the factors affecting individual action, this would still not be sufficient to predict group or institutional behaviour. The message is even stronger if we make the plausible assumption that it is not only social action that is complex in this sense, but also individual cognition (Conte and Castelfranchi 1995).

Emergence

A formal notion of emergence is one of the most important ideas to come from complexity theory. Emergence occurs when interactions among objects at one level give rise to different types of objects at another level. More precisely, a phenomenon is emergent if it requires new categories to describe it which are not required to describe the behaviour of the underlying components. For example, temperature is an emergent property of the motion of atoms. An individual atom has no temperature, but a collection of them does.

That the idea of emergence in the social sciences is not obvious is attested by the considerable debate among sociologists, starting with Durkheim (1895), about the relationship between individual characteristics and social phenomena. Durkheim, in his less cautious moments, alleged that social phenomena are external to individuals, while methodological individualists argued that there is no such thing as society (for example, Watkins 1955). Both sides of this debate were confused because they did not fully understand the idea of emergence. Recent social theorists (Kontopoulos 1993; Archer 1995; Sawyer 2001, forthcoming) are now beginning to refine the idea and work through the implications. Simulations can provide a powerful metaphor for such theoretical investigations.

There is one important caveat in applying complexity theory to social phenomena. It appears to leave human organizations and institutions as little different in principle from animal societies such as ants' nests (Drogoul and Ferber 1994) or even piles of sand. They can all be said to emerge from the actions of individuals. The difference is that while we assume that, for instance, ants have no ability to reason – they just follow instinct and in doing so construct a nest – people do have the ability to recognize, reason about and react to human institutions, that is, to emergent features. The institutions that result from behaviour that takes into account such emergent features are characteristic of human societies (for example, governments, churches and business organizations). The emergence of such reflexive institutions is called 'second-order emergence' and might be one of the defining characteristics of human societies, distinguishing them from animal societies (Gilbert 1995). It is what makes sociology different from ethology. Not only can we as social scientists distinguish patterns of collective action, but the agents themselves can also do so and therefore their actions can be affected by the existence of these patterns.

A theoretical approach that was originally developed within biology, but which is becoming increasingly influential because it takes this reflexive character of human interaction seriously, is known as autopoietic or self-organization theory (Varela *et al.* 1991; Maturana and Varela 1992). Autopoietic theory focuses on organisms or units that are 'self-producing' and self-maintaining. An autopoietic system is one that consists of a network of processes that create components that through their interactions continuously regenerate the network of processes that produced them. Social institutions and cognitive systems have both been analyzed in these terms by Maturana and Varela (see also Winograd and Flores 1986). The emphasis on process and on the relations between components, both of which can be examined by means of simulation, accounts for the developing link between this theoretical perspective and simulation research.

Simulation can also usefully be applied to theories involving spatial location and rationality, two topics that have often been neglected in social science, but which are increasingly recognized to have profound implications. Geographical effects can be modelled by locating agents on a simulated landscape, faithfully reproducing an actual terrain – see, for example, Lansing's (1991) simulation of the irrigation system in Bali – or on the regular grid of cells used with a cellular automata model. Rationality (Elster 1986) can be modelled using the artificial intelligence techniques described in Chapters 8 and 9, but often the main concern is not to model general cognitive capability, but to investigate the consequences of bounded rationality. For example, some theories about markets assume that traders have perfect information about all other traders and all transactions and are able to maximize their own profits by calculating their optimum strategy on the basis of all this information. In large markets, this is obviously unrealistic. What are the consequences for markets reaching equilibrium if the traders have limited information and limited capacity to process that information? Epstein and Axtell (1996: Chapter 4) describe a model they constructed to study the effect of decentralized markets where traders possess only local information and bounded rationality.

Conclusion

In the following chapters, we shall consider in turn the main techniques available for building simulations. These techniques each have their own specific characteristics and areas of application. In Table 1.1, the 'number of levels' refers to whether the techniques can model not just one level (the individual or the society) but the interaction between levels. A technique capable of modelling two or more levels is required to investigate emergent phenomena. Some techniques allow the modelling of communication (for example, the passing of messages) between agents and so are appropriate for modelling language and interaction; others do not. The techniques based on artificial intelligence (distributed artificial intelligence and learning models) are able to accommodate sophisticated agent designs; others derive some of their benefit from constraining the researcher to very simple agents. Finally, most techniques are able to handle the large number of agents that one would expect to find in social simulation, although the first to be considered here, system dynamics, is oriented to the development of models of a whole system, where the system itself is the one and only agent simulated.

Table 1.1: A comparison of social science simulation techniques

Chapter	Number of levels	Communication between agents	Complexity of agents	Number of agents
3 System dynamics	1	No	Low	1
4 Microsimulation	2	No	High	Many
5 Queuing models	1	No	Low	Many
6 Multilevel simulation	2+	Maybe	Low	Many
7 Cellular automata	2	Yes	Low	Many
8 Multi-agent models	2+	Yes	High	Few
9 Learning models	2+	Maybe	High	Many

We have suggested in this chapter that simulation has a number of valuable features for social science research. One of the clearest is that it is well adapted to developing and exploring theories concerned with social processes. In comparison with some other methods of analysis, computer simulations are well able to represent dynamic aspects of change. A second important feature of simulation is that it can help with understanding the relationship between the attributes and behaviour of individuals (the 'micro' level) and the global ('macro') properties of social groups. That is, it is possible to use simulation to investigate emergence.

Simulation is akin to an experimental methodology. One can set up a simulation model and then execute it many times, varying the conditions in which it runs and thus exploring the effects of different parameters. Experimental research is almost unknown in most areas of the social sciences, yet it has very clear advantages when one needs to clarify causal relationships and interdependencies. However, while simulation has similarities with experimentation, it is not the same. The major difference is that while in an experiment one is controlling the actual object of interest (for example, in a chemistry experiment, the chemicals under investigation), in a simulation one is experimenting with a model rather than the phenomenon itself.

We shall develop this idea further in the next chapter, which is concerned with the methodology of simulation research.

Chapter 2

Simulation as a method

This chapter is about the use of computer simulation as a method of social research: the logic behind the method, the stages that one needs to go through and the pitfalls to be avoided. To start, we need to define some terms.

We shall assume that there is some 'real world' phenomenon which you, the researcher, are interested in. This we call the *target* (Doran and Gilbert 1994; Zeigler 1985). The aim is to create a *model* of this target that is simpler to study than the target itself. We hope that conclusions drawn about the model will also apply to the target because the two are sufficiently similar. However, since our modelling abilities are limited, the model will always be simpler than the target. For example, we might model the real market for the wholesale supply of fish with a simpler system where both suppliers and purchasers are represented by computer programs standing in for complex and multifaceted businesses and their customers (cf. Weisbuch *et al.* 1997).

In the social sciences, the target is always a dynamic entity, changing over time and reacting to its environment. It has both structure and behaviour. This means that the model must also be dynamic. We can represent the model itself as a *specification* – a mathematical equation, a logical statement or a computer program – but to learn something from the specification, we need to examine how the behaviour of the model develops over time. One way of doing this is using an analytical method. This entails deriving the model's future structure from the specification by reasoning, perhaps using logic or more often by using mathematics. For example, we might have a model of the relationships between a set of macroeconomic variables and use algebra to derive the outcome if one of those variables changes over time.

With complex models, especially if the specification is nonlinear, such analytical reasoning can be very difficult or impossible. In these cases, simulation is often the only way. Simulation means 'running' the model forward through (simulated) time and watching what happens. Whether one uses an analytical technique or simulation, the *initial conditions*, that is, the state in which the model starts, are always important. Often, the dynamics are very different depending on the precise initial conditions used.

Figure 2.1: The logic of statistical modelling as a method (after Gilbert 1993)

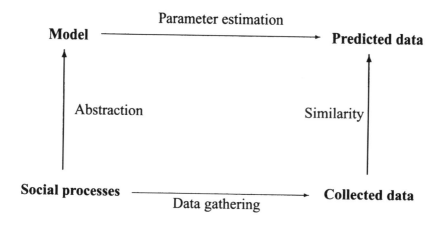

The logic of simulation

With statistical models, the relationship between model and target is quite well understood (see, for example, Gilbert 1993: Chapter 1). As Figure 2.1 indicates, the researcher develops a model (for example, a set of equations) through abstraction from the presumed social processes in the target. These equations will include parameters (for example, beta coefficients) whose magnitudes are determined in the course of estimating the equations (this is the step where a statistical package would normally be used). As well as developing a model, the researcher will have collected some data with which to perform the estimation (for example, survey data on the variables included in the equation). The analysis consists of two steps: first, the researcher asks whether the model generates predictions that have some similarity to the data that have actually been collected (this is typically assessed by means of tests of statistical hypotheses); and second, the researcher measures the magnitude of the parameters (and perhaps compares their relative size, in order to identify the most important).

Figure 2.2: The logic of simulation as a method

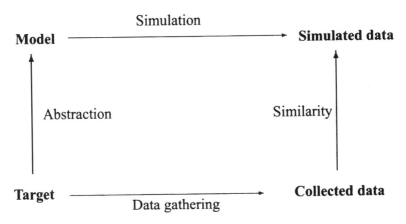

Much the same logic underlies the use of simulation models, as Figure 2.2 shows. Once again, the researcher develops a model based on presumed social processes. But this time, the model might be in the form of a computer program rather than a statistical equation. This model is run and its behaviour measured. In effect, the model is used to generate the simulated data. These simulated data can then be compared with data collected in the usual ways to check whether the model generates outcomes which are similar to those produced by the actual processes operating in the social world.

Both simulation models and statistical models can be used for explanation and prediction. The prime purpose may be to try to understand some particular social phenomenon: for instance, why one gets clusters of people all of whom share the same opinions (see Chapter 7). We may not be particularly interested in predicting how many people there are in a cluster and, indeed, the theory might suggest that forecasting the number is impossible (see the discussion of complexity in Chapter 1). A model that incorporates simulated processes which lead to clustering might suit the purpose of explaining the observed clusters. In other circumstances, we might be particularly concerned with making specific predictions and less concerned with understanding social processes. For example, there might be a requirement to predict the level of aggregate personal taxation flowing to the state in 20 years' time, taking account of demographic changes (see Chapter 4). The model we construct might have little in it about the social processes involved in defining taxation policy and only very simple assumptions about demographic trends, yet be useful in making predictions about aggregate fiscal changes.

While some statistical and simulation modellers emphasize the desire for understanding and others emphasize the need for making predictions, all simulations have in fact to satisfy both requirements: a successful predictive model will contribute to understanding at least to some degree, while an explanatory model will always be capable of making some predictions, even if they are not very precise.

While there are these strong similarities between statistical models and simulation models (and the boundary line between the two is not a hard-and-fast one), there are also important differences. As we noted in Chapter 1, simulation models are concerned with processes, whereas statistical models typically aim to explain correlations between variables measured at one single point in time. We would expect a simulation model to include explicit representations of the processes which are thought to be at work in the social world. In contrast, a statistical model will reproduce the pattern of correlations among measured variables, but rarely will it be modelling the mechanisms that underlie these relationships.

The stages of simulation-based research

With these basic ideas about the logic of simulation in mind, we can outline the 'ideal' set of steps in using simulation in the social sciences (cf. Doran 1997b). One starts by identifying a 'puzzle', a question whose answer is not known and which it will be the aim of the research to resolve. For example, we might be curious about the reasons for the pattern of Puebloan settlements which were established in Mexico from AD 900 to 1300 (Kohler *et al.* 1996). This leads us to the *definition* of the target for modelling (settlement dynamics in the Mesa Verde region). Normally, some *observations* of the target will be required in order to provide the parameters and initial conditions for our model. For the work of Kohler *et al.* (1996), these were obtained from detailed archaeological work by Van West (1994). One can then make some *assumptions* and design the model, probably in the form of a computer program. The simulation itself is performed by executing this program and the output of the simulation is recorded.

So far, the steps involved are fairly obvious, although of
to carry out. The remaining steps often receive less attention, ~~ ~~
crucial. We need to ensure that the model is correctly implemented and
working as intended. This is *verification* – in effect, a 'debugging' step.
Unfortunately, this process can be difficult to carry out with complex simulations and, in particular, it is difficult to know whether one has eradicated all
the remaining bugs. The difficulty is compounded by the fact that most social
science simulations are dependent on pseudo-random numbers to simulate
the effects of unmeasured variables and random effects (Gilbert 1996) and
so repeated runs can be expected to produce different outcomes.

Next, there is *validation*, ensuring that the behaviour of the model does
correspond to the behaviour of the target. If settlement patterns in the
Mesa Verde are being modelled, the simulation needs to reproduce to some
adequate degree the observed pattern of settlements. Unless there is some
correspondence, the simulation is unlikely to be a plausible model of the
processes which led to the formation of those settlements. Finally, one needs
to know how sensitive the model is to slight changes in the parameters and
initial conditions: *sensitivity analysis*. In the following we shall consider
some of these steps in more detail.

Designing a model

Every model will be a simplification – sometimes a drastic simplification –
of the target to be modelled. The most difficult step in designing a model
is to decide what needs to be left out and what needs to be included. The
more that is left out, the greater the conceptual leap required between the
conclusions drawn from the model and their interpretation in relation to the
target. The more that is put in, the more precisely the parameters have to be
measured or assumed, and each of them may have an effect on the validity
of the conclusions which are obtained. What one hopes for is a model
that embodies the minimum number of assumptions, but which applies as
generally as possible to many different circumstances. The choice of where
to place one's model on this continuum between the detailed and the abstract
is partly a matter of skill and experience, partly a matter of research style
and partly a matter of the amount of data one has available and how difficult
it is to collect more. In general, accuracy (in terms of the number of data
points and assumptions built into the model) is important when the aim is
prediction, whereas simplicity is an advantage if the aim is understanding
(Axelrod 1997a).

The temptation is to make a model more detailed than it really needs to be. Apart from the sheer labour of collecting and entering what can quickly amount to many thousands of data points, there is a danger that the additional complexity of dealing with substantial quantities of data will mean that the stages of verification and validity become very difficult to carry out. This in turn means that valid conclusions will be hard to draw from the research. The best map of the world is the world itself, but unfortunately such verisimilitude teaches us nothing about how the world works.

At the other end of the continuum from detailed to abstract modelling is research on 'artificial societies'. This is simulation without reference to any specific 'real world' target. The object of study is the set of possible social worlds, of which the actual world in which we live is just one (Conte and Gilbert 1995). As Epstein and Axtell (1996: 4) write:

> We view artificial societies as *laboratories*, where we attempt to 'grow' certain social structures in the computer – or *in silico* – the aim being to discover fundamental local or micro mechanisms that are sufficient to generate the macroscopic social structures and collective behaviours of interest.

At the heart of research on artificial societies is the goal of finding theories that apply not just to human societies but to societies of interacting agents generally. For example, there are results about the consequences of constraints on communication in markets in which there are some agents selling and others buying (see, for example, Alvin and Foley 1992). These apply regardless of whether the buyers and sellers are people, organizations or computers. Another example of the value of experimenting with artificial societies is Doran's (1997a) work on foreknowledge. His simulation studies the implications of agents having knowledge of future facts or events. Of course, most of us do not believe that people have foreknowledge, and experimentation with worlds in which there is foreknowledge necessarily involves the development of artificial societies. His work clarifies whether, in worlds in which there is foreknowledge, agents can still have choices about what to do. He shows that the answer is yes, there is still the possibility of freedom of will unless the agents' foreknowledge is total. Nevertheless, the choices they have are constrained by the need to include in their predictions of the future what is foreknown to occur. He is also able to investigate whether foreknowledge is beneficial to the survival of the agents in his artificial society (Doran 1998).

Building the model

Once the model has been designed, one can turn to its construction. This involves either writing a special computer program or using one of the many packages or toolkits that have been written to help in the development of simulations. It is almost always easier to use a package than to start afresh writing one's own program. This is because many of the issues that take time when writing a program have already been dealt with in developing the package. For example, writing code to show plots and charts from scratch is a skilled and very time-consuming task, but most packages provide some kind of graphics facility for the display of output variables. At least some of the bugs in the code of packages will have been found by the developer or subsequent users (although you should never assume that all bugs have been eliminated). The disadvantage of packages is that they are, inevitably, limited in what they can offer. There is a choice of several packages for some styles of simulation, but nothing at all is available for others. In subsequent chapters, we shall describe the available programs and comment on their merits as we consider each type of simulation.

If one has to program a simulation without the aid of a package, a question then arises about the best programming language to use. There are several desirable features for a programming language for simulation:

- The language should be well structured and allow for incremental refinement. Most simulation programming is exploratory, because usually the specification of the program develops as the problem becomes better understood. It is therefore important that the programmer can cycle easily and quickly between coding, testing and modifying the code. Interpreted languages (such as Java, Visual Basic, Python or Ruby) are often better than compiled languages (C, C++ or Pascal) in this respect, but modern compilers and programming environments mean that the difference between compilation and interpretation is now much less than it used to be.
- The language should allow easy and rapid debugging, programs should be easily instrumented and there should be good graphics libraries. Simulations generate lots of data and there needs to be an easy way of processing them into manageable form. Because so much time in writing simulation programs (as with other types of program) consists of debugging, the quality of the facilities available for testing and tracking down faults is very important.
- Once the program has been written and tested, many hundreds of runs

will be needed to carry out sensitivity analyses (see below). For this reason, the final simulation program needs to run as efficiently as possible; this implies that the language needs to be compiled rather than interpreted.

- The language should preferably be familiar to the modeller and to researchers in the simulation community, so that it is possible for others to replicate simulation results and to take over and adapt the program to their needs. It is also useful if the language is easily portable between different types of computer.

Unfortunately, these various desirable features are contradictory in their implications for the choice of a programming language for simulation. It is difficult to find one that is easy to debug, has a good graphics library, can be compiled efficiently and is portable across different computers. In practice, this means that many different languages are used for simulation, depending on the particular balance of attributes which modellers think is important for their research. However, Java, C, C++, Objective C, Prolog, Smalltalk and Lisp are probably the most common.

Verification and validation

Once one has a 'working' simulation, the next step is to check that the simulation is actually doing what one expects (Balci 1994). With a complicated computer program, it is all too easy to make errors and find that the output is the result of a mistake, rather than a surprising consequence of the model. The process of checking that a program does what it was planned to do is known as verification. In the case of simulation, the difficulties of verification are compounded by the fact that many simulations include random number generators, which means that every run is different and that it is only the distribution of results which can be anticipated by the theory. It is therefore essential to 'debug' the simulation carefully, preferably using a set of test cases, perhaps of extreme situations where the outcomes are easily predictable.

It is often useful to set up a suite of such test cases and rerun the simulation against them each time a major change is made, to check that further errors have not been introduced. To make this easier, it is also desirable to have a system that will automatically run the test suite and record the outputs, perhaps even highlighting differences between the previous run and this one, since it is these which will need attention. In order to keep a record of which version of the simulation program gave which results, a version control system, such as provided in some programming environments, can also be very useful. Chapter 9 considers these issues in more detail.

While verification concerns whether the program is working as the researcher expects it to, validation concerns whether the simulation is a good model of the target[1]. A model which can be relied on to reflect the behaviour of the target is 'valid'. Validity can be ascertained by comparing the output of the simulation with data collected from the target (see Figure 2.2). However, there are several caveats that must be borne in mind.

First, both the model and the target processes are likely to be stochastic (that is, based partly on random factors). Exact correspondence would therefore not be expected on every occasion. Whether the difference between simulation and data from the target is so large as to cast doubt on the model depends partly on the expected statistical distribution of the output measures. Unfortunately, with simulations, these distributions are rarely known and not easy to estimate.

Second, many simulations are path-dependent: the outcomes depend on the precise initial conditions chosen because these affect the 'history' of the simulation. In other words, the outcomes may be very sensitive to the precise values of some of the assumptions in the model.

Third, even if the results obtained from the simulation match those from the target, there may be some aspects of the target that the model cannot reproduce. An example is found in the world systems models considered in Chapter 3, where predictions about the growth of the world's population for the next 50 years looked plausible, but 'retrodiction' of the population to the situation 20 years in the past, using the same model and the same parameters, was completely wrong when compared with the actual world population then.

Fourth, one must not forget the possibility that the model is correct, but the data about the target are incorrect, or, more often, are themselves a result of making assumptions and estimates. For example, in Chapter 8 we shall discuss a model that aims to contribute to understanding the rise in social complexity in France 20,000 years ago. The only data against which this model can be validated are archaeological traces, which have to be subjected to a great deal of interpretation before they can be used for validation.

Another kind of difficulty arises when the model is intentionally highly abstract. It may be hard to relate the conclusions drawn from the model to any particular data from the target. For example, in Chapter 7 we shall

---

[1] A similar distinction is made in the philosophy of science, between internal validity (corresponding to verification) and external validity

encounter a model first proposed by Schelling (1971), which aims to explain one of the processes that could generate ethnic residential segregation. However, it is a highly abstract model and it is not clear what data could be used to validate it directly. The same issue arises with models of artificial societies, where the target is either intentionally remote from the simulation, or does not exist at all. For these models, questions of validity and of verification are hard to distinguish.

Once one has a model that appears to be valid, at least for the particular initial conditions and parameter values for which the simulation has been run, the researcher is likely to want to consider a sensitivity analysis. This aims to answer questions about the extent to which the behaviour of the simulation is sensitive to the assumptions which have been made. For example, for a model of the tax and benefit system, one might be interested in whether a small change in welfare benefit rates results in a small or a large change in the total benefits paid out by the government. It might be that if the rate of benefit is decreased, other poverty support arrangement cut in, so that the net effect on government expenditure is much smaller than the benefit decrease might suggest. Another issue that sensitivity analysis is used to investigate is the robustness of the model. If the behaviour is very sensitive to small differences in the value of one or more parameters we might be concerned about whether the particular values used in the simulation are correct.

The principle behind sensitivity analysis is to vary the initial conditions and parameters of the model by a small amount and rerun the simulation, observing differences in the outcomes. This is done repeatedly, while systematically changing the parameters. Unfortunately, even with a small number of parameters, the number of combinations of parameter values quickly becomes very large, and because each combination requires the simulation to be run again, the resources required to perform a thorough analysis can become excessive. In practice, the modeller is likely to have a good intuition about which parameters are likely to be the most important to examine.

One of the ways in which the modeller can obtain an understanding of the sensitivity of a simulation to the values of its parameters is to vary them at random, thus generating a distribution of outcomes. One or more parameters are set to values drawn from a uniform random distribution. Plotting the values of the outputs generated from many runs of the simulation will give an indication of the functional form of the relationship between the parameters and the outputs and will indicate whether small parameter changes give rise to large output variations. In effect, one is sampling the parameter space in order to build up a picture of the behaviour of the model over many different conditions.

Randomization of parameters in order to obtain a sample of conditions is one of several uses of random numbers in simulation.[2] Random numbers also have the following uses:

- They allow for all the external and environmental processes that are not being modelled (the exogenous factors) such as the effects of the job market in a simulation of household income over time. Here, the random value is substituting for an unmeasured (and perhaps unmeasurable) parameter and is equivalent to the modeller making a guess in the absence of more accurate information.

- For a similar reason, they are sometimes used to model the effects of agents' personal attributes, such as their preferences and their emotions.

- Some simulation techniques (for example, some kinds of cellular automata and agent-based models; see Chapters 7 and 8) yield different results depending on the order in which the actions of agents in the model are simulated. It is good practice to randomize the order to avoid such unwanted effects.

Whatever the reason for introducing randomness, the simulation will have to be run many times in order to observe its behaviour in a variety of conditions. Results from the simulation will need to be presented as distributions, or as means with confidence intervals. Once one has included a random element, the simulation needs to be analyzed using the same statistical methods as have been developed for experimental research (for a primer, see Box *et al.* 1978): analysis of variance to assess qualitative changes (for example, whether clusters have or have not formed) and regression to assess quantitative changes.

Publication

The final stage in simulation research is to publish the results, adding them to the stock of scientific knowledge. However, there are some particular difficulties in writing about simulation (Axelrod 1997a). Ideally, the reader

---

[2]Strictly speaking, computers provide only 'pseudo-random' numbers, rather than truly random numbers, but if a good generator is used there should not be any significant difference. Most simulations use large numbers of 'random' numbers and depend greatly on the accuracy of their distribution, so it is worth checking that the programming system being used for the simulation does have a good pseudo-random number generator (see Appendix C for more on this).

should be able to grasp the social science aspects of the research without being drowned in detail, but should also be able to replicate the simulation, if he or she wants to understand precisely how it works. These objectives are in tension with one another. Often, there is not space within the length of a conventional journal article or of a chapter in a book to describe a simulation sufficiently to enable replication to be carried out. One solution is to publish the code itself on the Internet. A more radical solution is to publish in one of the increasing number of electronic journals that, because they are not constrained by the costs of paper and printing, can include not only an article of standard length, but also the code, sample runs and other materials. An electronic journal also has no difficulty in publishing colour graphics, animations and other multimedia formats, which would be impossible or prohibitively expensive to reproduce on paper.[3]

Conclusion

There is still much to learn about the most effective methods for conducting simulation-based research. However, experience is growing and the lessons that have been learned can be summarized as follows:

- If the goal is understanding, use simulation to develop theories, not accurate models. Even complicated models are unlikely to reproduce the behaviour of the social world particularly well, are difficult to construct and the complexity can get in the way of discovering new relationships and principles.
- In the past, social scientists have tended to espouse either deduction (loosely, testing of sets of assumptions and their consequences) or induction (the development of theories by generalization of observations). Simulation provides a third possibility, in which one starts with a set of assumptions, but then uses an experimental method to generate data which can be analyzed inductively (Axelrod 1997a: 24). Keep in mind the need to iterate between a deductive and inductive strategy as one develops the model.
- Since many models incorporate random elements, the results of just one run cannot be relied on. It is necessary to establish that the results are robust with respect to different random values. In addition, for

---

[3]For an example of an electronic journal, see the *Journal of Artificial Societies and Social Simulation* at http://jasss.soc.surrey.ac.uk/. For an example of a multimedia report of a simulation, see the CD-ROM which accompanies the book by Epstein and Axtell (1996).

many simulations, it is important to conduct a sensitivity analysis of the effect of variations in the assumptions on which the model is based.

- While many models have the objective of simulating a specific target in the social world, it is also possible to develop models of artificial societies which may be used to investigate not just our present society, but also possible social worlds. This can be one way of developing social theories which apply generally to interacting agents.

In the following chapters, we shall be developing these methodological recommendations with respect to a number of approaches to simulation. These range from the use of 'world models' and microsimulation, which emphasize the value of simulation for prediction (for example, the effects of population growth and environmental degradation on the human world as a whole) to approaches based on multi-agent models, which emphasize the value of exploring artificial societies.

Chapter 3

System dynamics and world models

System dynamics has its roots in systems of difference and differential equations (Forrester 1980: Section 3.3). A target system, with its properties and dynamics, is described using a system of equations which derive the future state of the target system from its actual state. System dynamics is restricted to the macro level in that it models a part of reality (the 'target system') as an undifferentiated whole, whose properties are then described with a multitude of attributes in the form of 'level' and 'rate' variables representing the state of the whole target system and its changes, respectively.

The typical *difference* equation has the form

$$x_{t+1} = f(x_t; \vartheta) \tag{3.1}$$

where x_{t+1} is the state of the target system at time $t + 1$, which depends on its state at time t and on a parameter ϑ. Both x and ϑ may be vectors, that is, consist of several elements. f is usually a continuous function. Only in rare cases can the difference equation be solved explicitly to yield an expression for x_t as a function of t and x_0.

The typical *differential* equation has the form

$$\dot{x}(t) = \frac{dx}{dt} = g(x(t); \vartheta) \tag{3.2}$$

where $\dot{x}(t)$ is the state change of the target system within an infinitesimally short period of time dt. The amount of change depends on the state $x(t)$ at time t and on a parameter ϑ. Again, both x and ϑ may be vectors, and g is usually a continuous function. In simple cases, the differential equation can be solved explicitly, yielding an expression for $x(t)$ as a function of t.

Conceptually, there is a close relationship between difference and differential equations. In the case of difference equations, equidistant points of time are numbered or labelled by t, and nothing is said about the time scale. Hence, we could introduce a new time scale τ_t in which the distance of consecutively labelled or numbered points of time is $\Delta\tau$. If the right-hand side of a difference equation can be written in the following form:

$$x_{t+1} = f(x_t; \vartheta) = x_t + g(x_t; \vartheta) \tag{3.3}$$

meaning that the state at time $t + 1$ is equal to the state at time t, plus the change of state, or with the explicit distance Δt between points of time,

$$x_{\tau_t+\Delta\tau} = f(x_{\tau_t}; \vartheta) = x_{\tau_t} + \Delta\tau \cdot g(x_{\tau_t}; \vartheta) \tag{3.4}$$

(which is always possible), then the following transformation can be performed:

$$x_{\tau_t+\Delta\tau} - x_{\tau_t} = \Delta\tau \cdot g(x_{\tau_t}; \vartheta) \tag{3.5}$$

$$\frac{x(\tau + \Delta\tau) - x(\tau)}{\Delta\tau} = g(x(\tau); \vartheta) \tag{3.6}$$

Taking limits – that is, as $\Delta\tau$ is reduced to an infinitesimally short period of time ($\Delta\tau \to 0$) – we arrive at

$$\lim_{\Delta\tau \to 0} \frac{x(\tau + \Delta\tau) - x(\tau)}{\Delta\tau} = \frac{dx}{d\tau} = \dot{x}_\tau = g(x(\tau); \vartheta) \tag{3.7}$$

which is a differential equation. Note that the solution of a differential equation will be different from the solution of the corresponding difference equation. The simplest procedure for finding numerical solutions to differential equations uses the similarity between the two types of equations and a fixed Δt to approximate the differential equation. And this is exactly what system dynamics does, too. Thus, system dynamics differs from systems of differential equations mostly in two technical aspects: discrete time is used as a coarse approximation for continuous time to achieve numerical solutions; and functions of all kinds, not just continuous functions, can be used.

System dynamics also provides the modeller with a graphical description language, the system dynamics diagrams that describe the interdependencies between the attributes of the target system. The graphical symbols – see Figure 3.1 – are taken from the world of streaming water or steam which

flows between containers controlled by valves: heating is a favourite example for explaining the principles of feedback loops, and words referring to
bonding relations (Bunge 1979) are derived from words used for the same
target systems in many languages (for example, 'influence', according to
Webster's Dictionary was originally 'an ethereal fluid held to flow from the
stars and to affect the actions of humans').

Figure 3.1: System dynamics diagram (redrawn from Forrester 1980:
Fig. 2.2a)

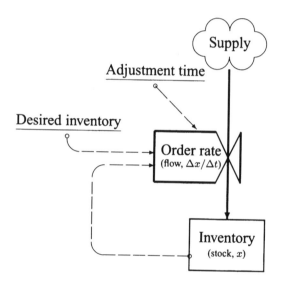

Figure 3.1 shows the supply flow (———) from the inexhaustible cloud
(source) into the 'inventory' through the valve 'order rate' which is controlled (– – –) by the actual 'inventory', the 'desired inventory', and the
'adjustment time'. Figures of the same kind may also be used to visualize
the control of more complex feedback loops, as in the case of models of
the dynamics of the world system. Such complex target systems and their
models show, however, that there are limits to the system dynamics diagram
technique: a diagram measuring 60 cm by 40 cm with a barely decipherable
legend (as on the back flap of Meadows *et al.* 1974) is hardly appropriate to
communicate an overview. This is because a whole system dynamics model
is represented by one single object with a vast number of attributes.

Software

DYNAMO was the first language especially designed for building system dynamics models. It is a functional simulation language that can handle an arbitrary number of equations for:

- levels – for example, `L inventory.k=inventory.j +dt*orderRate.jk`
- rates – for example, `R orderRate.kl= (desiredInventory-inventory.k)/adjustmentTime`
- constants – for example, `C desiredInventory=6000`
- initializations – for example, `N inventory=1000`

Auxiliaries can also be used as a shorthand for complicated expressions, as in the example below (see p. 39).

Over the years, a number of DYNAMO-like simulation languages and simulation systems have been developed. The best known of them include:

- Professional DYNAMO Plus^{TM};
- STELLA, originally developed for Macintosh, and much like DYNAMO, but with important additional features, including a graphical user interface (`http://www.hps-inc.com/`);
- PowerSim (`http://www.powersim.no` or `http://www.powersim.com`) is also equipped with a graphical user interface and allows for all types of system dynamics modelling.
- VenSim (`http://www.vensim.com`) comes in a so-called 'personal learning edition' that 'gets you started in system dynamics modeling' (quoted from the website) as well as standard and professional editions which allow for more complex models as well as for sensitivity analyses.

There are several other packages running DYNAMO or DYNAMO-like languages.

A DYNAMO program consists of expressions that are bound to names. Names do not refer to memory locations where values of variables are stored, but refer to the expressions to which they are bound. The DYNAMO interpreter will evaluate expressions at the time they are first used and store the result of the evaluation for further use. This is why the order of equations in a DYNAMO program is arbitrary (although it is good programming style to start with level equations and initializations of level variables, then place rate equations just below, have equations for auxiliaries follow and end up with constants).

In the example above, the first expression to be evaluated is inventory.k, the value that the level inventory will assume at this point in time (which always is marked by the suffix k). The related expression first contains inventory.j, the value that the level assumed at the former point in time (which is always marked by the suffix j) – this value will be known from earlier computations and, if not, will be taken from the initialization. In this case the initialization expression inventory = 1000 will be evaluated to 1000, where this branch of the evaluation will terminate. The next term in the expression for inventory.k consists of two factors, namely dt and orderRate.jk. dt means the length of one time step. The other factor orderRate.jk is a rate to which a rate expression is bound. The suffix jk denotes the fact that orderRate.jk is the rate of flow between j and k. Thus, inventory.k can be assigned a value.

The next step in the evaluation is the rate orderRate.kl, the rate of flow during the *next* time step (between k and l). Expressions for rates may contain references to the values of levels because these are either known or can easily be evaluated (as they must only depend on former values, .j and .jk). Expressions for auxiliaries are evaluated in the same manner. Auxiliaries, too, have a former and an actual value.

At the end of all evaluations for one point in time, all values of levels, auxiliaries and rates (with suffixes .k and .kl, respectively) replace the former values (possibly after these have been written to some output file). This means that at every point in time, only the rate and level values of the immediate past are accessible and values about the earlier past are lost. Special functions (for example, the delay function) are necessary to model influences from the remote past.

An example: doves, hawks and law-abiders

A differential equation model . . .

For an introductory example we take a model that was described by Martinez Coll, who tried 'to develop a formal model of the Hobbesian state of nature from the perspective of bioeconomics' (Martinez Coll 1986: 494). He defines Hobbes' state of nature as a society whose members are continually competing with each other to obtain a resource. All resources belong to someone, thus conflicts arise between resource owners and those who want an additional resource. Martinez Coll follows Maynard Smith (1982) in that he endows the members of his model society with one of three strategies: the hawk, the dove and the law-abiding strategies.[1]

- The *dove* never tries to get hold of others' possessions, but waits until they are given up, and himself abandons his resource as soon as he is attacked. If two compete for the same resource, one of them gets it (through persistence or luck) with equal probability.
- The *hawk* always tries to get hold of others' resources by means of aggression and gives up only if he receives serious injuries.
- The *law-abider* never tries to get hold of others' possessions, but waits until they are given up, and he defends his possession by counterattack until he either succeeds or is defeated.

In Hobbes' state of nature, the human population consists only of hawks, and in Hobbes' 'Commonwealth' only of law-abiders.

The strategies applied by the individuals may spread all over the population, by inheritance, imitation or education. In any case, in a situation defined by the distribution of strategies, the most profitable strategy is transmitted to other members of the population.

To operationalize what a profitable strategy is, we have to make some assumptions about the 'costs' and 'gains' of strategies. We assume that if an individual following strategy i (a hawk, dove or law-abiding strategy) meets an individual following strategy j, i's gain will be r_{ij} (if r_{ij} is negative, i makes a loss in the encounter). The values r_{ij} are given by the utility of possession minus the costs of the fight. Let the utility of possession be u (poss in the DYNAMO model), and the costs of fighting or waiting be c_H and c_D (coha and codo), respectively, and let $c_D < u < c_H$.

Thus, when an individual applying the strategy of any row of the table below meets an individual applying the strategy of any column, they receive the gains shown in the entries of the table (the first term is the gain of the 'row' individual, the second is the gain of the 'column' individual).

	Dove	Hawk	Law-abider
Dove	$\frac{u}{2} - c_D, \frac{u}{2} - c_D$	$0, u$	$\frac{0+\frac{u}{2}-c_D}{2}, \frac{u+\frac{u}{2}-c_D}{2}$
Hawk	$u, 0$	$\frac{u-c_H}{2}, \frac{u-c_H}{2}$	$\frac{u-c_H}{2}+u, \frac{u-c_H}{2}+0$
Law-abider	$\frac{u+\frac{u}{2}-c_D}{2}, \frac{0+\frac{u}{2}-c_D}{2}$	$\frac{u-c_H}{2}+0, \frac{u-c_H}{2}+u$	$\frac{u}{2}, \frac{u}{2}$

Division by 2 is interpreted as follows:

---

[1] We will return to a very similar model in later chapters of this book (Chapter 6, p. 123; see also Werner and Davis 1997).

- When two individuals applying the same strategy meet, each of them has the same chance of winning or losing. For example, if two hawks meet, one of them will get the resource (u), while the other will receive serious injuries ($-c_H$). Since both have the same chance of winning, the expected outcome will be $\frac{u-c_H}{2}$.
- When a law-abider meets another individual each of them may be the lawful owner of the resource competed for. For example, if a dove meets a law-abider and both compete for the same resource, then we have two equally probable possibilities:

  - If the law-abider is the lawful owner of the resource, it keeps the resource (u), and the dove takes nothing (0).
  - If the dove is the lawful owner of the resource, both have to wait until one of them gives up ($-c_D$) and then one of them gets the resource with equal probability, so the expected outcome of this case is $\frac{u}{2} - c_D$ for both of them.

Thus the overall outcome is $\frac{u+(\frac{u}{2}-c_D)}{2}$ for the law-abider and $\frac{0+(\frac{u}{2}-c_D)}{2}$ for the dove.

For our numerical example, we will take the following numbers: $c_D = 3$, $u = 10$ and $c_H = 20$, which yields the following payoff matrix:

	Dove	Hawk	Law-abider
Dove	2, 2	0, 10	1, 6
Hawk	10, 0	−5, −5	2.5, −2.5
Law-abider	6, 1	−2.5, 2.5	5, 5

Now we have to observe the average gain $y_i(t)$ of an individual applying strategy i at time t: it is given by the mean of possible gains, weighted by the proportions p_i of the population following each of the strategies, i:

$$y_i(t) = \sum_j r_{ij} p_j(t) \tag{3.8}$$

This average gain of strategy i must be compared with the mean gain of all strategies:

$$y(t) = \sum_i y_i(t) p_i(t) \tag{3.9}$$

The growth of the subpopulation applying strategy i is modelled as proportional to the difference $F_i(t)$ between its average gain and the overall mean gain of all strategies $y(t)$:

$$F_i(t) = y_i(t) - y(t) \tag{3.10}$$

If $F_i(t)$ is positive, then strategy i is more successful than the average and it is inherited, imitated or indoctrinated more often; that is, it spreads faster than the overall mean of the strategies. Thus, the relative growth of the strategies can be written as follows:

$$p_i(t+1) = p_i(t)[1 + F_i(t)] \qquad (3.11)$$

This difference equation can be transformed into a differential equation if we assume that within a time span of length Δt the effects on growth are reduced by this factor (compare equations (3.3)–(3.7)):

$$p_i(t+\Delta t) = p_i(t)[1 + \Delta t F_i(t)] \qquad (3.12)$$

$$\frac{p_i(t+\Delta t) - p_i(t)}{\Delta t} = p_i(t)F_i(t) \qquad (3.13)$$

Taking limits, we have

$$\lim_{\Delta t \to 0} \frac{p_i(t+\Delta t) - p_i(t)}{\Delta t} = \dot{p}_i = p_i F_i \qquad (3.14)$$

Inserting equations (3.10), (3.9) and (3.8) into equation (3.14) yields the relative growth of strategy i:

$$\dot{p}_i = p_i F_i \qquad (3.15)$$

$$= p_i(y_i - y) \qquad (3.16)$$

$$= p_i y_i - p_i \sum_k y_k p_k \qquad (3.17)$$

$$= p_i \sum_j r_{ij} p_j(t) - p_i \sum_k \sum_j r_{kj} p_j(t) p_k(t) \qquad (3.18)$$

which is a cubic differential equation of the same type as described by Eigen and Schuster (1979: 30–31) (selection under constrained growth with nonlinear growth rates) and used by Troitzsch (1994: 44).

... and its analytical treatment

Differential equation models of this type can be treated in three different ways:

- by linear stability analysis, where interest centres on whether the model can assume a stationary state (or equilibrium, a state in which the system will remain once it has reached this state) and how the system performs in an infinitesimally small region of its phase space around stationary states, that is, whether the equilibria are stable or unstable;

- by global stability analysis, which is concerned with whether stationary states are attractors or repellors, that is, whether the system approaches or escapes stationary states from arbitrary initial states;
- by numerical treatment, in which a large number of trajectories are calculated starting from different initial states.

The first question is whether and where a system has stationary states. This is addressed by determining those states in which the right-hand sides of the system of differential equations become zero. In these states, the derivatives, that is, the time-dependent changes of all state variables, are zero, and consequently, the system will remain one of these states once it has been reached. This means we equate the right-hand side of equation (3.18) to zero:

$$0 = p_i \sum_j r_{ij}p_j(t) - p_i \sum_k \sum_j r_{kj}p_j(t)p_k(t) \qquad (3.19)$$

Three first candidates for stationary states are all the states in which the whole population applies the same strategy. For $p_D = p_H = 0$ and, consequently, $p_L = 1$, equation (3.19) is satisfied for $i = D$ (dove) and $i = H$ (hawk); and for $i = L$ (law-abider) it simplifies to

$$0 = 1 \cdot r_{LL} \cdot 1 - 1 \cdot r_{LL} \cdot 1 \cdot 1 \qquad (3.20)$$

and the same is true for all permutations of indices.

There is a fourth stationary state, in which doves and hawks coexist and law-abiders are absent. To find this stationary state (and to do some mathematical derivations, which are necessary for the following discussion) it is convenient to express the system of differential equations in terms of the constants c_H, c_D and u, and to keep in mind that there are only two coupled differential equations, because at all times $p_L = 1 - p_D - p_H$. By several intricate transformations and insertions, this leads to the following system of differential equations:

$$\dot{p}_D = -\frac{p_H p_D^2}{2}(2c_D + c_H) + \frac{p_H p_D}{4}(2c_H + 2c_D - u) +$$
$$+\frac{p_D^2}{4}(2c_D + u) - \frac{p_D}{4}(2c_D + u) \qquad (3.21)$$

$$\dot{p}_H = -\frac{p_H^2 p_D}{2}(2c_D + c_H) + \frac{p_H^2}{4}(c_H - u) +$$
$$+\frac{p_H p_D}{4}(4c_D + c_H + u) - \frac{p_H}{4}(c_H - u) \qquad (3.22)$$

Both right-hand sides of this system reduce to zero for

$$p_D = \frac{c_H - u}{2c_D + c_H} \qquad p_H = \frac{2c_D + u}{2c_D + c_H} \qquad (3.23)$$

This means that the system will be in equilibrium if the proportion of doves in the population is $\frac{c_H - u}{2c_D + c_H}$ and the proportion of hawks is $\frac{2c_D + u}{2c_D + c_H}$ (and no law-abiders are present).

To find out what happens in an immediate (infinitesimal) neighbourhood of the stationary states we have to approximate the nonlinear system of differential equations (3.21) and (3.22) by a linear system. We leave this analysis to Appendix B (p. 267) which will also give a first introduction to the analytical treatment of equation-based models. Its result is that the only stable state is the state with only law-abiders surviving. The states with only doves, with only hawks, and the mixed state in equation (3.23) are all unstable, so that even minimal fluctuations that import a small fraction of law-abiders into the population will lead to an ever growing proportion of law-abiders. A population starting with an arbitrary mixture of only hawks and doves into which some law-abiders are inserted will first approach the mixed stationary state of equation (3.23) and then the proportion of law-abiders will grow until the law-abiders have driven out all the hawks.

Intuitively, we may assume that the law-abiders are fitter than both hawks and doves. They avoid the additional costs of fighting which the hawks have to bear when they attack others, and they avoid the unnecessary losses the doves have to bear when they do not defend their possessions against attacks by hawks. In a world with a large majority of hawks, law-abiders are not much better off than hawks, because they will behave much like hawks in most encounters (in that they at least start counterattacks), and in a world with a large majority of doves, law-abiders are not much better off than doves, because they will behave like doves in most encounters (in that they wait for a possession until it is given up). But in a mixed world they enjoy their adaptive strategy: in encounters with hawks they have a better expected outcome than doves because they give up less easily than doves, and in encounters with doves they have the better expected outcome than doves because they take the resources away without waiting.

A DYNAMO model

The equations with which we described our model mathematically, (3.8)–(3.11), can easily be transformed into a DYNAMO model. The

Table 3.1: Correspondence between the system of differential equations and the DYNAMO code

$p_D(t+1)$
$p_H(t+1)$
$p_L(t+1)$
	`dove.k`
	`hawk.k`
	`lawa.k`

$p_D(t)$ . . .	`dove.j` . . .
$y_D(t) = \sum_j r_{Dj} p_j(t)$ . . .	`dove.k*rdd+hawk.k*rdh+lawa.k*rdl` . . .

$y_D(t) p_D(t)$
 	
. . .
	`yieldd.kl=(dove.k*rdd+hawk.k*rdh`
	`+lawa.k*rdl)*dove.k`
	. . .

$y(t)$	`yields.kl=yieldd.kl+yieldh.kl` `+yieldl.kl`
$p_D(t) F_D(t) = p_D(t)\left(y_D(t) - y(t)\right)$	`yieldd.jk-dove.j*yields.jk`

correspondence between the mathematical formulation and the DYNAMO code is given in Table 3.1 (i is replaced by D, H and L, respectively).

Thus, we arrive at a first formulation of the DYNAMO model:

```
dove.k=dove.j+dt*(yieldd.jk-dove.j*yields.jk)
hawk.k=hawk.j+dt*(yieldh.jk-hawk.j*yields.jk)
lawa.k=lawa.j+dt*(yieldl.jk-lawa.j*yields.jk)
yieldd.kl=(dove.k*rdd+hawk.k*rdh+lawa.k*rdl)*dove.k
yieldh.kl=(dove.k*rhd+hawk.k*rhh+lawa.k*rhl)*hawk.k
yieldl.kl=(dove.k*rld+hawk.k*rlh+lawa.k*rll)*lawa.k
yields.kl=yieldd.kl+yieldh.kl+yieldl.kl
. . .
```

This DYNAMO program is correct, but it does not reflect the fact that the sum of the level variables (`dove.k+hawk.k+lawa.k`) always remains constant. In a population of constant size, there are no flows to and from outside, but only flows among the subpopulations. Observe, however, that a direct flow between the doves' and the law-abiders' populations need not be explicitly modelled. Only net flows via the rates for the doves' and the law-abiders' populations can and need be modelled, since Martinez Coll's explication of his model does not give any clue to the individual flows between the subpopulations. His description is only about growing and shrinking subpopulations, not about individuals changing their strategies – hence we cannot determine how many individuals (or which proportion) 'flow' from, for example, dove to lawa.

To visualize this fact, one would need a system dynamics diagram without sources and sinks,[2] like that in Figure 3.2 – which, however, is not a systems dynamics diagram in the sense of Forrester, but a diagram that is generated in the first step of STELLA modelling.

A STELLA model

With the help of the STELLA software one does not start with equations, but with graphic symbols that are arranged on screen to yield a diagram that is much like the diagrams invented by Forrester. The STELLA software then converts the diagram into program code, which is similar to, but not identical with DYNAMO code. The main difference between the two formalisms is that STELLA uses a more mathematical notation instead of the cryptic JKL denotation of the time points – as is shown in the program code below.

The terminology of STELLA is quite similar to DYNAMO, but levels are called *stocks* in STELLA, while rates are *flows* and auxiliaries (such as yieldd in the following example) are *converters*. Stocks are connected by flows, either between each other (as in this example) or with sinks and sources (as in the next example below). *Connectors* connect stocks and converters with the valves in the flows.

In our example, the diagram consists of three stocks, each standing for one of the populations, and two bidirectional flows called ddove and dlawa both of which can be either negative or positive (and this is why dhawk need not explicitly be modelled). ddove and dlawa have to be calculated in a way that reproduces Martinez Coll's original ideas (see the program code generated by STELLA). Of course, STELLA cannot formulate the right hand sides for ddove, for example, instead the STELLA user is given a chance to write down this right hand side. The panel popping up when the ddove line in STELLA's code window is double-clicked (see Figure 3.3) lists the required inputs for the right hand side of the ddove equation (this list is derived from the arrows pointing into the ddove valve) and gives the user the opportunity to enter his or her code.

The full STELLA code derived from the diagram of Figure 3.2 is the following:

---

[2] A 'sink' in system dynamics terminology is a never-overflowing basin to which flows may be directed that leave the system; thus it is the opposite of a 'source'. Note that in linear stability analysis (see Appendix B) 'sink' and 'source' have a different meaning, namely stable and unstable stationary state, respectively.

Figure 3.2: System dynamics diagram of the dove–hawk-law-abider model

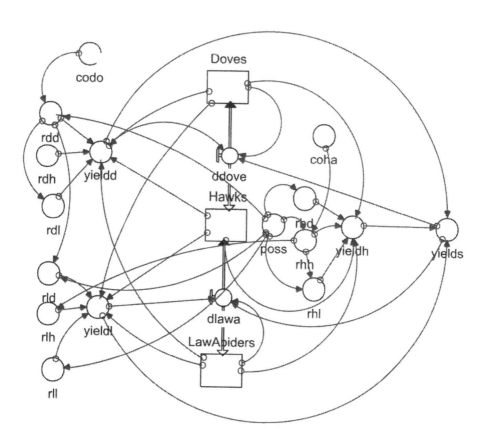

```
Doves(t) = Doves(t - dt) + (- ddove) * dt

INIT Doves = (1-InitialHawks)/2
ddove = Doves*yields-yieldd

Hawks(t) = Hawks(t - dt) + (ddove - dlawa) * dt

INIT Hawks = InitialHawks
ddove = Doves*yields-yieldd
dlawa = yieldl-LawAbiders*yields

LawAbiders(t) = LawAbiders(t - dt) + (dlawa) * dt
INIT LawAbiders = (1-InitialHawks)/2
dlawa = yieldl-LawAbiders*yields
```

Figure 3.3: Entering flow equations in STELLA

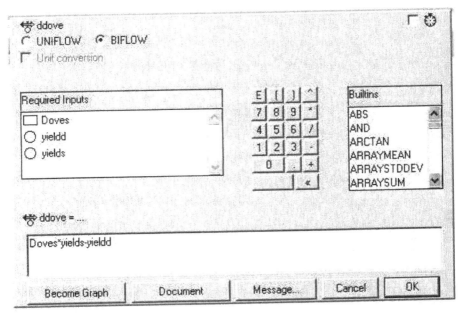

```
codo = 3
coha = 20
InitialHawks = 0.9
poss = 10
rdd = poss/2-codo
rdh = 0
rdl = rdd/2
rhd = poss
rhh = (poss-coha)/2
rhl = (rhh+poss)/2
rld = (rdd+poss)/2
rlh = rhh/2
rll = poss/2
yieldd = (Doves*rdd+Hawks*rdh+LawAbiders*rdl)*Doves
yieldh = (Doves*rhd+Hawks*rhh+LawAbiders*rhl)*Hawks
yieldl = (Doves*rld+Hawks*rlh+LawAbiders*rll)*LawAbiders
yields = yieldd+yieldh+yieldl
```

yieldd, ..., yields are converters (in DYNAMO: auxiliaries) which
are used as shorthand for a longish expression such as (Doves*rdd
+ Hawks*rdh + LawAbiders*rdl)*Doves which could have replaced

`yieldd` in line 3 of the above program code (but then with any change of this expression, one would have needed to change it several times).

Running this simulation with the payoffs from the table on p. 34 and an initial distribution of 90 per cent hawks and 5 per cent of both doves and law-abiders, we obtain the results in Figure 3.4. With 99.9 per cent hawks, we obtain Figure 3.5. Figure 3.6 shows the results with 99 per cent doves at the start. This model displays the following behaviour:

- The proportion of hawks rapidly decreases (or increases) to about 61 per cent, whereas the proportion of doves rises (or falls) to about 38 per cent. This level persists for quite a while (this is much more clearly visible in Figure 3.5 and Figure 3.6 than in Figure 3.4; see the discussion below, in the commentary section). Afterwards the proportions of both hawks and doves decrease, first slowly, then more rapidly. A mixture of about 61.5 per cent hawks and about 38.5 per cent doves makes up a stationary state – see equation (3.23) – which is stable in the absence of law-abiders (that is, it is a saddle point state, which is left if there is even a minute proportion of law-abiders).
- After the stationary state, the proportion of law-abiders increases very slowly.
- Later on, the proportions of both hawks and doves decrease (and eventually they become extinct), while the proportion of law-abiders rises to 100 per cent.

Of course, any population with only one strategy extant is at a stationary state. With the parameter values as applied above, only the last mentioned state – the extinction of hawks and doves – is a stable state. Even if the simulation starts with 99 per cent doves and 0.5 per cent of hawks and law-abiders each, only the latter survive (see Figure 3.6).

For Hobbes' theory we have two consequences:

- As soon as the law-abiding strategy, which is superior to the other two, was invented, it would necessarily prevail, and it would so by nature, not by covenant and only because of the individuals' capacity to inherit, imitate or learn.
- The law-abiding strategy prevails only after a considerable time. The time it takes until it first grows is the longer, the larger the initial proportion of hawks. The eventual success is rather sudden, the more so, the larger the initial proportion of hawks (compare Figure 3.4 to Figure 3.5).

Figure 3.4: Result of a STELLA run of the dove–hawk–law-abider model with 90 per cent hawks at the start

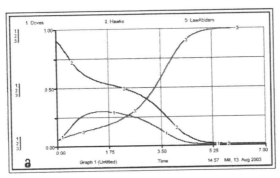

Figure 3.5: Result of a STELLA run of the dove–hawk–law-abider model with 99.9 per cent hawks at the start

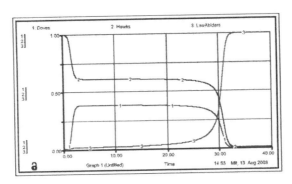

Figure 3.6: Result of a STELLA run of the dove–hawk–law-abider model with 99 per cent doves at the start

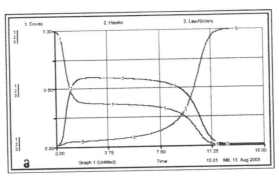

Commentary

Neither the mathematical treatment nor the simulation allowed a convincing qualitative overall description of the model. While mathematics taught us that, regardless of the initial conditions, there is only one stable state, the equations did not say much about the path taken through the state space. Simulation, on the other hand, showed the behaviour of the model, but only for one initialization at a time. Hence, the comparison of a large number of simulation runs is necessary to complete the qualitative description of a model's behaviour, larger than the number of runs we could present here.

To overcome this gap between mathematical analysis and single-run simulation, we choose next another kind of visual representation, namely the representation of the model's behaviour in its state space. For this we draw 20 of the paths the model takes through its state space (see Figure 3.7 – the state space is spanned by the proportions of doves and hawks, and every point on one of the curves represent a state explicitly defined by the proportions of doves and hawks; the representative point of a population

Figure 3.7: Behaviour of the dove–hawk–law-abider model in its state space

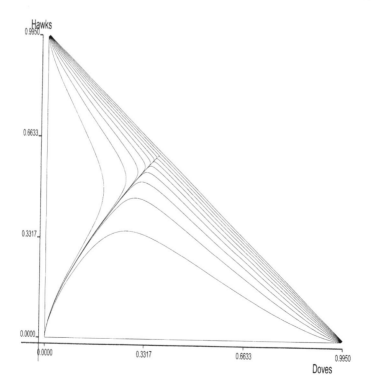

moves towards the origin, which in turn represents a state with no doves and no hawks, but only law-abiders). Note that this diagram does not indicate the speed with which the model changes state.

When the model starts with a large proportion of doves (and consequently with a tiny proportion of both hawks and law-abiders), that is to say, from the lower right-hand corner of the state space, first the number of hawks rises while the number of doves decreases. The number of law-abiders remains small for quite a time, until the proportions of doves and hawks approach the fourth stationary state (see equation (3.23)). From then on, the numbers of both doves and hawks decrease, and the proportion of law-abiders increases until in the end both doves and hawks die out. If we have a larger number of law-abiders and only very few hawks from the beginning, that is, if we start from the middle of the bottom of the state space, the number of hawks initially increases only slightly and afterwards decreases, while the number of doves decreases from the very beginning. If we start with many hawks and few doves and law-abiders (top left-hand corner of the state space), then the number of hawks decreases fast, the number of doves first increases and then decreases again, while the number of law-abiders only begins to grow after the model has approached the saddle point.

So we are able to generalize the conclusions of the previous section, and this generalization would not have been possible from the few simulation runs we described there:

- The law-abiding strategy prevails only after a considerable time. The more homogeneous the population at the start (a large majority of doves *or* hawks before the first law-abiders are born), the later its success, and the more sudden its rise (start from the bottom right-hand corner of the state space).
- If the first law-abiders are born into a mixed society of doves and hawks, they begin to multiply very soon (start from the saddle point).

World models

System dynamics and DYNAMO received widespread interest mainly because they were used to build large world models such as WORLD2 (Forrester 1971); WORLD3 (Meadows *et al.* 1974); and WORLD3 revisited (Meadows *et al.* 1992). Forrester's WORLD2 was the first and simplest of these. We will use it now to discuss some problems of large system dynamics models.

Figure 3.8: Main features of Forrester's world model

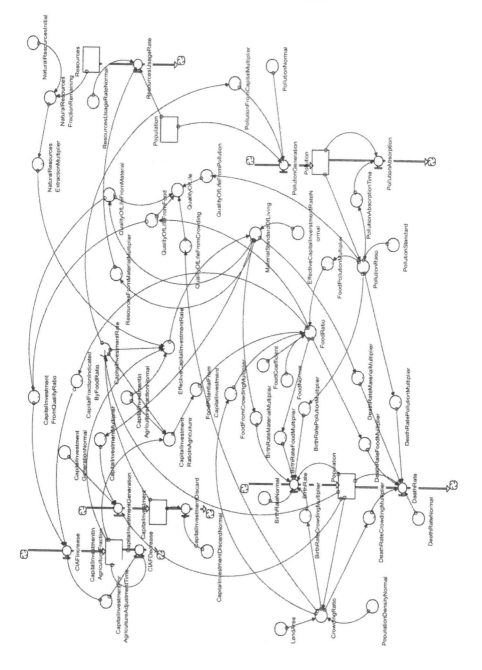

Figure 3.8 shows a STELLA version of Forrester's world model with its population sector, pollution sector, natural resources sector and capital stock sector. All these sectors contain one or two internal feedback loops. They are tied together by numerous auxiliaries and controlled by numerous constants.

The bottom part of Figure 3.8 shows some of the feedback mechanisms between the population and the pollution sectors. The corresponding lines of Forrester's program are shown below in a STELLA version:

- The population increases and decreases according to the birth and death rates:

```
Population(t) = Population(t - dt) + (BirthRate -
                DeathRate) * dt
```

- The birth rate depends on the actual population size, on a constant 'normal birth rate' and on several auxiliaries ('birth rate multipliers') for food supply, material life standard, crowding and pollution:

```
BirthRate = Population*BirthRateNormal*
            BirthRateFoodMultiplier*
            BirthRateMaterialMultiplier*
            BirthRateMaterialMultiplier*
            BirthRateCrowdingMultiplier*
            BirthRatePollutionMultiplier
BirthRateCrowdingMultiplier = GRAPH(CrowdingRatio)
(0.00, 1.05), (1.00, 1.00), (2.00, 0.9), (3.00, 0.7),
(4.00, 0.6), (5.00, 0.55)
CrowdingRatio = Population/(LandArea*
                PopulationDensityNormal)
LandArea = 135E6
PopulationDensityNormal = 26.5
BirthRatePollutionMultiplier = GRAPH(PollutionRatio)
   (0.00, 1.02), (10.0, 0.9), (20.0, 0.7), (30.0, 0.4),
   (40.0, 0.25), (50.0, 0.15), (60.0, 0.1)
```

The latter two (BirthRateCrowdingMultiplier and BirthRate-PollutionMultiplier) are determined by so-called table functions (see below). BirthRateCrowdingMultiplier and BirthRatePollutionMultiplier depend on CrowdingRatio (crowding) and PollutionRatio (pollution rate), respectively. CrowdingRatio is defined as proportional to the actual population size (for the latter, see below).

- The death rate also depends on the actual population size, on a constant death rate and, like the birth rate, on multipliers for food supply, material life standard, crowding and pollution:

```
DeathRate = Population*DeathRateNormal*
            DeathRateMaterialMultiplier*
            DeathRatePollutionMultiplier*
            DeathRateFoodMultiplier*
            DeathRateCrowdingMultiplier
DeathRateFoodMultiplier = GRAPH(FoodRatio)
    (0.00, 30.0), (0.25, 3.00), (0.5, 2.00), (0.75, 1.40),
    (1.00, 1.00), (1.25, 0.7), (1.50, 0.6), (1.75, 0.5),
    (2.00, 0.5)
DeathRateMaterialMultiplier =
    GRAPH(MaterialStandardOfLiving)
    (0.00, 1.80), (0.5, 1.80), (1.00, 1.00), (1.50, 0.8),
    (2.00, 0.7), (2.50, 0.6), (3.00, 0.53), (3.50, 0.5),
    (4.00, 0.5), (4.50, 0.5), (5.00, 0.5)
DeathRateCrowdingMultiplier = GRAPH(CrowdingRatio)
    (0.00, 0.9), (1.00, 1.00), (2.00, 1.20), (3.00, 1.50),
    (4.00, 1.90), (5.00, 3.00)
DeathRatePollutionMultiplier = GRAPH(PollutionRatio)
    (0.00, 0.92), (10.0, 1.30), (20.0, 2.00), (30.0, 3.20),
    (40.0, 4.80), (50.0, 6.80), (60.0, 9.20)
```

Again, the death rate multipliers (DeathRateFoodMultiplier, DeathRateMaterialMultiplier, DeathRateCrowding-Multiplier and DeathRatePollutionMultiplier) are determined by table functions different from the ones used for the calculation of birth rate multipliers.

- The pollution rate is calculated from the actual pollution level by a simple division:

```
PollutionRatio = Pollution/PollutionStandard
PollutionStandard = 3.6e9
```

- The level of pollution is determined by the rates of its generation and absorption:

```
Pollution(t) = Pollution(t - dt) + (PollutionGeneration -
               PollutionAbsorption) * dt
```

- Pollution generation depends on the population size, on a switchable constant, and on `polcm`, the 'pollution capital multiplier' determined by the capital sector, which we will not discuss here:

```
PollutionGeneration = Population*PollutionNormal*
                          PollutionFromCapitalMultiplier
```

- Pollution absorption depends only on the actual level of pollution, but in so intricate a manner that a table function is again used:

```
PollutionAbsorption = Pollution/PollutionAbsorptionTime
PollutionAbsorptionTime = GRAPH(PollutionRatio)
   (0.00, 0.6), (10.0, 2.50), (20.0, 5.00), (30.0, 8.00),
   (40.0, 11.5), (50.0, 15.5), (60.0, 20.0)
```

Table functions were DYNAMO's (and graph functions are STELLA's) means of modelling those nonlinear relationships between two variables that cannot be written down as a single equation. In most cases, these nonlinear relationships are taken from empirical data. In STELLA, function tables are defined with the help of a special window which is shown in Figure 3.9.

The value that `table` returns is calculated as a linear interpolation. The

Figure 3.9: Evaluation of table functions in STELLA

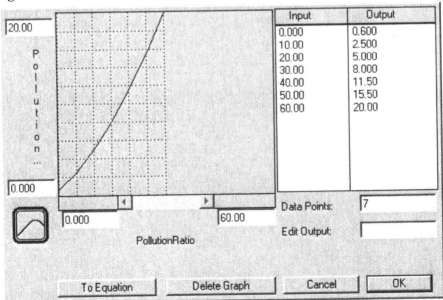

table function used in the calculation of pollution absorption is evaluated as indicated by Figure 3.9: function values when its argument is within the first interval are interpolated between the first and second table entries, function values when its argument is within the second interval are interpolated between the second and third table entries, and so on. Thus, the table must have $n + 1$ entries for n intervals.

The table function technique makes a large number of numerical values necessary in a STELLA program. With WORLD2's 22 table functions, this amounts to 151 numerical values.

Figure 3.10 shows its predictions for births, deaths and world population size. The latter is predicted to have its maximum about the year 2035 when, for the first time since the early twentieth century, the number of deaths will exceed the number of births.

Figure 3.10: Prediction results of Forrester's WORLD2 model for births, deaths and population size

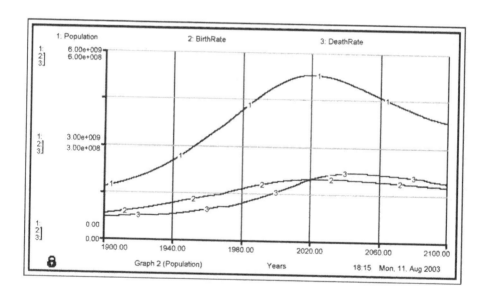

Problems and an outlook

It is interesting to see what happens when Forrester's world model, with its standard parameter set, is used to 'retrodict' births, deaths and world population backwards in time (see Figure 3.11). We see immediately that there is a problem, because during the last two decades of the nineteenth century the world population is 'predicted' to have decreased from 6 billion in 1880 to the historical 1.7 billion in 1900, which was obviously not the case.

Figure 3.11: Retrodiction of Forrester's WORLD2 model back to 1880

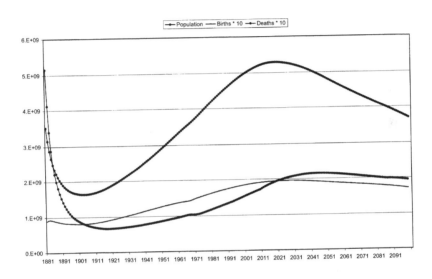

It is difficult to find the cause of this erroneous 'retrodiction'. Zwicker (1981: 481) points out that with a slight modification of the dependence of the death rate multiplier for material life standard (DeathRateMaterial-Multiplier) on the material life standard (MaterialStandardOfLiving) the retrodiction is much more plausible. He changed the first entry in the DeathRateMaterialMultiplier table function from 3 to 1.8,

```
DeathRateMaterialMultiplier = GRAPH(MaterialStandardOfLiving)
    (0.00, 1.80), (0.5, 1.80), (1.00, 1.00), (1.50, 0.8),
    (2.00, 0.7), (2.50, 0.6), (3.00, 0.53), (3.50, 0.5),
    (4.00, 0.5), (4.50, 0.5), (5.00, 0.5)
```

and obtained a more or less correct 'retrodiction' of the total population for 1880 and, moreover, a birth rate above the death rate back to 1888 (see Figure 3.12).

The high dependence of DeathRateMaterialMultiplier on

Figure 3.12: Retrodiction of Forrester's WORLD2 model back to 1880, with a slight correction of `DeathRateMaterialMultiplier`

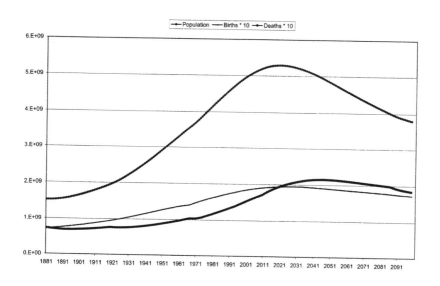

`MaterialStandardOfLiving` for low values of `MaterialStandard-OfLiving` (at the eve of the twentieth century) is responsible for this effect. Eliminating this high dependence cancels the effect without changing the model for the twentieth and twenty-first centuries.

Table functions can thus be dangerous – we should not forget that a table function is a fairly raw means of representing the dependence of one variable on another. In many cases, modellers have only a rough notion of this dependence and a notion such as 'the more of *x*, the faster *y* increases' may be represented by an infinite number of different continuous or table functions. Hence, modellers may fall into the 'trap of tractability' (Doran and Gilbert 1994: 13) when they select their representation of a monotonic dependence: a linear dependence is always the simplest form of a monotonic dependence, and it is easily tractable by mathematical algorithms, but solutions will usually be different for linear dependencies as compared with different nonlinear ones. This was one of the reasons for introducing so-called 'qualitative differential equations' (Kuipers 1994: 3) into the modelling and simulation scene. The only type of knowledge used in qualitative simulation is in terms of intervals between 'landmarks' – for example, the interval between the melting point of ice and the boiling point of water – and in terms of monotonically increasing and decreasing functions. Qualitative simulation has so far mostly been applied to physical phenomena ('naïve physics'), and only seldom to social phenomena (but see Brajnik and Lines 1998), so we will not go into the details of this new approach.

Another shortcoming of Forrester's WORLD2 is the fact that the population is always seen as a whole and that its age structure is not considered at all. A changing age structure, however, will affect both birth and death rates. Thus, Meadows' WORLD3 was a step forward in so far as this world model contained four different level variables for the age groups 0–14, 15–44, 45–64 and 65+, with different death rates and birth rates depending only on the population aged between 15 and 44. However, the model did not distinguish between men and women.

What is still missing even in WORLD3 is a differentiation between regions of the world. Birth and death rates as well as many other variables vary greatly between different continents, countries and even regions within countries. This is why as early as in the mid-1970s a new effort was launched under the name of GLOBUS: 'the construction of an all-computer, nation-based, political world model from empirical data – something which did not then exist anywhere in the world' (Deutsch 1987: xiv). GLOBUS is a model that consists of interacting component models for each of 25 different nations with their own demographic, economic, political and government processes whose interactions are separately modelled. This type of model is far beyond system dynamics, so we will not discuss it in any further detail.

GLOBUS overcomes one of the most important shortcomings of the system dynamics approach. System dynamics describes the target system as a single entity or object. A system dynamics model is an indivisible whole. If we happen to find parts in the target system (like continents or countries in the world) we have to describe their properties as attributes of the world model and thus leave the system dynamics approach – as GLOBUS did.

Although the GLOBUS group never continued their research after their book appeared and after MicroGLOBUS (a DOS-based demonstration model) had been distributed, there are other groups who followed similar approaches. The 'International Futures' Group (Hughes 1999) developed a model encompassing all major states of the world (which can be aggregated arbitrarily into regions.[3] Population is modelled in five-year cohorts, several economic sectors, food types, land types, energy types and types of government spending can be distinguished. Thus the International Futures model is, of course, much more detailed than the classical world models by Forrester and Meadows, and even more detailed than the GLOBUS model in so far

---

[3]The downloadable demonstration and student version, http://www.du.edu/~bhughes/ifswelcome.html, comes with nine individual countries, the European Union and seven regions such as 'Other Europe'.

as the latter encompasses only 25 nations plus the 'rest of the world', has a coarser-grained age structure, which is exogenously determined, just to name a few differences.

Further reading

There are many books dedicated to the system dynamics simulation approach, beginning with

- Forrester, J. W. (1980): *Principles of Systems*, 2nd preliminary edn. MIT Press, Cambridge, MA (1st edn 1968).

which first introduced the technique. It includes a number of technical details about an early version of DYNAMO and some simple examples. This technique was first applied by

- Forrester, J. W. (1971) *World Dynamics*. MIT Press, Cambridge, MA

to world models of the type we discussed earlier in this chapter, and

- Forrester, J. W. (1969) *Urban Dynamics*. MIT Press, Cambridge, MA

applied system dynamics to 'the problems of our ageing urban areas', introduced a model of an urban area and predicted over 250 years its future development in the unemployment, labour, managerial and professional sectors as well as in the housing, industry, tax and town planning sectors. Forrester's first book on related topics,

- Forrester, J. W. (1961) *Industrial Dynamics*. MIT Press, Cambridge, MA

has enjoyed a wide readership and stimulated research on complex systems. The original DYNAMO manual was

- Pugh, A. L. III (1976) *DYNAMO User's Manual*. MIT Press, Cambridge, MA

which has since been superseded by more modern versions of the DYNAMO language.

Another influential group of books began with the introduction of a far more sophisticated world model in

- Meadows, D. L. *et al.* (1974) *Dynamics of Growth in a Finite World*. MIT Press, Cambridge, MA.

This described the world population in different age groups, distinguished between industrial and service capital, and went into more detail concerning land use and fertility. Its results are discussed from a 1990s perspective in

- Meadows, D. H. *et al.* (1992) *Beyond the Limits.* Chelsea Green, Post Mills, VT.

This book states that the original model needed only very few corrections, after the data produced by the target system – the world as it behaved in the 1970s and 1980s – were taken into consideration.

A comprehensive description of system dynamics oriented simulation methods in the social sciences is provided by

- Hanneman, R. A. (1988) *Computer-Assisted Theory Building. Modeling Dynamic Social Systems.* Sage, Newbury Park, CA.

He does not so much address a special target system (like Forrester and Meadows always did, writing about urban or industrial or world development), but rather has 'the immodest goal of reorienting how many social scientists go about building and working with theories' (p. 9), thus making simulation a new methodological paradigm for the social sciences, restricting himself, however, to macro and other equation-based models throughout the book.

An extensively comprehensive description of system dynamics oriented simulation mostly, but not only, in business research was recently published as

- Sterman, J. D. (2000) *Business Dynamics: Systems Thinking and Modeling for a Complex World.* McGraw-Hill, New York, NY.

It comes with a CD-ROM with modelling software from Vensim, ithink and PowerSim dedicated to 'issues such as fluctuating sales, market growth and stagnation, the reliability of forecasts and the rationality of business decision making.' (from the blurb)

More recent world models are presented and discussed in

- Bremer, St.A. ed. (1987) *The GLOBUS Model. Computer Simulation of Worldwide Political and Economic Developments*, Campus/Westview Press, Frankfurt/M. and Boulder, CO.

which is the summary of work done in the GLOBUS project which developed a world model 'based on nation-states, not regions' while

- Hughes, B.B. (1999) *International Futures: Choices in the Face of Uncertainty*, Westview Press, Boulder, CO.

in a way continues this work in so far as it presents a more modern (Windows compatible) type of multi-nation world model which can be downloaded from http://www.du.edu/~bhughes/ifswelcome.html.

The qualitative simulation approach briefly mentioned on page 52 is discussed in detail in

- Kuipers, B. (1974) *Qualitative Reasoning. Modeling and Simulation with Incomplete Knowledge*, MIT Press, Cambridge, MA.

Chapter 4

Microanalytical simulation models

As discussed in the previous chapter, system dynamics models its target systems as indivisible wholes and does not take into account the fact that for the social scientist target systems usually consist of individual persons, groups, classes, subpopulations and so on. Social scientists will therefore be interested in modelling approaches on several levels – an aggregate level and at least one lower level. The first approach that tried to solve this problem was the classical microsimulation approach. It has been used to predict the individual and group effects of aggregate political measures that often apply differently to different persons. For instance, a tax formula that imposes taxes only on persons with incomes above a certain threshold might be changed by moving this threshold. If we want to calculate the gross effect on the total tax revenue, a simulation on the macro level cannot help. We must instead go back to the individual cases, calculate their taxes due before and after the tax revision, and reaggregate the tax revenue.

Another example can be taken from demography. Changing age structures of a population can be simulated on a macro level – see the discussion on page 53 in Chapter 3. We would have several level variables with the sizes of a number of sex/age groups to which we would apply age-group-specific death rates, and we would calculate births from the sizes of the female age groups between 15 and 45 years of age, applying age-dependent fertility rates. If we were only interested in the age structure of a population, this deterministic macro model might be sufficient because, with a very large number of persons, all random influences on individual births and deaths (and other events that might be of interest) would be averaged out. But if we wanted to use additional information, say on different fertility rates for different education levels, we would need a very complicated system dynamics model with a large number of level and rate variables that could not be decomposed or otherwise simplified.

The microsimulation approach overcomes this problem by going to the individual level, modelling individual persons with a number of attributes (such as sex, age, marital status, education, employment) and a number of transition probabilities. This makes up a stochastic micro model, as opposed to the deterministic macro model of the system dynamics approach. In simple cases, especially in demography, both approaches will produce approximately the same result – both models would yield the same prediction for the age structure, given that the birth and death probabilities of the macro model are compatible with the respective probabilities of the micro model.

Most microanalytical simulation models (MSMs) aim to predict the effects of (and thereby support) social and financial policy (for a number of examples, see the 'Further Reading' section of this chapter).

In general, the MSM procedure is as follows (see Figure 4.1, cf. also Figure 2.2). We start with a target population from which we draw a representative sample and collect data about some selected properties of its members.

Figure 4.1: General features of microanalytical simulation models

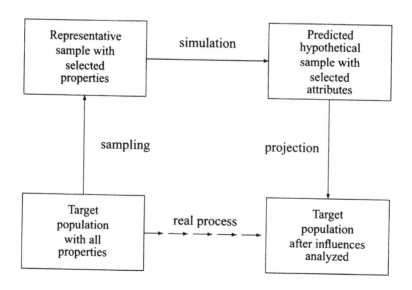

This sample serves as a model of the population. The data are entered into a database (the microdata file). Its rows ('cases' or 'objects') correspond to the individual members of the sample, and its columns ('variables' or 'attributes') correspond to the selected properties. Then the microdata file is updated ('simulated'), that is to say, transition probabilities are applied to the individual cases. For each simulation step, this procedure yields a predicted hypothetical sample. After a number of steps, the microdata file is projected (or 'grossed up'). This projection yields an estimation of the structure of the target population after some time has passed.

Microanalytical simulation models consist of at least two levels: the level of individuals or households (or the level of enterprises) and the aggregate level (for example, the population or national economy level). More sophisticated MSMs distinguish between the individual and the household levels, thus facilitating models in which persons move between households and can create and dissolve new households (for instance, by marriage and divorce).

Since MSMs usually use 'available detailed information about the initial state of microunits such as persons and families' (Orcutt 1986: 14), they are not only extremely data-based but also very demanding as far as the data collection requirements and the necessary computing and data storage capacity are concerned. A representative sample of a population will easily contain several thousand households because its subsamples with respect to all property combinations relevant to the purpose of prediction have to be large enough to allow projection. All the members of these households have to be interviewed and the data have to be stored, taking into account that some of the relevant properties have to be represented by household attributes, whereas others have to be represented by individual attributes. The necessary storage capacity is proportional to the number of microunits represented in the model, and computing time may be proportional to the square of this number, at least where marriage and kinship relations are simulated. In the 1970s and early 1980s, these demands resulted in a small number of MSMs, which were then run on large mainframe machines, making them accessible only to a few specialists. As a result, user-friendly tools to perform microanalytical simulation have not been developed until very recently. Only 20 years ago, the state of the art was described as follows: 'There is no universal general-purpose microsimulation software available ... most MSMs are developed in a conventional way from scratch' (Klösgen 1986: 485–486). Microanalytical simulation models had to be programmed in a general-purpose language such as FORTRAN or PL/1 (because general-purpose language programs can be fine-tuned for computational efficiency). The use of general-purpose languages and mainframe computers made maintenance a task for programming specialists. Nowadays, however, workstations and even personal computers are sufficiently powerful to run quite large MSMs and more user-friendly software has begun to emerge.

Methodologies

Models simulating the household (individual) sector begin from microdata collected from a representative sample of the population, often including several thousand households. The microdata file typically includes data about age, marital status, participation in education and employment, income from various sources, consumption, wealth and taxes for every member of a household at the time the data were collected.

Before a microdata file can be used for simulation it has to be updated – the microdata file may be several months or even years old when it is used for simulation purposes, and the percentages of income classes, age cohorts and so forth may have changed (or the sample may have been biased from the very beginning, due to different response rates in the respective classes). This is typically done by reweighting the individuals or households in the sample so that the weighted samples represent the current distributions of the attributes in question.

There are several different methodologies for MSMs.

Static microsimulation

In static microsimulation the demographic structure of the model population is changed by reweighting according to external information – that is, each individual data record in the microdata file is given a different weight for different years, so that the weighted file displays the age structure for all years; the same can also be done for other classifications, such as income.

Static microsimulation is usually applied to short-term predictions of the immediate impact of a policy change. It answers questions such as 'What increase in government revenues is to be expected if the income tax rate is changed in a certain manner?' All other influences are kept equal in this case. Static microsimulation may include hypotheses about how people's behaviour changes in response to the policy change. For example, if the tax on luxury goods were sharply increased, people might abstain from buying goods of this type, which would in turn reduce the government's revenue instead of increasing it.

Dynamic microsimulation

In dynamic microsimulation the demographic structure of the model population is changed by ageing the model persons individually (and by having them give birth to new persons, and by having them die) according to life tables. Individuals and households change their attributes at every time step, and birth and death can be explicitly modelled. Hence, the demographic structure of the microdata file changes endogenously, and the same applies to all the other attributes in question such as participation in education, employment and income.

Dynamic microsimulation is usually applied to the long-range prediction of demographic change and its effect on social security expenditures and incomes, and the redistributive impact of the social security system.

Longitudinal microsimulation

In longitudinal microsimulation simulation is done on an age cohort and over the whole life of this cohort, thus omitting a population's age structure (but children of the cohort members may still be simulated).

Longitudinal microsimulation (or dynamic cohort) models are quite similar to dynamic population models. However, they start from a microdata file that includes only one age cohort. The microunits of this file are then aged such that an entire life cycle is simulated. This might be sufficient to detect the redistributive impact of the social security system. The model would for instance give answers to questions about whether and to what extent the mean individual is a winner or a loser over his or her entire lifetime, and which type of individual is a loser or a winner.

Subprocesses within household MSMs

Simulating a population sample dynamically over a number of years is only possible if a number of different processes are modelled (see Figure 4.2 for a rough sketch of these processes in six households with 15 individuals). The simplest process to be modelled is *ageing*: in each simulated year, every individual's age is increased by one year (assuming that it survives during this year). Age-dependent *death* probabilities are then applied to decide whether a particular individual survives during the actual simulation year. *Birth* is considerably more intricate, because births have to occur within a

Figure 4.2: Subprocesses within households

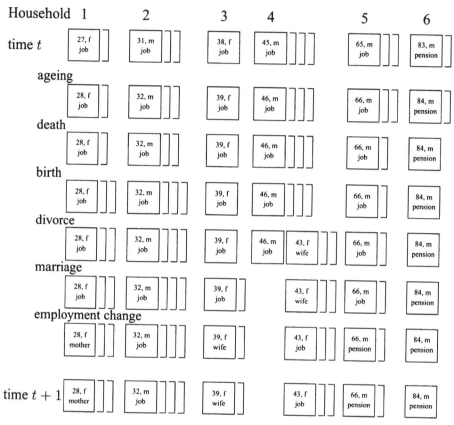

At the beginning of year *t*, the situation is represented by the households shown in the top row. In the *ageing* step, all persons' ages are increased by one. In the *death* step, two people, in households 5 and 6, die. In the *birth* step, children are born into households 1 and 2. In the *divorce* step, household 4 is dissolved into a single male and a new household consisting of his ex-wife and their two children. In the *marriage* step, the two singles form a new household. In the *employment change* step, the new mother in household 1 and the newly married wife give up their jobs, the newly divorced wife gets a job, and the two older persons retire. Thus at the end of the simulated year, the situation is as in the bottom row.

sample household. A simulated child is born into a household with a certain probability depending on (among other things) the age, nationality and social status of the potential mother. *Divorce* is also modelled on a stochastic basis: divorce rates may depend on the duration of the marriage, on the ages of the spouses, on their social status, and on their religion. Divorce will result in the dissolution of one household into two new households. Modelling *marriage* is even more complicated, because typically a new simulated household has to be built from two individuals who have in turn to leave their former households, and the two simulated spouses have to be selected from all marriageable individuals.

During their lifetimes, the simulated individuals have to change their educational and *employment* status. They will enter school with different probabilities when they are 5–7 years old, and they will leave school with different probabilities when they are between 14 and 20 years old, they will be employed in different jobs, lose their jobs, earn an income that depends on their type of job, and eventually retire with different probabilities depending on their ages.

Simulated individuals will receive social transfers, according to their income and employment status, and pay taxes and social security according to their income. They will use their income for consumption purposes or save part of it.

All probabilities applied in the model have to be calculated from empirical data; they may be kept constant over the simulation run, or change over time. Calculating these transition probabilities may be very difficult. The probability of pregnancy depends on such factors as age, marital status, employment status and education, but while birth statistics in most countries will indicate how many children were born to women of different ages and marital status, they might fail to give information about their employment status and their education; hence the interaction between these attributes cannot completely be adjusted for. The probability of death also depends on age and a number of other attributes, but while an age-dependent death probability may easily be estimated from available tables, this is not the case for most other attributes. Birth and death probabilities may change over time due to cultural and technological changes and to progress in medicine. For example, age-specific fertility rates have changed considerably over the last 30 years, an effect that cannot be explained by only taking into account changes in women's education and employment. Some transition rates can only be obtained from longitudinal data.

Subprocesses within enterprise MSMs

In the case of enterprise MSMs, the microunits are firms. Starting from a sample of firms and their most recent balances, for every firm a number of subprocesses have to be run: the potential sales on the product market have to be estimated as a function of prices; the production capacity is calculated; and the production is adapted to the expected sales. Investment has to be done if the production capacity does not cover the expected demand, invention and innovation may occur, and products have to be bought and sold on the market.

Initialization

The initial states of MSMs are read from databases in which individual and/or household and/or enterprise characteristics are derived from an empirical sample.

If a microsimulation model is to include both households and enterprises, it is difficult to obtain representative data for both household and enterprise sectors at the same time. With a fixed household sample, enterprise data would be collected from those enterprises that employ the members of the household sample. Typically, this enterprise sample would not be representative of the economy as a whole, and the same would apply if one started with an enterprise sample and collected data for all the employees of the sample enterprises (and their household members). This is why, in the rare combined models, the household sector is linked to econometric macrodata (see below).

In a number of countries, it is becoming easier to obtain time series data for individuals and households (for example, the German Socio-Economic Panel since 1984, and similar panels in Belgium, the United Kingdom, the Netherlands, Luxembourg, Hungary, the United States, Sweden and, recently, Russia). If data are available from household panels, then it is possible to calibrate model parameters and algorithms using these data. The representativeness of panels is, however, a greater problem than in the case of simple one-time samples because the drop-out of panel members usually induces bias. Evidence from the German Socio-Economic Panel shows that over the first seven waves (1984 to 1990), 61.2 per cent of the interviewees of the first wave remained in the sample and are available for 'complete case analysis' (Hauser *et al.* 1994b: 94–98).

Linkage between macro models and MSMs

MSMs restricted to the household sector must be linked to econometric macro models that make their data available to the individual level. For example, the probability of losing one's job depends not only on individual or household attributes but also on macroeconomic effects that might not be apparent from the MSM itself; individual consumption characteristics may also depend on macroeconomic factors. The same is true for pure enterprise sector MSMs and for combined household–enterprise models.

Software

Microanalytical simulation models were originally developed as general-purpose language programs that could only be written, changed and maintained by programming specialists, but in recent years several MSMs have been developed which can be run on workstations and personal computers. Some examples are

- MICSIM 3.x, for Windows 3.x/NT/95, using Visual C++ and ORACLE (Merz 1996);
- UMDBS, for Windows NT/2000/XP, with its own programming language (MISTRAL) and query language 2002 – see below and `http://www.fh-friedberg.de/sauerbier/umdbs` (Sauerbier 2002) – which was developed from the older Darmstadt Micro Macro Simulator (Heike *et al.* 1996);
- STINMOD (Lambert *et al.* 1994) and DYNAMOD (Antcliff 1993), for Windows (National Center for Social and Economic Modeling, see `http://www.natsem.canberra.edu.au/index.html` and Brown and Harding 2002);
- CORSIM (Caldwell 1993); see also `http://www.strategicforecasting.com/corsim/`.

Most of these follow the updating procedures described above, stepping from one year (or month) to the next. DYNAMOD seems to be the first MSM to use discrete event simulation features (see Chapter 5) – components of the model are only evaluated when there is a change in attributes. To put it more explicitly, take a person in the microdata file who is employed in a certain job. Instead of applying a probability to decide whether this person loses his or her job in each given year, the time until he or she she loses his or her job is taken from an appropriate random distribution (which, of course, has to be estimated from empirical data) at the time he or she starts his or her job, and without any annual calculation he or she is removed from his or her job at the 'predicted' time (for more details, see Antcliff 1993; Galler 1997).

Examples

A static microsimulation of the impact of a tax reform

Our first example looks at what might be the impact of an income tax reform. We start with a sample of households of which only the yearly taxable income (and information relevant to taxation, such as marital status and number of children) need be known, and we require the gross effect of the change in tax rates and the effects of the tax reform on different types of households. We will use data from 1995 wave of the German Socio-Economic Panel (GSOEP).[1] The sample consists of 6214 persons whose income distribution is similar to the real income distribution of Germany in the mid-1990s.

In more detail, GSOEP 1995 consists of 13,511 records of individual interviewees in 6894 households. Of these interviewees, 6214 were taxable persons according to German tax law (married couples count only as one taxable person, see below) and gave sufficient information about their personal income (including, if applicable, their spouse's income). Only these 6214 interviews were reweighted according to the national tax statistics of 1995, as published in the German statistical yearbook (Statistisches Bundesamt 2001: 544). The statistical yearbook contains a table which lists the numbers of taxable people in different (gross) income classes. Since even in this detailed survey not all information on income and taxes is given, data taken from GSOEP and data from the national tax statistics are not fully comparable, but for the purpose of an example the difference is negligible. In terms of the German tax declaration conventions, 'gross income' is the sum of all types of income (whereas the data include only labour income) minus the sum of all costs related to earning one's income (for instance, public transport tickets for commuting or the subscription to professional journals and so forth), 'income' is gross income minus reductions for contributions to pension funds, health insurance etc., whereas 'taxable income' is income

---

[1] The data used in this chapter were made available by the German Socio-Economic Panel Study (GSOEP) at the German Institute for Economic Research (DIW), Berlin.

minus reductions for children.[2] The GSOEP data do not contain precise information on all types of reductions, so the three stages of income are estimated from the gross income reported by the interviewees, the relation between gross income and income in the national statistics, and the number of children.

Taxable persons are divided into 18 classes. For the purpose of this example the upper six classes are grouped together. Hence, our simulation considers only 13 classes (see Table 4.1).

Table 4.1: Taxable persons 1995 in the German national statistics and in the GSOEP sample: total income

Tax class	Total gross income (DM)	Cases		Mean gross income (DM)	
		National statistics	Sample	National statistics	Weighted sample
1	1–4,999	1,145,008	581	2,580	1,515
2	5,000–9,999	1,274,868	369	7,593	7,414
3	10,000–14,999	1,489,169	405	12,481	12,354
4	15,000–19,999	1,309,984	461	17,412	17,197
5	20,000–24,999	1,227,877	633	22,497	22,611
6	25,000–29,999	1,333,681	586	27,528	27,343
7	30,000–39,999	3,136,635	1,265	35,197	35,052
8	40,000–49,999	3,619,401	959	44,999	44,829
9	50,000–59,999	3,105,688	457	54,758	54,340
10	60,000–74,999	3,252,768	376	66,997	66,588
11	75,000–99,999	3,383,398	149	86,117	86,285
12	100,000–249,999	3,126,897	70	134,452	127,219
13	250,000+	277,705	4	571,686	376,011
All classes		27,683,079	6,315	59,609	56,644
All classes, total income in billion DM				1,650	1,568

Sample households have to be weighted because the income structure of the sample differs from the income structure of the total taxable population as given in the statistical yearbook. In class 4, for instance, the weighting factor will be 1,309,984/237 = 5527.35865 – which roughly means that 237 interviewees in this income class represent 1,309,984 taxable persons in the

[2]German tax law is in fact much more complicated, but these three stages might do for the purpose of an example.

national statistics. Even after reweighting, there remains a difference in the mean incomes of about 8.5 per cent, due to the fact that the top income class is only sparsely represented,[3] but the estimates in classes 2 to 11 are quite reasonable (with biases below 3 per cent). The reweighted sample can now serve as a rough approximation to the total taxable population.

If we now apply the tax regulations that were in force in 1995 we should arrive at an estimate of the total and individual tax loads (see Table 4.2). And if we apply the tax regulations that came into force for 1996 (with a minor tax reform in October 1995) or 2004 (with a major tax reform in December 2002) or that are currently being discussed for the longer-term future we should be able to predict the impact of those proposals.

Let us assume we have prepared our data file with the necessary weight variable as explained above and that we analyze it with the help of the well-known Statistical Package for the Social Sciences (SPSS). SPSS is normally used for statistical analysis, rather than for microsimulation. Nevertheless, because it will be available to most readers and appropriate at least for a simple microsimulation example, we use it here. The SPSS variable taxinco represents the adjusted taxable income (which is less than the total household income because there are many allowances that need to be taken into account).

The complicated German tax and social security laws do not really allow an estimation of gross and taxable income if one only knows the gross income from the GSOEP data. To calculate the taxable income, the gross income has to be reduced by a large number of allowances and deductions which differ between types of persons and households. These allowances and deductions include, for instance, part of the social security contributions, but also allowances for children (the only allowance which will be considered here), old age, the cost of education, expenditure on commuting between home and job, and many more.

Hence, taxinco is constructed by using the information from the national tax statistics about total income and taxable income. After adjusting for all the allowances that we are not considering separately in our simulation, Table 4.1 has to be modified – see the 'mean taxable income' column in Table 4.2 which reproduces exactly the national statistics in the adjusted sample.

This step, which leads to the variable taxinco, allocates taxable income values to all the sample households which conform to the national statistics.

---

[3] In fact, there are only 13 households with an income above DM 250,000 in the GSOEP sample. Since the 2002 wave an extra high-income sample was interviewed, but data from the national tax statistics for 2002 will only be available in a couple of years.

Table 4.2: Taxable income and taxes 1995 (DM) due according to the 1990–5 tax laws (national statistics and GSOEP sample)

Tax class	Total gross income	Mean taxable income National statistics	Mean tax due National statistics	Mean tax due Sample
1	1–4,999	1,230	14	0
2	5,000–9,999	4,145	76	0
3	10,000–14,999	7,338	264	271
4	15,000–19,999	10,362	750	645
5	20,000–24,999	13,827	1,467	1,246
6	25,000–29,999	18,133	2,273	2,148
7	30,000–39,999	25,283	3,763	3,676
8	40,000–49,999	33,255	5,543	5,313
9	50,000–59,999	40,770	7,214	6,875
10	60,000–74,999	51,622	9,655	9,408
11	75,000–99,999	68,891	13,839	13,605
12	100,000–249,999	112,946	27,825	27,766
13	250,000+	520,758	213,860	235,589
All classes				
	National statistics	46,867	10,303	
	Sample	44,245		10,354
Total income and tax revenue (billion DM)				
	National statistics	1,297	285	
	Sample	1,297		287

Hence, our microdata file could be considered to be 'semi-synthetic' in so far as each household is allocated a taxable income which is only loosely related to its gross income as reported in the GSOEP sample. On the other hand, each household still bears all characteristics (such as marital status and number of children) from the original sample.

In the next step, tax calculation is done. The applicable formula depends on the number of children and the marital status of the taxable person. For each child there is a certain allowance. For married couples (most of whom are taxed together) the tax formula is applied in a special way. German tax law assumes that all the earnings of wife and husband are equally divided between them (even if one of them has no income at all), then each is taxed according to the general formula, and finally their taxes are summed, so that the tax is twice the amount that would result if the formula had been applied to half the taxable income.

In SPSS, this is formulated as follows (married is 1 for households with a married couple and 0 for singles, children is the number of children in the household, x1 is the taxable income after children's allowances have been deducted,[4] x and tax90 are temporary variables used to model the tax split procedure for married couples, and y90 is another temporary variable used to model the progressive tax rates in the so-called progression zone of the German tax rate):

```
* if (married = 0) x1 = taxinco-children*1512.
* if (married = 1) x1 = taxinco-children*3024.
compute x1 = taxinco .
if (x1<0) x1 = 0.
if (married = 1) x = x1/2.
if (married = 0) x = x1.
if (x<=5616) tax90 = 0.
if (x>5616 & x<=8153) tax90 = 0.19*x - 1067.
if (x>8153 & x <= 120041) y90 = (x - 8100)/10000.
if (x>8153 & x <= 120041) tax90 = (151.94*y90 + 1900)*y90 +
472.
if (x>120041) tax90 = 0.53*x - 22842.
if (married = 1) tax90_1 = tax90*2.
if (married = 0) tax90_1 = tax90.
```

This piece of code models the tax rates. Taxable incomes below DM 5616 are not taxed. Between DM 5616 and DM 8153 there is a proportional tax zone with a 19 per cent marginal tax rate. Between DM 8153 and DM 120,041 there is a progressive tax zone with a marginal tax rate rising from 19 to 53 per cent (the increase in the marginal tax rate is quadratic), while above DM 120,041 another proportional tax zone begins with a 53 per cent marginal tax rate.

Table 4.2 shows that the GSOEP sample is fairly representative, although the mean tax dues in the lower-income classes differ considerably from the mean tax dues from the official statistics. This is due to the fact that the

---

[4]Note that the first two lines of the code are not actually used because the calculation of taxinco has already taken account of this type of deduction, but if we want to redesign children's allowances we will have to recalculate x1.

distribution of marital status in some of the tax classes of the sample differs from the distribution in the entire taxable population. On the other hand, the total income tax revenue is estimated with an error of only about 3 per cent. This will do for our example.

The 1995 tax reform (which was approved by the national parliament in 1995 and came into force in 1996) made the tax schedule more complicated in so far as the progressive zone was split into two such zones (after they had been combined in 1988 with effect for 1990), with a maximum marginal tax rate of 53 per cent; the first DM 12,095 were exempt from taxes. We model this as follows:

```
if (x <= 12095) tax95 = 0.
compute y95 = (x - 12042)/10000 .
compute z95 = (x - 55674)/10000 .
if (x > 12096 & x <=  55727) tax95 = ( 86.63*y95 + 2590)*y95 .
if (x > 55727 & x <= 120041) tax95 = (151.91*z95 + 3346)*z95 +
12949.
if (x > 120041) tax95 = 0.53*x - 22842.
if (married = 1) tax95_1 = tax95*2.
if (married = 0) tax95_1 = tax95.
```

Applying the 1995 tax regulations to our semi-synthetic household data yields Table 4.3. The total income tax revenue was reduced by DM 20 billion. All income classes (except the highest) profited from the tax reduction: classes 3 and 4 gained from the extension of the 'no taxation' zone, classes 7 to 10 gained most because the difference between the two progressive tariffs had the greatest effect here, and so on – only class 13 experienced no changes since the tariff for taxable incomes beyond DM 120,041 had not been changed. Generally speaking, this type of static simulation allows detailed analyses of distribution effects of tax revisions.

If we were only interested in simulating the impact of tax regulation changes on child allowances, marital status, and the formula for calculating individual tax rates, this simple model would meet all our requirements (although a larger sample with data for all individual household members would yield a better representation). Considering all the other allowances available in the German tax system would necessitate much more information about the households, information which is typically not given in general surveys (not even in the GSOEP data), but which is available from the tax offices' databases and documented at the aggregate level in the statistical yearbook.

Table 4.3: Taxable income and taxes 1995 (DM) due according to the 1990 and 1995 tax laws (GSOEP sample)

Tax class	Total gross income	Mean taxable income (statistics)	Mean tax due (sample)	
			1990	1995
1	1–4,999	1,225	0	0
2	5,000–9,999	4,140	0	0
3	10,000–14,999	7,324	269	0
4	15,000–19,999	10,362	645	0
5	20,000–24,999	13,827	1,246	321
6	25,000–29,999	18,133	2,148	1,102
7	30,000–39,999	25,283	3,677	2,472
8	40,000–49,999	33,255	5,313	4,154
9	50,000–59,999	40,770	6,875	5,786
10	60,000–74,999	51,622	9,408	8,553
11	75,000–99,999	68,891	13,605	13,073
12	100,000–249,999	112,946	27,766	27,730
13	250,000+	520,758	235,589	235,589
All classes		46,832	10,346	9,630
Total tax revenue (billion DM), sample		1,298	287	267

We can now play with alternatives. Table 4.4 gives the results of two modifications of the 1990 tax law. In the 'DCA' column we have doubled the allowance for children. This makes no difference for poorer households: if there are no children in such a household, no difference occurs, and if there are, then in most cases the split rule will be used. Hence up to an income of DM 10,000, even the normal children's allowance reduces the taxable income below the tax threshold. In the higher-income classes the tax reduction is quite considerable. The overall loss for the treasury would be about DM 14.4 billion (most of which would go to rich people with children).

In the 'no split' column we have only the standard children's allowances, but here we abolish the split rule for married couples. This alternative leads to a considerable increase in taxes for all income classes. The overall gain with this measure for the treasury is DM 67 billion, most of which is paid by richer married couples, while singles are of course not affected.

We have seen in this subsection that it is quite difficult to prepare a microdata file for use even with static microsimulation. Reweighting –

Table 4.4: Taxable income and taxes 1995 (DM) due according to the 1990 tax law with two modifications (GSOEP sample)

Tax class	Total gross income	Mean taxable income	Mean tax due (sample)		
			1990	DCA 1990	No split 1990
1	1–4,999	1,225	0	0	0
2	5,000–9,999	4,141	0	0	0
3	10,000–14,999	7,325	269	170	325
4	15,000–19,999	10,362	645	528	911
5	20,000–24,999	13,827	1,246	1,068	1,611
6	25,000–29,999	18,133	2,148	1,891	2,532
7	30,000–39,999	25,283	3,677	3,357	4,193
8	40,000–49,999	33,255	5,313	4,852	6,220
9	50,000–59,999	40,770	6,875	6,302	8,307
10	60,000–74,999	51,622	9,408	8,722	11,640
11	75,000–99,999	68,891	13,605	12,783	17,686
12	100,000–249,999	112,946	27,766	26,725	37,486
13	250,000+	520,758	235,589	233,247	253,160
All classes		46,832	10,346	9,832	12,767
Total tax revenue (in billion DM), sample		1,297.5	286.6	272.2	353.7

making the sample representative of income distribution – does not suffice to yield a representative distribution of household types with respect to other characteristics of the household, such as marital status and number of children. Thus for serious purposes, readers are recommended not to use general surveys, but special surveys prepared for the purpose of tax (and social security) simulation, such as the German Socio-Economic Panel (Hauser *et al.* 1994b: 70–112), which we used here, and the Family Expenditure Survey (conducted by the British Office for National Statistics and available from the Economic and Social Research Council's Data Archive at the University of Essex (Eason 1996)). Once microdata files are prepared, static microsimulation can be done by means of quite straightforward algorithms.

A dynamic microsimulation enquiring into future nursing demand

For an example of dynamic microsimulation we will use UMDBS mentioned earlier. To give an impression of how this type of simulation is done and what kind of results can be expected, we use data from the German Socio-Economic Panel (2002 wave) and with the help of this toolbox we will give an answer to the question how many people 60 years or older will have adult near relatives who could nurse them if they needed care in the middle of the twenty-first century (to be precise: in the year 2040). To answer this question, a simple demographic simulation will not do. It is quite easy to predict the future age structure of a population with a system dynamics simulation with level variables for the size of a large number of age classes, but this simulation would not answer the question how many old people would be able to rely on their near relatives' nursing.

Table 4.5: Adult relatives of persons above 60, 2002 and 2040 (simulation results calculated from 2002 panel data and 1985 transition rates)

	Year	Age group			
		60+	*60–69*	*70-79*	*80+*
Cases	2002	7,871	4,040	2,072	759
	2040	7,577	3,081	3,118	1,378
Persons with					
partner	2002	63.3	74.6	59.7	27.7
	2040	43.4	56.8	40.9	18.0
children	2002	72.3	71.5	74.5	70.5
	2040	59.6	58.9	66.9	44.6
daughter	2002	51.5	52.0	52.4	47.2
	2040	44.0	37.7	48.7	47.5
Persons without					
partner/children	2002	13.9	11.8	13.6	22.9
	2040	22.4	23.5	21.3	22.4

So for our purpose, we have to simulate a complete kinship network. All persons must be modelled in a way that allows the recording of who their children and their brothers and sisters are. The algorithm described on page 61 and in Figure 4.2 can be used for this purpose, provided we attribute information about children, brothers and sisters to every person who ever 'lived' in this model.

The algorithm is even easier than in Figure 4.2 because we do not need to consider households. Instead we use only individual data and apply birth, death and marriage probabilities to update the microdata file year by year. Birth enters a new individual record into the database (with information about mother and father) and updates the father's and mother's record with information about the newborn child. Death marks a person as dead and removes him or her from the database. Marriage and divorce (or, more generally, entering and dissolving partnerships) update both partners' information. Then, after a number of simulation steps, we can trace kinship relations back and tell how many living children, brothers, sisters and cousins a person has at a given time. We can cross-tabulate these numbers of relatives with the person's age and arrive at an answer to our question. SPSS could not easily be used to solve this task although it was adequate for the simpler example on static microsimulation above. A relational or object-oriented database would be the appropriate tool, and UMDBS provides us both with a database and a database manipulation language.

A calculation like this was originally done in a large research project carried out at the Sonderforschungsbereich 3 (Sfb3) (Galler 1990; Hauser *et al.* 1994a: 130–133). It tried to answer the question for the year 2050. The simulation started from an ALLBUS sample drawn in 1986 and applied death, birth and marriage rates estimated from 1982–3 data (Hauser *et al.* 1994a: 132).

In our own example, the numbers for 2002 are taken from the GSOEP 2002 wave. In contrast to the Sfb3 model not only are relatives living in the same household considered, but so are all children who were ever born to women in the sample, no matter whether they were part of the panel or not.

The most striking result of this simulation is that some 40 years from now the percentage of persons above 60 years of age without a partner and without children will be two times the current percentage, except for the oldest cohort whose children were already born at the time of the interviews.

Commentary

Although in the context of this book only a brief overview of microsimulation models has been given, the discussion in the first section of this chapter and the two examples should have shown that microanalytical simulation models are a powerful means to predict both the short-term and long-term effects of taxes and transfer policy as well as micro effects of demographic processes. None of these can be studied with macro methods alone. Unlike the first efforts in microanalytical simulation in the 1970s, this type of simulation can be done on workstations, but – with the exception of UMDBS – toolboxes that could be used in the classroom are still not available. Hence, building microanalytical simulation models is still a task for specialists. Nowadays object-oriented languages such as C++ are used which enhance portability and maintenance. Models need not be written from scratch but can at least partially be reused. On the other hand, it would be quite difficult to design a toolbox for microanalytical simulation which could cope with the quite different requirements arising from quite different tax and transfer systems in a large number of countries. The most recent approach, EUROMOD, funded by the European Commission under its Targeted Socio-Economic Research Programme from 1998 to 2000, constructed a Europe-wide benefit–tax model which, again, is a model, but not a toolbox (see http://www.econ.cam.ac.uk/dae/mu/emodconstr.htm, Sutherland 2001 and Mitton *et al.* 2000: Chapter 6).

Further reading

There are a number of collections, mostly conference proceedings, which include articles about microsimulation models, such as:

- Harding, A. (ed.) (1996) *Microsimulation and Public Policy*, Contributions to Economic Analysis, vol. 232. Elsevier, Amsterdam.

This contains five chapters on static microsimulation from the United Kingdom, Canada, Belgium, the Netherlands and Finland, which cover both tax and social policy problems. Four chapters incorporate behavioural response, that is, reactions of the microunits to the political measures simulated in the respective models taken from Denmark, Sweden, Germany and the United Kingdom. Another part, with five chapters, addresses the estimation of lifetime and retirement incomes; examples are taken from Australia, the Netherlands, Germany, Sweden and Norway. Enterprise microsimulation is included in four chapters, with examples from Australia, Canada and Sweden. The last part of the collection addresses the problem of data quality and the reliability of microsimulation results.

Ten years earlier, another collection of papers devoted to microsimulation appeared:

- Orcutt, G. H. *et al.* (eds) (1986) *Microanalytic Simulation Models to Support Social and Financial Policy*, Information Research and Resource Reports, vol. 7. North-Holland, Amsterdam.

Besides four introductory chapters and seven concluding chapters on data, methods and software, it contains 12 chapters on social policy and tax simulation in the United States, Israel, Germany and Sweden.

In a number of countries, specialist institutes carry out microanalytical studies on a regular basis and publish part of their results. In Australia, the National Centre for Social and Economic Modelling publishes several series of booklets describing methods, software and simulation results (see http://www.natsem.canberra.edu.au/index.html).

Another Australian microsimulation group documents their results in

- Creedy, J., and Duncan, A. S. (2002) *Microsimulation Modelling of Taxation and the Labour Market: The Melbourne Institute Tax and Transfer Simulator.* Edward Elgar, Cheltenham.

This book discusses the rationale for the basic modelling approach adopted and provides information on econometric methods used to estimate behavioural relationships. Secondly, it describes the Melbourne Institute Tax and Transfer Simulator (MITTS) in detail, explaining its main features, installation and use.

For 12 years, the German Science Foundation funded a Special Collaborative Program (Sonderforschungsbereich) on the microanalytical foundations of social policy, whose final report was published in two volumes:

- Hauser, R. *et al.* (1994a) *Mikroanalytische Grundlagen der Gesellschaftspolitik. Ausgewählte Probleme und Lösungsansätze. Ergebnisse aus dem gleichnamigen Sonderforschungsbereich an den Universitäten Frankfurt und Mannheim*, vol. 1. Akademie-Verlag, Berlin.

- Hauser, R. *et al.* (1994b) *Mikroanalytische Grundlagen der Gesellschaftspolitik. Erhebungsverfahren, Analysemethoden und Mikrosimulation. Ergebnisse aus dem gleichnamigen Sonderforschungsbereich an den Universitäten Frankfurt und Mannheim*, vol. 2. Akademie-Verlag, Berlin.

British tax policy is analyzed in

- Redmond, G., Sutherland, H. and Wilson, M. (1998) *The Arithmetic of Tax and Social Security Reform: A User's Guide to Microsimulation Methods and Analysis.* Cambridge University Press, Cambridge.

This book serves as an introduction to the authors' POLIMOD microsimulation system and is based on the 1991 Family Expenditure Survey. The interesting thing about this book is that it tries to find out who were the winners and losers of British tax reforms since the mid-1970s.

A textbook on microsimulation models was designed to guide future investment in modelling and analysis capability on the part of the (US) government agencies that produce policy estimates:

- Citro, C. F. and Hanushek, E. A. (eds) (1991) *The Uses of Microsimulation Modelling. Vol. 1: Review and Recommendations.* National Academy Press, Washington, DC.

Another reader takes stock of the state of microsimulation models by looking carefully at those in use by US and Canadian government policy offices:

- Lewis, G. H. and Michel, R. C. (eds) (1989) *Microsimulation Techniques for Tax and Transfer Analysis.* Urban Institute Press, Washington, DC.

A more general view on microsimulation is given by

- Mitton, L., Sutherland, H., and Weeks, M. (eds) (2000): *Microsimulation Modelling for Policy Analysis: Challenges and Innovations.* Cambridge University Press, Cambridge.

It brings together examples of microsimulation modelling that are at the frontiers of developments in the field, either because they extend the range of techniques available to modellers, or because they demonstrate new applications for established methods. It represents the state of the art with chapters on the use of microsimulation for comparative policy research and for challenging conventional assumptions, combining microsimulation with other types of economic models and the much-neglected subjects of model alignment and validation. Data and case studies are taken from regions including Asia-Pacific, Europe and North America.

Chapter 5

Queuing models

Queuing models or discrete event models have a long tradition in a wide variety of sciences. In engineering, workflow management and several other disciplines, discrete event modelling is nearly synonymous with simulation. From the point of view of discrete event simulation, a model is a representation of a system 'in terms of its entities and their attributes, sets, events, activities, and delays' (Kheir 1988: 98). The notion of a system as 'a collection of entities that interact together over time to accomplish a set of goals or objectives' (Kheir 1988: 98) is quite common (see, for example, Bunge 1979), but the role of the 'event' as 'an instantaneous occurrence in time that alters the state of the system' is not central in all the other approaches to simulation introduced in this book. Differential equation models are continuous-time models, and system dynamics and microanalytical simulation models proceed in discrete and equidistant time steps, as is the case in difference equation models and in the modelling approaches presented in later chapters. Of course, these time steps are instantaneous occurrences in time that alter the state of the system, but since they are equidistant, there is nothing special about them. At each time step event all the system's state variables are changed, and the same state transition functions are applied. In discrete event modelling, events usually change only part of the system's state, in many cases just one or very few of the state variables of the system, leaving all other state variables of the system constant.

As in the rest of this book, the components of a system are called entities, and these are represented by model objects, and have properties that are represented by object attributes. The system state is defined by the values of all attributes of all objects, although for some purposes some aggregation of these attributes or a subset of these attributes might also be sufficient to describe the state of the system. The system state will only be changed by an event. Between two consecutive events nothing changes, not even implicitly.

Characteristics of queuing models

In a queuing model, time is neither continuous nor does it pass in equidistant discrete steps, but it proceeds from event to event. Events are scheduled in a so-called agenda, a list of all those future events which can be predetermined at a given time. Past events are removed from this list, and events may generate new events and insert them into the agenda.

In terms of the queuing metaphor of discrete event models, there are at least three different kinds of objects, namely *servers*, *customers* and *queues*. Technically speaking, there is one additional object, the *agenda*, which keeps track of the events and schedules them.

Queuing models are stochastic. In the queuing metaphor, the time between customers' arrivals as well as the time needed to serve a customer are random, following a certain random distribution.

Discrete event models are dynamic: states of servers, queues and customers depend on past states.

Areas of application of queuing models

Table 5.1 gives a few examples of the application of queuing models. Consider, for instance, a bank with a number of counters and clerks serving customers. At some time there might be more customers than can be served by the available personnel at the counters. In this case, a new customer, who arrives at an unpredictable time, queues up in front of a counter and waits until this counter is free. Then he or she is served – which takes a certain amount of time that neither the customer nor the clerk knows in advance. The question that arises is, given some statistical evidence about the distribution of arrival and service times, how many counters and clerks should be available to minimize both the customer's average waiting time and the clerks' idle time?

The same considerations apply to the other examples in Table 5.1: programs wait for the processor to be free, printing jobs wait for the printer to be free, aircraft wait for the runway to be free for the next take-off or landing,

Table 5.1: Areas of application of queuing models

Area	Server	Customer
Bank	counter, clerk	customer
Computer	processor, I/O device	program, printing task, user
Airport	gate, counter	passenger
	runway	aircraft
Publishing	journal	manuscripts
Auction	auctioneer	bids
Law	court	cases
Public administration	counter, officer	client, customer document, application

and in all cases we want to predict how long – on average – a program, a printing job, or an aircraft must wait until it is served, given certain mean arrival and service times.

While these are simple examples, we may imagine more complex situations. A passenger might first queue up in front of the information desk to enquire about the check-in counter he has to go to. The passenger will then move to the appropriate check-in counter (which takes some time, the average of which may be known in advance) where he or she again has to queue, together with a number of other passengers whose average arrival time may depend on the number of passenger requests the information desk can handle per hour. Service at the check-in counter takes some time which depends on whether the passenger has baggage to check in. After being served the passengers are sent to the appropriate gate where they arrive after some time, and so on.

Given that we know the statistical characteristics of all the arrival and service processes mentioned above, we can set up a schedule of prospective events of the type 'passenger A arrives at the tail of the queue in front of the information desk', or 'information desk starts serving passenger C' or 'check-in counter ends serving passenger D'. With a large number of events of this type, a realistic simulation of a working day in an airport can be established. Such a model proceeds from event to event:

- The event 'customer arrives' puts this customer in a queue, and at the same time schedules the event 'next customer arrives' at some time in the future.
- The event 'start serving next customer from queue' takes this customer from the queue up to the server, and at the same time schedules the

event 'customer served' at some time in the future.
- The event 'customer served' triggers the next event 'start serving next customer from queue'.

Between events, nothing relevant happens. Since most events schedule other events (as in the examples above), the event list is updated every time: the scheduled event is inserted into the event list at its appropriate position, and the actual event is removed from the head of the event list.

Ordinary discrete event simulation treats all events separately. In complex models, there will be lots of event routines (which describe what is to happen at this event) and lots of interactions between event routines (that is, one event will schedule another). This makes this type of simulation program difficult to read, to debug, to change and to maintain. More complex programming styles have been designed to avoid this 'fragmentation of model logic' (Kreutzer 1986: 58):

- Process orientation: the structure and behaviour of one (type of) customer are encapsulated in a process which is a life cycle of events; a process combines all events for one customer; processes are suspended and resumed at event times.
- Activity orientation: an activity clusters descriptions of state transitions at the start and finish of some time-consuming activity ('enter queue' and 'leave queue', or 'start serve' and 'finish serve').

Principles of queuing theory

Queuing models are often represented by diagrams like that in Figure 5.1. A source (much like the source in system dynamics diagrams) generates new customer objects which arrive in the system, join the queue in front of a server where they wait until they are served by the server. After being served they leave the system at the sink. Queues and servers are called *static objects* or *resources*, while customers are *dynamic objects*. Sources and sinks represent the environment of the target system.

Figure 5.2 visualizes the airport example. The 'source' represents the world outside the airport from which passengers arrive by car, bus or train. Their arrival times follow a certain distribution (more below) of which at least the mean will be known. Considering that arrival times cannot be negative, some initial assumptions about this distribution are possible. Once the distribution is known (or reasonably assumed), a random number generator can output the time of the next arrival event, and this event can be inserted

Figure 5.1: Diagram of a simple queuing model

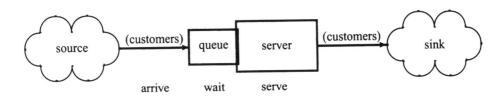

Figure 5.2: Diagram of a SIMPROCESS queuing model of an airport (parallel check-in counters and passport counters are not shown)

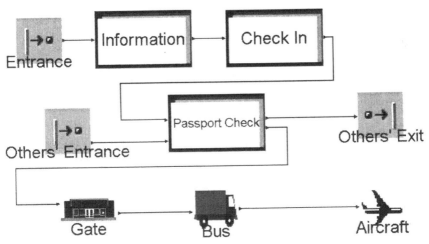

This model is designed from the point of view of one carrier which is responsible for a number of check-in counters and one gate and which has to take into account that other airlines share part of the facilities of the airport (here: the passport check and transport means); thus other airlines' passengers meet this carrier's passengers only at the passport check.

in the list of pending events. The same is true for the time the information desk needs for the average passenger. Hence the random number generator can output the time at which the service at the information desk will be completed for this passenger (which is equal to the time at which the next passenger in the queue can be served).

There will be several check-in counters in a typical airport, so the information desk must know where to send clients. The minimum time between end of service at the information desk and queuing up in front of the appropriate check-in counter will depend on the distance between the two entities (this time might be considered to be constant, but a normal distribution with a certain mean and a relatively small standard deviation might also be reasonable). Service time at the check-in counter depends on whether a passenger wants to check in any baggage.

There will also be several gates in a typical airport. Check-in counters will send their clients to one of several different gates, and clients arriving at a certain gate will have been sent from one of several counters (think of first-class, business and economy check-in counters that serve passengers for different flights at the same time). Check-in counters must know where to send their clients, and the minimum time between leaving the check-in counter and arriving at the gate will depend on the distance between the two entities. The maximum arrival time is when the aircraft leaves, and the actual arrival time will be some time between the earliest possible and the maximum arrival time. Service time for the gate might also depend on, for example, the passengers' hand baggage. At the end of the whole process the passenger is released to the sink, which in this case is the aircraft (where the passenger leaves the airport and enters the outer world).

Subprocesses

After this more elaborate example, we can return to a more systematic description of the subprocesses of a discrete event model. Three subprocesses may be distinguished.

In the *arrival process* we can distinguish

- between a finite (and fixed) number of arriving customers, and an unspecified (mathematically speaking, an infinite) number which is the usual case;
- between having only one or several types of customers (first-class, business and economy passengers);
- between the case of only one or several types of customer demands (for example, passengers with and without luggage);
- whether the arrival distance is deterministic or stochastic (for example, exponentially distributed), the latter being the usual case (the arrival rate – arrivals per time unit – is usually called λ, $\frac{1}{\lambda}$ being the mean time between arrivals);
- whether the arrival rate depends on the queue length (passengers who

only want to buy a ticket for a trip next week might return home – that is, 'not arrive' – if they think the queue is too long).

In the *waiting process* we can distinguish

- whether the length of the queue is finite and fixed, or infinite (the latter is the usual case);
- among several different orders of service, the most usual case being first in first out (FIFO), where new customers are appended to the tail of the queue while the customer at the head of the queue is served next. Another common order of service is the LIFO principle (last in first out). Service may also be ordered by priorities borne by the customers, or at random.

Finally, in the *service process* we have to distinguish

- whether only one or several servers are available at the same time and for the same type of customers and customer demands; the usual case is with one server per queue, but the case with one queue and several servers (each of whom calls the next customer from the head of the queue when it becomes free) is also quite common;
- whether there is only one or a number of types of servers (in a more complex model we will have many different types of servers in line, or in parallel, as in the airport example above, where information desk, check-in counter and gate are different types of counters, and parallel check-in counters may also be different, for example for first-class, business and economy passengers);
- between a constant serving rate and a serving rate dependent on customer demands (for example, different serving rates at the check-in counter for passengers with and without baggage);
- between a fixed (deterministic) serving time and a stochastic (random) serving time (which might be exponentially distributed). The serving rate (number of customers per time unit) is usually called μ, $\frac{1}{\mu}$ being the mean serving time.

Depending on the combination of alternatives realized in a particular model, some types of queuing models have an analytical solution. The mean system load can be determined by $\rho = \frac{\lambda}{\mu}$. Other interesting parameters are:

$\bar{N}$	mean number of objects (customers) in the system;
$\bar{N}_q$	mean number of objects in queue;
$\bar{N}_s$	mean number of objects being served;
$\bar{W}$	mean waiting time;

$\bar{W}_q$ mean waiting time in queue;
$\bar{W}_s$ mean waiting time at server.

In simple cases, these values can be calculated analytically, but otherwise they must be determined by simulation experiments. To be analytically solvable, queuing models must fulfil the following conditions. The arrival rate must be lower than the serving rate (otherwise queues might grow endlessly). Arrival and service processes must obey particular distributions. For instance, a model with Markov arrival and service processes and any number of parallel servers has an analytical solution, as has a model with Markov arrival and general service process and only one server. A Markov process is a process where 'the probability of any particular future behaviour of the process, when its present state is known exactly, is not altered by additional knowledge concerning its past behaviour' (Karlin and Taylor 1975: 29; more details will be found throughout this book).

Software

There are a large number of simulation tools for discrete event simulation. The earliest tools originated from subroutine libraries in general-purpose programming languages such as FORTRAN (Schmidt 1987) and PASCAL (Kreutzer 1986). Later, simulation languages were developed, among them GPSS, SimScript and CSL. In recent years, there has been a preference for simulation systems that allow a graphical specification of a model as well as a number of (possibly animated) simulation experiments and the statistical and graphical analysis of their results. The following list gives a few examples:

- SimScript (now in version II.5), SimLab, MODSIM II and SIMPRO-CESS (http://www.caciasl.com, CACI Products Company 2003 and the examples below);
- SIMPLEX 3 (http://www.or.uni-passau.de/english/3/simplex.php3 – freeware from the University of Passau and successor to SIMPLEX II);
- SIMPLE++, now known as emPlant (http://www.emplant.de/simulation.html);
- Extend 6.0.5 (http://www.imaginethatinc.com/);
- AnyLogic (http://www.xjtek.com/).

Examples

The airport example

The following shows a SimLab queuing model which includes most of the features of the airport example above.[1] We use it to introduce some features of the SimScript II.5 language. SimScript applies the process-oriented simulation paradigm briefly discussed above. The simulation program consists of a number of modules. Some of them are used to describe the different entities and processes of the model, while others are only used to display graphics on the screen (we will not discuss these here). SimScript is quite a straightforward language. Readers with programming experience in general-purpose languages will be able to build a SimScript model like our airport model in little more than an afternoon.

The important declarations have to be made in a preamble, which in our case contains the following statements:

```
preamble
  processes include generator and passenger
  resources include InformationDesk, CheckInCounter,
    and Gate
  accumulate AVG.InformationDesk.Queue.Length as the
    average and MAX.InformationDesk.Queue.Length as the
    maximum of N.Q.InformationDesk
  accumulate AVG.CheckInCounter.Queue.Length as the
    average and MAX.CheckInCounter.Queue.Length as the
    maximum of N.Q.CheckInCounter
  accumulate AVG.Gate.Queue.Length as the average
    and MAX.Gate.Queue.Length as the maximum
    of N.Q.Gate
  accumulate InformationDesk.Utilization as the average
    of N.X.InformationDesk
  accumulate CheckInCounter.Utilization as the average
    of N.X.CheckInCounter
  accumulate Gate.Utilization as the average of
    N.X.Gate
'' several definitions needed for graphic output
'' omitted
  define ServedCounter as an integer, 1-dimensional
    array
  define .First to mean 1
  define .Business to mean 2
```

---

[1] Note that AnyLogic comes with a demonstration model of an airport simulation that is much more sophisticated than the one we discuss here.

```
define .Economy to mean 3
end
```

The first two lines declare the processes and the resources, and the next lines (accumulate ...) declare a number of output variables. These declarations of average and maximum queue lengths and the average resource utilizations are readily understandable. With the declaration of a resource, the number of requests currently waiting, that is, the length of its queue (N.Q.*resource*), and the number of requests currently being satisfied (N.X.*resource*) are also defined.

The main module initializes the resources (create every ...) with a number of instances (let U.*resource name* = *number*), activates the first process, which is the generator, and starts the simulation. At this point, control is given to the generator process and its child processes.

```
main
  reserve ServedCounter(*) as 5
'' an array is declared to hold the number of
'' passengers served by each resource
  create every InformationDesk(1)
  let U.InformationDesk(1) = 1
  create every CheckInCounter(3)
'' we need three different kinds of check-in counters
  let U.CheckInCounter(.First) = 1
  let U.CheckInCounter(.Business) = 2
  let U.CheckInCounter(.Economy) = 4
'' two Business and four Economy counters are created
  create every Gate(1)
  let U.Gate = 1
'' all resources are ready
  activate a generator now
  start simulation
'' The print statement starts here and extends to the end
'' of this code segment. 'thus ...' is a template for the
'' printed output.
  print 14 lines with AVG.InformationDesk.Queue.Length(1),
    MAX.InformationDesk.Queue.Length(1),
    InformationDesk.Utilization(1)
    * 100./U.InformationDesk(1),
    ServedCounter(1),
    AVG.CheckInCounter.Queue.Length(.First),
    MAX.CheckInCounter.Queue.Length(.First),
    CheckInCounter.Utilization(.First)
    * 100./U.CheckInCounter(.First),
    ServedCounter(2),
    AVG.CheckInCounter.Queue.Length(.Business),
```

```
MAX.CheckInCounter.Queue.Length(.Business),
CheckInCounter.Utilization(.Business)
* 100./U.CheckInCounter(.Business),
ServedCounter(3),
AVG.CheckInCounter.Queue.Length(.Economy),
MAX.CheckInCounter.Queue.Length(.Economy),
CheckInCounter.Utilization(.Economy)
* 100./U.CheckInCounter(.Economy),
ServedCounter(4),
AVG.Gate.Queue.Length(1),
MAX.Gate.Queue.Length(1),
Gate.Utilization(1) * 100./U.Gate(1),
ServedCounter(5)
thus
Airport with different check-in counters
  average queue waiting for information desk is ***.*** passengers
  maximum queue waiting for information desk is **** passengers
  information desk was busy **.** per cent of the time, served ****
  passengers

  The queues for the check-in counters were as follows:
  type      average      maximum      utilization    passengers served
  First     *.***        *            *.** per cent  ****
  Business  *.***        *            *.** per cent  ****
  Economy   *.***        *            *.** per cent  ****

  average queue waiting for the gate is ***.*** passengers
  maximum queue waiting for the gate is **** passengers
  gate was busy **.** per cent of the time, served **** passengers.
end
```

The last (`print 14 lines with ...`) statement is executed after the simulation has stopped. It outputs the result of a simulation run.

The generator process generates a number of passenger processes. Remember that in process-oriented discrete event simulation, all events belonging to the same type of dynamic object ('customer') are encapsulated in a 'process'. The following code segment activates a (new) passenger and then waits for some time – the inter-arrival time – until it activates the next passenger. In our example, the inter-arrival time is an exponentially distributed random number with mean 1.5 minutes. For a more thorough discussion of random numbers for simulation see Appendix C.

```
process generator
  for i = 1 to 1000,
  do
    activate a passenger now
```

```
    wait exponential.f(1.5, 1) minutes
  loop
end
```

The passenger process contains most of the description of our model:

```
process passenger
  define luggage as an integer variable
  define randLugg as a real variable
  define grade as an integer variable
  define randPass as a real variable
'' determine the class the passenger is booked on
  let randPass = random.f(3)
  if randPass < 0.10     '' ten per cent of all passengers
    let grade = .First    '' fly first class
    if randLugg < 0.70    '' 70 per cent of first class
      let luggage = 1     '' passengers have luggage
    else
      let luggage = 0
    always '' this is the end of the if clause
  else
    if randPass < 0.40 '' another 30 per cent fly business
      let grade = .Business
      if randLugg < 0.30 '' 30 per cent of business
        let luggage = 1  '' passengers have luggage
      else
        let luggage = 0
      always
    else '' and the rest, 60 per cent, fly economy
      let grade = .Economy
      if randLugg < 0.70   '' 70 per cent of economy
        let luggage = 1    '' passengers have luggage
      else
        let luggage = 0
      always
    always
  always
'' now the passenger is ready to enter the airport
  request 1 InformationDesk(1)
  work exponential.f(1.0, 2) minutes
  let ServedCounter(1) = ServedCounter(1) + 1
  relinquish 1 InformationDesk(1)
  wait uniform.f(5.0, 8.0, 2) minutes
  request 1 CheckInCounter(grade)
  if luggage = 1
    work uniform.f(5.0, 20.0, 2) minutes
  else
    work uniform.f(2.0, 4.0, 2) minutes
```

```
always
  let ServedCounter(grade+1) = ServedCounter(grade+1) + 1
  relinquish 1 CheckInCounter(grade)
  wait uniform.f(10.0, 20.0, 2) minutes
  request 1 Gate
  work uniform.f(1.0, 2.0, 2) minutes
  let ServedCounter(5) = ServedCounter(5) + 1
  relinquish 1 Gate
end
```

The first part of the passenger process code segment determines which class the passenger is booked in and whether he or she has luggage to check in. Here we have assumed that business class passengers have luggage in 30 per cent of the cases whereas 70 per cent of first-class and economy passengers have luggage.

Passengers first walk to the information desk where they queue up, and when it is their turn to be served, they spend an exponentially distributed random time with mean 1.0 minutes ('work' means that the information desk has to work for the passenger). After leaving the information desk ('relinquish') passengers walk to their check-in counters which takes them between 5 and 8 minutes. From the point of view of the simulation program, this walking time is waiting time. When passengers arrive at their check-in counters they can either be served at once or they have to queue up. In our example there will be only one queue for the four economy class check-in counters and only one for the two business counters (in most airports, however, there is a queue for each individual counter). When it is their turn, passengers with luggage will be served, which may take them between 5 and 20 minutes, while passengers without luggage will be served in between 2 and 4 minutes. After leaving the check-in counter, passengers take another walk of 10–20 minutes before they arrive at the gate, where a security check is taken, which lasts between 1 and 2 minutes. After having passed the gate, they leave our system.

The lines beginning with let ServedCounter ... are used to count how many passengers have been served by the different resources.

The simulation stops when all passengers generated by the generator process have been served. Then the print statement in the main module is executed, yielding the following result:

```
Airport with different check-in counters
  average queue waiting for information desk is    .874 passengers
  maximum queue waiting for information desk is   9 passengers
  information desk was busy 62.48 per cent of the time, served 1000
    passengers
```

```
The queues for the check-in counters were as follows:
type      average    maximum    utilization    passengers served
First      .359       4         52.52 per cent  105
Business   .331       6         50.77 per cent  294
Economy   5.058      19         92.87 per cent  601

average queue waiting for the gate is  10.978 passengers
maximum queue waiting for the gate is   26 passengers
gate was busy 97.39 per cent of the time, served 1000 passengers.
```

As defined in the code of the passenger module, about 10 per cent of all passengers (exactly 10.5 per cent in this run) are first-class passengers, 29.4 per cent fly business, and 60.1 per cent fly economy.

We see that the bottleneck of this system is the gate, with its average queue length of about 11 passengers (for which there might not be enough room). The queue length in front of the check-in counters seems tolerable, even with an average of five and a maximum of 19 economy passengers waiting to be served. First-class and business class passengers were served at once in most cases, and their counters were idle about half the time. So the only measure that would need be taken would be to increase the capacity of the gate.

The airport model in a graphical environment

The following shows another version of the airport model, which was designed with the help of the graphical user interface of SIMPROCESS, which again includes most of the features of the airport example above. We use it to introduce some features of 'an object-oriented process modeling and analysis tool that combines the simplicity of flowcharting with the power of simulation and statistical analysis' (this is SIMPROCESS's self-description on the first page of its built-in help system). SIMPROCESS, too, applies the process-oriented simulation paradigm briefly discussed above.

Even readers with little or no programming experience will be able to build a SIMPROCESS model like our airport model in little more than an afternoon. No programming in a general-purpose or specialized programming language is necessary, because (nearly) the whole modelling process is performed by copying and pasting graphical symbols on the computer screen (and giving these symbols names and some attributes when at a right mouse click windows open to allow editing of processes, activities and entities), as is true, for example, for STELLA too (see Chapter 3).

Figure 5.2 shows the top-level view of the airport model. Symbols are 'activities' in terms of SIMPROCESS, and rectangular boxes are (the default icons for) 'processes' which consist of lower-level processes and, eventually, of activities. The process boxes can be opened to allow a view into their internal structure – see Figure 5.3 for an example of the internal structure of the passport check process.

Figure 5.3: Internal structure of the information, the check-in and the passport check processes of the airport model

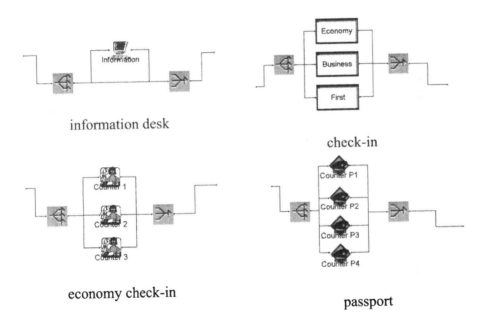

information desk

check-in

economy check-in

passport

Figure 5.2 shows that the passengers of the carrier in question and those of other airlines are generated by two separate 'generators' (or sources, as we called them above, named 'Entrance' and 'Others' Entrance'). These sources generate different types of passengers at different arrival rates which may be constants or random variables (distributed according to any of about 27 distributions).

We are interested in the 'other passengers' only in so far as they have to pass the same passport check as 'our' passengers, so we concentrate on what happens to 'our' passengers – who come as first-class, business class and economy class passengers. First they go to an information point (which they can use or not, see Figure 5.3, top left), then they are directed to the check-in area where they will queue up in front of the appropriate type of check-in counter (which is equipped with 'resources' of type clerk in this model). The server to which they move next is the passport check (equipped with 'resources' of type officer) where they are mixed up with the 'other' passengers (from which they are separated immediately after the passport check), then they proceed to the gate, from which they are transported by a bus to their aircraft which serves as a sink in the terms introduced earlier.

Branch and merge activities (with appropriate symbols shown in Figure 5.3) serve to send passengers to their appropriate destinations. They are defined in editor windows and attributed the necessary parameters, for example to send passengers (bottom left) to the respective economy check-in counters with equal probability, or (top right) to the class-specific check-in counter areas according to the passengers' tickets. The same applies to the definitions of delay activities. Delays usually use resources to serve a customer's needs, and also represent the queues of customers waiting in front of a server when the delay activity is not endowed with sufficient resources to serve all customers. Two examples of editor windows for delays are shown in Figure 5.4.

Figure 5.4: Editor window for specifying attributes to activities

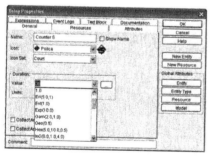
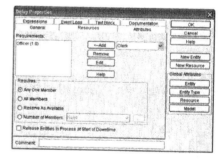

Delay properties: general   Delay properties: resources

In the left-hand window, the name and icon of the activity can be chosen, and the duration can be defined. The pop-down list at 'Duration' allows a wide choice among various random distributions[2] and units (from nanoseconds to years) can be chosen. In the right-hand window in Figure 5.4,

---

[2]Constant, Erlang, Evl(), Exponential, Gamma, Hyperexponential and Inverse Gaussian can be seen in the pop-down list; Evl() permits the insertion of an arbitrary expression that will de evaluated whenever a customer enters this activity, the constant being the simplest

resources can be allocated to the activity. In this example, exactly one officer per counter was chosen, but it would also have been possible to allocate two or more resources of the same kind or different kinds and to define any or all of them as required (with the radio buttons below the 'Requirements' text field). Editor windows for other purposes (for defining generate, branch, merge and dispose activities, to name the most important activities) look much the same.

SIMPROCESS, besides offering graphical output (time series of various, user-definable counters and measures), collects most of the relevant information in a so-called standard report, which, in contrast to SimLab/SIMSCRIPT II.5 does not need to be defined by the modeller. Part of this standard report is shown and commented on in the following:

```
SIMPROCESS Standard Report for Airport
Simulation Initiated at Thu Jun 03 12:34:02 2004
Simulation Concluded at Thu Jun 03 12:34:19 2004
```

The report first identifies the simulation run with a time stamp and then continues with the numbers of generated entities of each type. This run simulated 19 hours (from 4 a.m. to 11 p.m.) where 'our' airline served approximately 1,800 passengers (and the airport as a whole saw 15,500 passengers), as is shown in the next portion (in which 'Replication 1' reminds us of the fact that SIMPROCESS allows experiments with a number of simulation runs executed in parallel; in this case statistics of the parallel runs are also calculated).

```
Entity : Total Count - Observation Based : Replication 1
```

Entity Names	Total Generated	Remaining In System	Total Processed
First	82	2	80
Business	224	2	222
Economy	1520	22	1498
Other Passengers	13716	6	13710

This segment also tells that a few passengers remained in the system when the simulation run was stopped at 11 p.m. of simulated time. The next portion gives an overview of how much time the different entities spent in the system for different purposes:

---

expression, while the others are probability distributions whose density and distributions can also be viewed after pressing the '...' button next to the pop-down list.

```
Entity : Cycle Time (in Minutes) By State - Observation Based : Replication 1
```

		Total In System-----		Processing-----		Wait For Resources		Hold For Conditions	
Entity Names	Observed	Average	Maximum	Average	Maximum	Average	Maximum	Average	Maximum
First	80	25.257	46.871	5.714	21.321	2.935	14.508	16.608	39.358
Business	222	23.838	48.472	5.814	17.148	2.815	14.354	15.210	36.429
Economy	1498	25.211	57.917	6.922	27.150	2.900	19.351	15.388	39.529
Other Passengers	13710	0.502	0.667	0.499	0.500	0.003	0.167	0.000	0.000

Passengers spent up to an hour (slightly less than half an hour on average) in the system (first and business class passengers considerably less), of which – on average – only a few minutes were spent being serviced at counters, but processing could last up to nearly half an hour; waiting in a queue ('wait for resources') lasted 3 minutes on average and up to 20 minutes at most, while most of the time was spent waiting in the gate for being transported to the aircraft. The next portion shows the average work load of the two types of resources: at peak times, all of them were busy, but on an average 8.3 per cent of the clerks and 15 per cent of the passport check officers were idle.

```
Resource : Number of Units By State - TimeWeighted : Replication 1
```

		--------Idle--------		--------Busy--------	
Resource Names	Capacity	Average	Maximum	Average	Maximum
Clerk	10.000	0.831	10.000	9.169	10.000
Officer	8.000	1.204	8.000	6.796	8.000

A more detailed part of the standard report lists all types of entities and their time spent during the various processes and activities. Only a short segment of this report is reproduced here (and the 'hold for conditions' columns are discarded because the only entry is in the last line, saying that the mean waiting time for a bus was 15.42 minutes and at most 39.529 minutes):

```
Activity : Entity Cycle Time (in Minutes) By State at Selected Activity - Observation Based :
Replication 1
```

		Total In Process		Processing-----		Wait For Resources	
Activity Names	Entity Names	Average	Maximum	Average	Maximum	Average	Maximum
Information	First	5.057	18.961	3.149	16.321	1.909	7.400
Information	Economy	5.201	21.150	3.021	21.150	2.179	11.585
Information	Business	5.241	15.522	2.780	12.148	2.461	9.167
First Counter	First	6.441	14.491	4.000	4.000	2.425	10.491
Business Counter	Business	6.085	13.043	4.000	4.000	2.085	9.043
Economy Counter 3	Economy	7.260	16.771	5.000	5.000	2.260	11.771
Economy Counter 2	Economy	7.288	17.148	5.000	5.000	2.284	12.148
Economy Counter 1	Economy	7.161	16.428	5.000	5.000	2.153	11.428
Passport Check		0.504	0.667	0.000	0.000	0.000	0.000
Passport Check Counter 1		0.504	0.667	0.500	0.500	0.004	0.167
Passport Check Counter 2		0.504	0.667	0.500	0.500	0.003	0.167
Passport Check Counter 3		0.503	0.667	0.500	0.500	0.003	0.167
Passport Check Counter 4		0.504	0.667	0.500	0.500	0.004	0.167
Passport Check Counter 5		0.504	0.667	0.500	0.500	0.004	0.167
Passport Check Counter 6		0.504	0.667	0.500	0.500	0.004	0.167
Passport Check Counter 7		0.503	0.639	0.500	0.500	0.003	0.139
Passport Check Counter 8		0.504	0.667	0.500	0.500	0.004	0.167
Gate		0.500	0.500	0.500	0.500	0.000	0.000
Bus		15.118	39.529	0.000	0.000	0.000	0.000

We see that this run does not show any serious bottlenecks, instead one could think that the number of officers serving in the passport check could be reduced, since they were idle 15 per cent of the time. So we might reduce their number to seven and see what happens:

```
Resource : Number of Units By State - TimeWeighted : Replication 1
```

		--------Idle--------		--------Busy--------	
Resource Names	Capacity	Average	Maximum	Average	Maximum
Clerk	10.000	0.831	10.000	9.169	10.000
Officer	7.000	0.204	7.000	6.796	7.000

As expected, the average number of idle officers is decreased by one. And this is what happens to the passengers:

```
Activity : Entity Cycle Time (in Minutes) By State at Selected Activity - Observation
Based : Replication 1
```

		Total In Process		Processing-----		Wait For Resources	
Activity Names	Entity Names	Average	Maximum	Average	Maximum	Average	Maximum
Passport Check	Counter 1	0.552	0.849	0.500	0.500	0.052	0.349
Passport Check	Counter 2	0.552	0.833	0.500	0.500	0.052	0.333
Passport Check	Counter 3	0.554	0.833	0.500	0.500	0.054	0.333
Passport Check	Counter 4	0.552	0.750	0.500	0.500	0.052	0.250
Passport Check	Counter 5	0.553	0.833	0.500	0.500	0.053	0.333
Passport Check	Counter 6	0.555	0.833	0.500	0.500	0.055	0.333
Passport Check	Counter 7	0.552	0.833	0.500	0.500	0.052	0.333
Passport Check	Counter 8	0.551	0.833	0.500	0.500	0.051	0.333

The constant processing time of half a minute is of course not changed, the maximum time passengers had to wait in the queue is slightly increased – from about 10 seconds to some 20 seconds, which seems still tolerable.

SIMPROCESS models are designed graphically, so no code has to be written (at least not for models of a complexity comparable to our example), so no code can be published. But SIMPROCESS models are stored in XML, and they can be published both in XML and HTML. The code of the airport example is available at the Web site of this book.

Commentary

The examples will have shown that the discrete event simulation approach is appropriate for a class of problems which in the wider sense belong to the social sciences (business and public administration, management science, the analysis of workflow and business processes) where it is tempting to model entities in the target system as customers, servers and queues. This approach is used to detect bottlenecks and to redesign workflow and business processes. The information necessary for modelling and simulation consists of two parts: the structure of the target system (which resources a customer will use, which ways a customer will take through the system, stepping from resource to resource) and the empirical data for inter-arrival and serving times. Bottlenecks can, of course, be detected in the target system itself, but to develop strategies to avoid bottlenecks, simulation can be helpful because the structure of the model can be changed until bottlenecks disappear or become tolerable. When a satisfactory solution is found, the target system can be re-engineered. In the case of our first example, we might try to open a second security check post that would reduce the average queue length and waiting time at the gate.

The discrete event methodology can also be used in other contexts. In microanalytical simulation models (cf. Chapter 4), it may be used to avoid recalculating states of microunits which are known to be constant for a long time, such as the marital status of a person; so far, this has only been done in the DYNAMOD model (see p. 65 and Antcliff 1993). In multi-agent simulation it can be used for the same purpose (see, for example, Troitzsch 2004a).

What is beyond the methodology of discrete event models is adaptive behaviour on the part of the customers. Although customers are called 'dynamic objects' in discrete event simulation, they do not change their behaviour during the simulation. For example, they do not decide to leave a queue when they have waited for too long a time, or to change to a shorter queue (in our first example: to upgrade from economy to business to avoid long waiting times in front of the economy check-in counter). In a target system where each counter has a queue of its own, customers may even change queues without upgrading – which cannot be modelled at all.

Further reading

There is a vast literature on discrete event simulation. For the beginner, we recommend:

- Kreutzer, W. (1986) *System Simulation. Programming Styles and Languages*. Addison-Wesley, Sydney.

This describes discrete event simulation at an introductory level and with a number of examples written in the widespread PASCAL language. Most textbooks on simulation contain chapters on discrete event simulation, among them:

- Zeigler, B. P. (1985) *Theory of Modelling and Simulation*, pp. 125–196. Krieger, Malabar. Second edition: Zeigler, B. P., Praehofer, H., and Kim, T. G. (2000) *Theory of Modelling and Simulation. Second Edition. Integrating Discrete Event Continuous Complex Dynamic Systems*, Academic Press, San Diego, CA;

- Kheir, N. A. (ed.) (1988) *Systems Modeling and Computer Simulation*, pp. 97–135 and 567–596. Marcel Dekker, New York, NY. ;

- Pidd, M. (1984) *Computer Simulation in Management Science*, pp. 33–178. Wiley, Chichester;

- Bratley, P. *et al.* (1987) *A Guide to Simulation*, 2nd edn. Springer-Verlag, New York, NY.

All of these include the fundamentals of queuing systems, and although they were published a decade ago, they still provide the basic insights into this type of modelling.

Although other simulation techniques beside discrete event simulation have been used in many scientific disciplines, there are still lots of books on discrete event simulation which are just titled 'simulation', such as

- Chung, C. A. (2003) *Simulation Modeling Handbook: A Practical Approach.* CRC Press, Boca Raton, FL;

- Rubinstein, R.Y. and Melamed, B. (1998) *Modern Simulation and Modeling.* Wiley Interscience, New York, NY;

- Banks, J. (ed.) (1998) *Handbook of Simulation: Principles, Methodology, Advances, Applications, and Practice.* Wiley, New York, NY

where the latter starts with the remark 'The purpose of this handbook is to provide a reference to important topics that pertain to discrete event simulation' (Banks 1998: 3), while the back cover describes the handbook as 'the only complete guide to all aspects and uses of simulation'.

Chapter 6

Multilevel simulation models

In the 1980s and early 1990s, the first simulation environment – MIMOSE – was developed for simulating interacting populations. Figure 6.1 shows the template for this kind of simulation model. The typical case is that there is a population with its attributes (for example, its size, its birth and death rates and its gender distribution), homogeneously consisting of a possibly great number of individuals with their own attributes (such as sex, age, political attitudes or annual income). Population attributes depend on aggregated individual attributes, and these in turn depend on the population attributes. For example, the gender distribution of the population depends on how many individuals are male and how many female, and whether an individual is born or dies depends on the population's birth and death rates, which in turn may depend on the population size and sex ratio (see p. 47).

For computational reasons, a cyclic dependence within the same time step is forbidden, hence typically in each simulation step individual attributes are evaluated as depending on the values that the population attributes had in the previous simulation step, and population attributes are evaluated after all individual attributes in the same simulation step. From the outset, MIMOSE allowed an unrestricted number of object types (which may, but need not, be seen as levels in the sense of Bunge 1979: 13).

Hence, MIMOSE is also capable of performing classical microsimulation (see Chapter 4) where we often have a large number of persons, each belonging to a household, all of them making up a (sample of a) population. Earlier microanalytical simulation models did not include a complete feedback loop between persons or households and population in both directions.

Figure 6.1: Objects, attributes and their relations in *multilevel modelling* (including some direct interactions between objects of the same type)

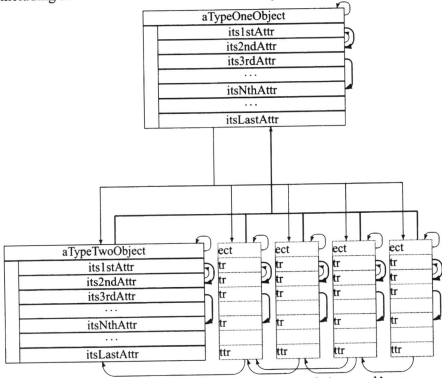

'a ⟶ b' means 'b's present depends on a's past', 'a ⟶ b' means 'b's present depends on a's present'. Note that some objects of type two depend on the past of some other objects of the same type.

In the terms of Figure 6.1, thick arrows (⟶) were used to aggregate data to the population level, but these aggregate attributes were then not used to control individual behaviour – there is no feedback from the reactions of microentities on to the macro policies. Microentities respond to changed tax laws, but within a microanalytical simulation model macro policies are not changed because of this response, only by the experimenter. This is why microanalytical simulation models were sometimes classified as static (Henize 1984: 571) – which is a little misleading because microanalytical simulation models are themselves classified as either static or dynamic (see p. 60).

The multilevel modelling technique described so far allows only for an indirect interaction between individuals. Each individual evaluates his or her environment as a whole and reacts to it, changing the environment by his or her behaviour. This is sufficient for models like the ones described in the next few paragraphs. In these we assume large populations whose members are influenced to change their attitudes by some factor such as the media and that personal interaction leading to opinion change is of less impact. Although it can be shown that models of this kind explain some interesting phenomena, they cannot explain effects in social networks or small groups where interactions are not only global, but also local, between individuals. Local, or direct, interactions necessitate an extension of the 'interacting populations' approach to include 'direct interactions', which is also possible in MIMOSE (again see Figure 6.1).

Multilevel simulation proceeds in six steps, as most simulation does:

1. Identify some part of reality as a 'real system' consisting of elements of different 'natural kinds' (Bunge 1977: 143); that is, define the target for modelling (as we put it in Chapter 2), and represent its elements by model objects.
2. Identify relations defined on the 'natural kinds' of these elements ('what depends on what?').
3. Identify the properties of the elements and represent them by model object attributes.

These three steps – steps 2 and 3 are easily interchangeable – are, by the way, also covered by the static entity-relationship approach to database modelling (Chen 1976) in computer science.

4. Detect – or rather reconstruct – the laws governing that part of reality we are about to model ('what are the dependences like?', 'system representation' (Kreutzer 1986: 2) – making assumptions in the terms of Chapter 2).
5. Combine our notions of the laws governing reality into a model written down in a formal language (a computer programming language), thus representing real-world elements and their properties with (programming language) objects and their attributes, and empirical laws with program invariants.
6. Run the simulation program.

Some synergetics

The classical example of a formal model of interacting populations is concerned with a single population of people whose decision on a certain issue may be either 'yes' or 'no' (Weidlich and Haag 1983); at the beginning, the most probable majority is 50 per cent. Depending on how strongly individuals' opinions are coupled (κ) to the prevailing majority, after a while the proportion of 'yes' decisions may be bimodally distributed, with most probable 'yes' percentages being either about 10 or 90 per cent. Figure 6.2 shows two results (for low and high κ, respectively) of a numerical evaluation of the model yielding the time-dependent probability distribution of finding the population with a certain 'yes' percentage.

Figure 6.2: Opinion formation in a homogeneous population (left: $\kappa = 0.5$, right: $\kappa = 1.5$; horizontal axis, 'yes' percentage; diagonal axis, time; vertical axis, probability of finding a population with a certain percentage at a certain time)

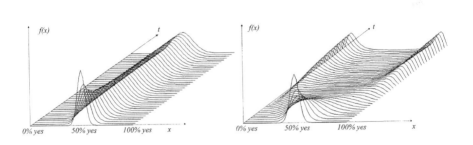

This model was one of the first published under the heading of synergetics (Weidlich 1972), 'an interdisciplinary field of research, [which] is concerned with the cooperation of individual parts of a system that produces macroscopic spatial, temporal or functional structures', as Haken (1978: ii), who coined the term, put it.[1] In Weidlich's example, the 'individual parts' are the members of the population (the 'system'), 'cooperation' is achieved through the coupling between individual opinion formation and the prevailing majority, and in the end, a 'macroscopic structure' may arise in so far as a very strong majority may develop out of a small initial majority. Another example of a phenomenon that can be described by synergetics is the phenomenon of clapping in time or the synchronous clapping of an enthusiastic audience which suddenly starts from 'white noise' applause when a certain level of intensity is reached (but to describe this phenomenon, synergetic techniques other than those described in this section must be used – see Babloyantz 1980; an der Heiden 1992).

---

[1] Meanwhile, synergetics is more or less embraced by the sociophysics movement.

We can describe the opinion formation model mathematically as a stochastic process – which means that at least some of the state changes in the model come about only with a certain probability. Thus, the core of this mathematical model is made up of the individual transition probabilities from 'yes' to 'no' and vice versa. These probabilities may be written down as follows:

$$
\begin{aligned}
\mu_{yes \leftarrow no} &= \nu \exp(\pi + \kappa x) \\
\mu_{no \leftarrow yes} &= \nu \exp\left[-(\pi + \kappa x)\right]
\end{aligned}
\tag{6.1}
$$

$$
x = \frac{n_{yes} - n_{no}}{n_{yes} + n_{no}}
\tag{6.2}
$$

The parameters in the individual transition probabilities have the following meaning ('exp' is the exponential function, which in the context of this model has the advantages of never being negative and of easy mathematical treatment):

- ν is a general 'flexibility' parameter; the higher it is, the higher will be both transition probabilities, and the more often will opinion change happen, regardless of the direction of the change.
- π is a preference parameter; the higher it is, the higher will be the probability of changing to 'yes', and the lower will be the probability of changing to 'no'; $\pi = 0$ means neither 'yes' nor 'no' is preferred in the absence of coupling, and $\pi < 0$ means a bias in favour of 'no'.
- x is a scaled variable that describes the majority in a population: $x = -1$ means 'all no', $x = 0$ means 'split half', and $x = 1$ means 'all yes'. Some mathematical derivations are easier with this scaled variable than with the numbers of 'yes' (n_{yes}) and 'no' (n_{no}).
- κ is a coupling parameter; if it is high, then the influence of a 'yes' majority on an individual change to 'yes' is high (and the same is true for the influence of a 'no' majority on an individual change to 'no'; with low κ this influence is also low). If $\kappa = 0$, then neither individual transition probability depends on the opinion distribution.
- N is half the total number of individuals in the population (which might seem a little strange but brings some convenience in deriving the mathematical results).

If n is defined as:

$$
n = \frac{n_{yes} - n_{no}}{2}
\tag{6.3}
$$

then we obtain equation (6.2), which we can also write as

$$
x = \frac{2n_{yes}}{2N} - 1
\tag{6.4}
$$

Note that:

$$-N \leq n \leq N$$
$$-1 \leq x \leq 1$$
$$n_{yes} - n_{no} = 2n$$
$$n_{yes} + n_{no} = 2N$$

from which a 'master equation' – a system of differential equations for the time-dependent distribution of populations – may be derived.

Let $p(n; t)$ be the probability that the population attains state n at time t. Then, for all times t,

$$\sum_{n=-N}^{N} p(n; t) = 1$$

Now we analyze the changes in $p(n; t)$ during a time span Δt which is designed to be so short that at most one individual has an opportunity to change its opinion; that is to say, the population can only attain a neighbouring state (from n to $n + 1$ or to $n - 1$) or stay in its former state n. Then we can calculate the probability that the population is still in state n at time $t + \Delta t$. We first define the transition probability rates for the population:

$$w[(n+1) \leftarrow n] = w_\uparrow(n) = n_-\mu_{yes \leftarrow no} = (N - n)\mu_{yes \leftarrow no}$$
$$w[(n-1) \leftarrow n] = w_\downarrow(n) = n_+\mu_{no \leftarrow yes} = (N + n)\mu_{no \leftarrow yes}$$
$$w[j \leftarrow i] = 0 \qquad \text{for} \quad |i - j| > 1$$

Multiplication by Δt yields the probability that the population will undergo the transition within a time span of this length. The probability that nothing happens within Δt is

$$w[n \leftarrow n]\Delta t = w_0(n) = 1 - w_\uparrow(n)\Delta t - w_\downarrow(n)\Delta t$$

Then the probability that the population is still in state n at time $t + \Delta t$ is given by the sum of the probabilities of being in one of the neighbouring states $n + 1$ and $n - 1$ at time t, multiplied by the respective transition probabilities $w_\uparrow(n - 1)$ and $w_\downarrow(n + 1)$, and of the probability of being in the actual state n multiplied by the probability $w_0(n)$ of staying there:

$$p(n; t + \Delta t) = p(n + 1; t)w_\downarrow(n + 1)\Delta t$$
$$+ p(n; t)w_0(n)\Delta t$$
$$+ p(n - 1; t)w_\uparrow(n - 1)\Delta t$$

Further simplifications lead to

$$\frac{p(n; t + \Delta t) - p(n; t)}{\Delta t} = p(n + 1; t)w_\downarrow(n + 1)$$
$$-p(n; t)(w_\uparrow(n) + w_\downarrow(n))$$
$$+p(n - 1; t)w_\uparrow(n - 1)$$

which, by taking the limit $\Delta t \to 0$ and further simplification, yields the system of linear differential equations[2] consisting of $2N + 1$ functions $p(n; t)$:

$$\dot{\mathbf{p}}(t) = \mathbf{L}\mathbf{p}(t)$$

where $\mathbf{p}(t)$ is a vector of the probabilities $p(n; t)$ for all the possible population states, and $\mathbf{L}$ is a matrix which has non-vanishing elements only in the main diagonal and in the two adjacent diagonals, and all its elements are constant:

$$
\begin{aligned}
l_{ii} &= -w_\downarrow(i) - w_\uparrow(i) \\
l_{ij} &= w_\downarrow(j) & j = i + 1 \\
l_{ij} &= w_\uparrow(j) & j = i - 1 \\
l_{ij} &= 0 & |i - j| > 1
\end{aligned}
$$

This, by the way, leads to $\sum_i \dot{p}(i; t) = 0$ for all t, which also fulfils the condition $\sum_i p(i; t) = 1$.

This is linear and could be solved by analytic means, although it is solved numerically here because for a population size of $2N$ we have $2N + 1$ coupled differential equations. By analytic means, however, the stable equilibrium distribution of populations for $t \to \infty$ may be calculated approximately, where the approximation is fairly good for population sizes above 50.

κ is the most important parameter of this model, since it represents the strength of the coupling of the individuals to the majority. κ determines whether a population is likely to have a fifty-fifty distribution of 'yes' and 'no' ($\kappa < 1$ for $\pi = 0$) or is likely to have a strong majority of either 'yes' and 'no' ($\kappa > 1$ for $\pi = 0$). With $\pi \neq 0$ and small κ, the most probable majority in a population would be different from 50 per cent (and with high κ the probability maxima in the right-hand part of Figure 6.2 would be of different height). ν is a frequency parameter but it is of little interest: it affects only the time scale of the structure-building process, because with higher ν the breakthrough of either 'yes' or 'no' comes faster. For $\pi = 0$ and

---

[2]A numerical solution of this system of differential equations is a simulation of the macro object 'population' with the vector-valued attribute 'probability of being in one of the possible states'.

$\kappa > 1$ the distribution of populations develops into a bimodal distribution – the probability of finding the population with a strong majority of either 'yes' or 'no' is very high. For $\kappa < 1$ the probability of an evenly split population is very high (see Figure 6.2 – for $\pi \neq 0$ the threshold for κ is different).

Models of this kind may be extended to the case of several interacting populations and to cases where members of the populations can decide between more than two alternatives (Weidlich 1991). Simulation is necessary for these kinds of models for two reasons. First, it is required to generate graphical representations of the time-dependent probability distribution – this is only a numerical treatment of the master equation, that is, of a system of ordinary differential equations. The second purpose of simulation becomes clear for extensions of the model. An analytical treatment of the master equation and the approximation of its stable solution is only possible for individual transition probabilities of the form of equation 6.1. Other, and perhaps theoretically more interesting, individual transition probabilities (or 'assimilation functions' as analyzed by Lumsden and Wilson 1981: 135) cannot be treated analytically. For these, only single realizations of the stochastic process may be found with the help of simulation (for an example with a varying number of interacting populations and individual transition probabilities which is much more intricate than the one discussed here; see Troitzsch 1994).

Software: MIMOSE

The MIMOSE simulation software package derives its name from 'micro and multilevel modelling and simulation environment'. It was originally planned as a model specification language in the early 1980s, but during the decade of its development, it grew into a more-or-less complete simulation tool with a graphical user interface both for model input and for representing results.

Model description in MIMOSE

Models must still be described in a textual manner, using the functional language described below. Experiments have been carried out to support users with graphical tools for model specification (Klee and Troitzsch 1993), but they are not part of the MIMOSE version currently distributed (for SunSparc, LINUX/X-Windows and (meanwhile obsolete) NeXTStep systems; a Java interface for use on the Internet is executable under WIN-DOWS (but still needs a UNIX or LINUX based server, consult http://www.uni-koblenz.de/~sozinf/projekte/mimose). Model description is done by specifying one or more object classes representing 'natural kinds' of things within the target system:

```
object1 := { ... }
object2 := { ... }
```

and then defining these object classes by specifying one or more attributes representing the properties of the things represented by MIMOSE objects:

```
object1 := {
  attr1 : <type> := <state change function>;
  ...
  constattr2 : <type>;
  ...
}
```

where *<type>* may be one of the basic types int (integer numbers, which may also be used for nominally scaled attributes like 'yes' and 'no') or real (non-integer numbers for metrical attributes) or a list type such as list of int or list of *<user-defined object type>*.

Initialization is done in a later step.

Constant attributes may also be specified. State change functions are expressions that must not be constant and may contain function applications of the form *<function name>*(*<arguments>*) as well as the common arithmetic operators $(+ - */)$. They may refer to the current or former values of attributes, attr and attr_n, respectively.

Functions may be user-defined (outside object type definitions). They are useful in more complex models than those introduced in this chapter, because if the same function is used in more than one place it need only be written once – which enhances understandability and the maintenance of the model.

A MIMOSE model description may be entered via a text editor or within MIMOSE's model description window. Figure 6.3 shows this window in the WINDOWS client environment. Even if the description is read from file, the model description window is opened and the description file is loaded. This is why it is possible to correct typing or modelling errors that may have been found during the model check or during runtime – it is not necessary to return to one's editor to correct the file and restart the simulator.

Figure 6.3: MIMOSE's model description window

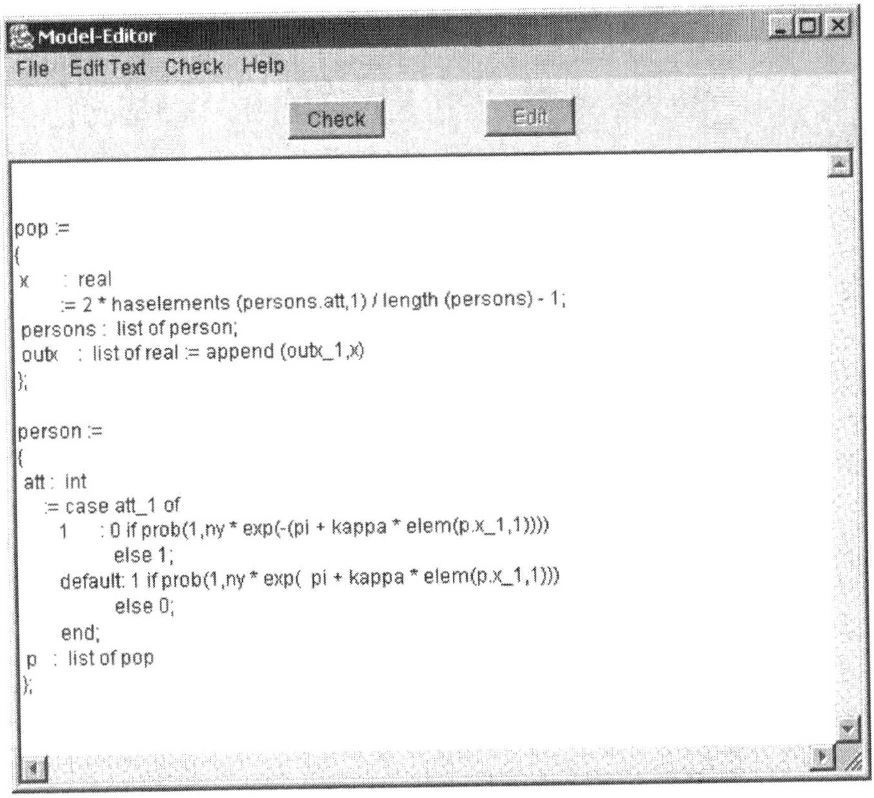

Model initialization

Although MIMOSE models may be initialized textually, using a text editor, the MIMOSE system allows for initialization from a graphical user interface. Once the model description has been checked, MIMOSE (or rather its graphical user interface) opens an initialization window in which all necessary initializations must be entered. Figure 6.4 shows this window in the WINDOWS client environment.

This window is only opened after the model description has successfully been checked (in fact, it can, of course, only be displayed after the simulation system knows about all objects, attributes and parameters). The initialization window remains open during the model's runtime. On interruption, values may be altered, for instance to analyze the effect of a sudden change in a parameter.

Objects and attributes are initialized on the objects register card, and the

Figure 6.4: MIMOSE's initialization windows

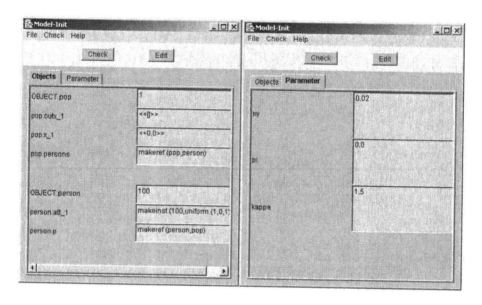

parameters register card allows parameter values to be entered.

Some new syntactical elements and built-in functions of the MIMOSE model description language show up in the initialization window: *numbers of instances* have to be inserted in the lines marked with the object type names alone, and *attribute initializations* have to be inserted in the lines marked with type names and attribute names, separated by '.'

In the example shown in Figure 6.4, makeref(list1, list2) is a function that generates references from all objects of list list1 to all objects of list list2 – in order that current values of attributes of the objects of type list2 can be accessed by objects of type list1 – and makeinst(<*number*>, <*function*>) is a function that initializes a certain attribute for <*number*> instances to the values returned by <*function*>. In our example, the att attribute of all 100 instances of object type person is initialized to the next 100 values generated by the random number generator uniform (in fact, it is the first instance of the random number generator – the first '1' in the argument list – and since the next two arguments are integers, random numbers are taken from the set of the integer numbers 0 and 1 meaning 'no' and 'yes'). [...] is a list constructor for attributes of type list of ... and <<...>> is a constructor for object lists.

Thus, in the pop.outx_1 textfield, <<[]>> means: initialize the 'old value' of attribute outx in the only instance of object class pop to the empty list [] (if there were two instances of class pop, the entry would be <<[] , []>>). Note here that the '<<...>>' operator applies to lists of objects, whereas the '[...]' operator applies to list type attributes. Even though there is only one instance of pop, its internal representation is a one-element list.

In the same manner, person.att_1 is initialized to 100 values returned by the function uniform with its seed no. 1 and on the interval $[0, 1]$. And the list of pop type attribute p of each of the 100 instances of object class person is initialized to the one-element list of references to the only instance of class pop.

Simulation initialization

MIMOSE separates the initialization and parametrization of the model from the initialization of a specific simulation run where the length of a time step (DT), break and stop conditions as well as random number generator seeds can be specified. Figure 6.5 shows this window in the NextStep/OpenStep environment. This window looks much the same in all MIMOSE implementations. The break condition in this example is fulfilled whenever the expression (count % 100) = 0 (the modulus of count with respect to 100) returns true, count being a built-in parameter that is incremented at each simulation step. The X-Windows and Java implementations also allow initialization of the random number generator with user-specified seeds.

Result presentation

The MIMOSE graphical user interface allows for a graphical representation of the results of simulation runs. Figure 6.6 shows the window from which graphs may be designed. With the two boxes on the left-hand side of the window, the x- and y-axes of the graph can be defined. The x-axis has to be identified with one attribute or parameter (e.g. $time or $count), whereas the y-axis can be identified with several attributes. In both boxes, first 'parameters' or an object have to be selected from the drop-down menu, and then particular parameters or attributes of the chosen object may be selected. Graphs are scaled (and in some interfaces may be rescaled at the user's discretion).

Graphs are automatically labelled (text fields at bottom left) and can be saved to disk or sent to the printer via the file menu. Figure 6.6 shows the

Figure 6.5: MIMOSE's simulation run initialization window

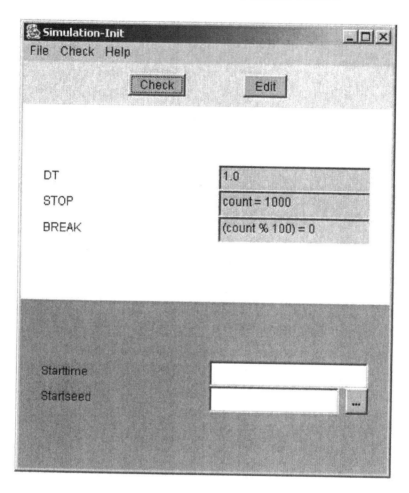

window in the Windows environment. In other implementations it looks a little different and has several subwindows for selecting objects, attributes, scales, line styles and colours.

Beside two-dimensional plots of single or multiple attributes against time (or step count, as in Figure 6.6), two- or three-dimensional plots of two or three attributes may be requested from the result presentation design window where this seems applicable. The attributes used for plotting must be of type list of real or list of int and these lists must be of the same length – which, of course, holds in our example where $count is the list of all values count ever had and where pop.outx is the list of all values pop.x ever had. Since at each simulation step count is incremented (starting, of course,

Figure 6.6: MIMOSE's result presentation design window for 2D-graphics

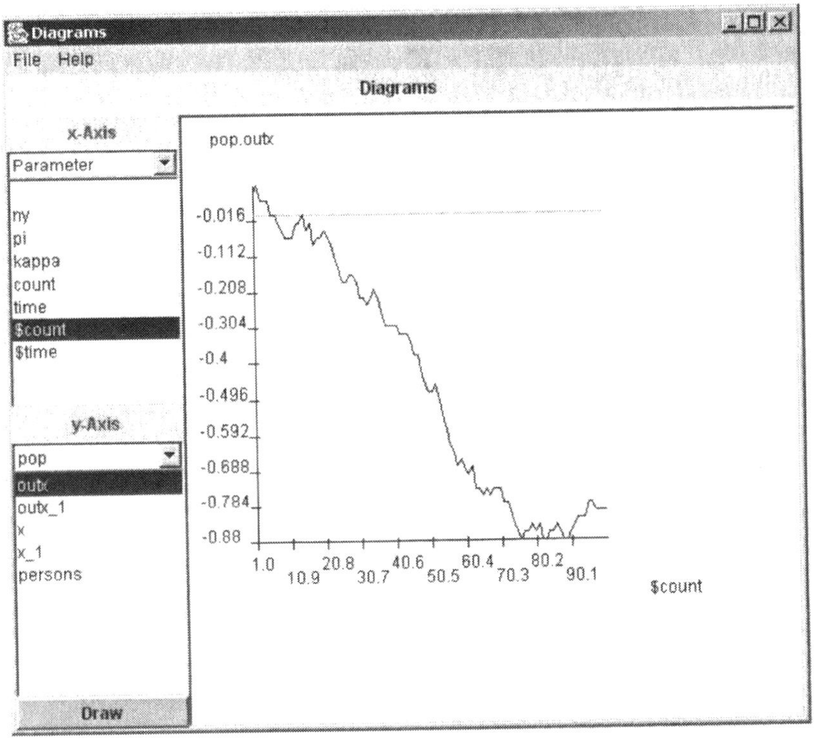

from 0) and since pop.x is appended to pop.outx (which was empty in the beginning), both lists must always have the same length. We will discuss this below with the help of the first example.

Examples

Opinion formation

The following example simulates the opinion formation model already used for the purpose of introducing basic synergetics (see page 102). It comprises two types of objects, namely the object representing the population as a whole (pop), and an object type for the persons this population consists of.

```
pop :=
{
```

```
x           :  real
            := 2 * haselements (persons.att,1)
               / length (persons)
               - 1;
persons :   list of person;
outx    :   list of real := append (outx_1,x)
};
```

At every time step, the number of persons holding attitude 1 ('yes') is counted, and the x-value for the population is calculated (recall that N is *half* the number of people in the population):

$$x = \frac{2n_{yes}}{2N} - 1$$

This value is then appended to the output list. This list has to be initialized as empty (see Figure 6.4), because only in this case will it have the same length as the (automatically generated) lists $time and $count, the latter being used in Figure 6.6.

```
person :=
{
 att :   int
        := case att_1 of
           1 :0 if
                 uniform(1,0.0,1.0) <
                 nu * exp(-(pi + kappa * elem(p.x_1,1)))
               else 1;
           default:1 if
                 uniform(1,0.0,1.0) <
                 nu * exp(  pi + kappa * elem(p.x_1,1))
               else 0;
           end;
 p   :   list of pop
};
```

A person holding attitude 1 ('yes') changes to attitude 0 ('no') with probability $\nu \exp[-(\pi + \kappa x)]$, and a person with any other attitude (default, the only alternative is, of course, 0 or 'no') changes to 1 or 'yes' with probability $\nu \exp[\pi + \kappa x]$, where x is the first element (elem(., 1)) of the list of p's old values (_1) of the attribute x: p is the local name of the one-element list of objects of type pop. The probable event is described explicitly here: a uniformly distributed random number in the interval $[0, 1]$

(uniform's second and third arguments) is drawn from the first random number stream – uniform's first argument. If this number is less than the respective probability, the attitude change happens. (MIMOSE also supplies a Boolean-valued function named prob with the desired probability as an argument.)

After the mathematical treatment of this model (see p. 102) the behaviour of the simulation model does not come as a surprise. Figure 6.7 shows time paths for 20 independent and (nearly) identical experiments for populations consisting of 100 persons each. This example shows that MIMOSE enables one to design multiple experiments: 2000 individuals were distributed among 20 populations with equal parameters and initialized randomly to the 'yes' and 'no' attitudes. All the populations started near (but not at) $x_0 = 0$ – which is why the 20 experiments are not fully identical.

There are only a few lines of MIMOSE code, which must be added to the model description to allow for multiple experiments:

```
experiment :=
{
 pops : list of pop;
 mean : real := pluslist(pops.x)/length(pops.x);
 outmean : list of real := append(outmean_1, mean);
}
```

Due to an idiosyncrasy of the MIMOSE system, we have to introduce at least one variable attribute in the definition of experiment, otherwise the object would never be evaluated. mean is an attribute that contains the mean of all x-values, but this is not used (nor very useful) in this context, because the mean value of the population distribution is a local minimum for $\kappa > 1$, as we saw earlier. outmean collects these means for all time steps.

Figure 6.7 shows that ten of the model populations develop into a large 'yes' majority ($x > 0.7$), while another eight display a similarly large 'no' majority ($x < -0.7$). Which majority evolves is obviously decided during the very first steps of the simulation runs, at least in most cases. Only two populations seem undecided ($x = -0.26$ and $x = 0.50$) after 200 simulation steps.

This example shows that a single run of a computer simulation does not yield more than one (or, within reasonable computing time, at most a few) realizations of a nonlinear stochastic process, and – in contrast to the case of linear models – we may never be sure that these realizations are near a maximum likelihood path. A single simulation of the development

Figure 6.7: Time series from 20 simulation runs with $\pi = 0$ and $\kappa = 1.5$, $2N = 100$, and all populations starting with approximately $n_{yes} = n_{no}$

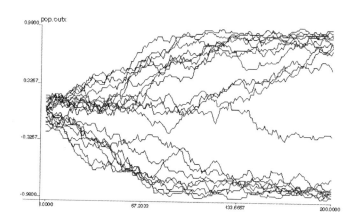

of one population of the type of this example might lead to the erroneous conclusion that our model always generates high 'yes' majorities. In more complex models, which would consume much more computing time, we might be tempted to run only one simulation (or, at most, very few) – and we would remain misled since no mathematical approximation would teach us better. Thus, to avoid erroneous conclusions, a large number of runs is always necessary to judge the behaviour of a stochastic model.

Models of this kind can easily be extended to the case of several interacting populations (see the next example) and to cases where members of the populations can decide among more than two alternatives.

Empirical applications have been suggested by several authors – see Haken (1996) and the discussion in the same issue of *Ethik und Sozialwissenschaften*; see also Helbing (1994a) – the most instructive perhaps being a model where the 'opinion' is which of two (or more) substitutable goods (such as competing computer operating systems, or competing video-tape systems, or competing cigarette brands) is preferred by consumers. A strong majority for one system or brand and the extinction of the competitor may be expected when cohesion is high ($\kappa > 1$) – for example, where compatibility is needed or is advantageous for using the good (as is the case for computers and their operating systems and for video-tape recorders). In contrast, an equal share may be expected when cohesion is low ($\kappa < 1$) – for example, where compatibility is unnecessary (as in the case of brands of cigarettes).

Gender segregation

Our second example has a sound empirical background. It is a formal recon-
struction of the process by which gender segregation in German *Gymnasien*
(high schools) was overcome after the Second World War. In 1950, there
were 59 single-sex and 56 coeducational *Gymnasien* in the federal state of
Rhineland-Palatinate; in 1990 these numbers had changed to 10 single-sex
and 130 coeducational *Gymnasien*. Although even in 1950 not only same-
sex teachers were assigned to single-sex schools, same-sex teachers were
in a large majority in single-sex schools. The process we consider here is
the process of assigning male and female teachers to both single-sex and
coeducational schools – for a more detailed description of the development
of gender proportions among teachers and pupils see Wirrer (1997). As the
process of changing a single-sex into a coeducational school often lasted
many years, it seems justified to model the process as a whole – for a more
detailed model see Kraul *et al.* (1995).

The two graphs in Figure 6.8 show the distribution of percentages
of women among teachers at some 150 secondary schools in Rhineland-
Palatinate from 1950 to 1990. The left-hand graph represents the empirical
data, and the right-hand graph is the output of a simulation based on a few
simple assumptions:

- All teachers leaving their jobs are replaced by men and women with
  equal overall probability. This could be considered to be positive
  discrimination, but for most of the period considered, the proportion
  and qualifications of women among newly graduated teachers were
  high enough to make positive discrimination unnecessary.
- Men stay in their jobs twice as long as women.
- New women are assigned to an individual school with probability
  $P(W|\xi) = \nu(t)\exp(\kappa\xi)$ according to the proportion ξ of women
  among its teachers – which for high κ would mean that there is a
  high preference for women to be sent to girls' schools with a high
  percentage of women teachers while for $\kappa = 0$ there would be no such
  preference.

κ is 0.5 in this simulation run, and $\nu(t)$ is such that at all times men and
women have the same overall probability of replacing retired teachers. The
simulation is initialized with a gender distribution close to the empirical
distribution in 1950. With $\kappa > 1$, gender segregation would continue and
become even stronger as in the right-hand plot in Figure 6.2.

Below is the MIMOSE code for this model. To enhance readability, the

Figure 6.8: Distribution of percentages of women among teachers at 150 secondary schools in Rhineland-Palatinate from 1950 to 1990: left, empirical data; right, three-level simulation (teachers–schools–state)

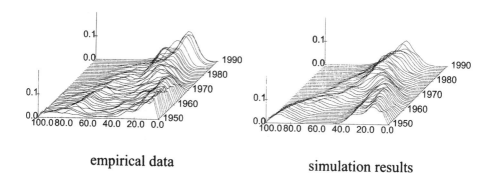

empirical data   simulation results

variability of nu (ν) is not considered in this program until later (see p. 122). The only attribute of interest for output is school.sexRatioList, which collects each school's gender ratio for consecutive time steps (years).

```
system :=
{
  schooltypes    : list of schooltype;
};


schooltype :=
{
  schools : list of school;
};


school :=
{
  lteacher       : list of teacher
                 := updateref(lteacher_1,
                            friend(teacher.position));
  sexRatio       : real    /* sex=0: male, sex=1: female! */
                 := haselements(lteacher.sex,1) / length(lteacher);
  sexRatioList   : list of real
                 := append(sexRatioList_1, sexRatio);
  prob1          : real
                 := nu * exp(kappa * sexRatio_1);
};
```

```
teacher :=
{
  position :  list of school;
  sex      :  int;
  age      :  int
              := age_1 + 1;
  duration :  int
              := (normal(1,15,5) if sex else normal(1,30,5))
                 if count = 1 else
                 duration_1 - 1;
  cond     :  int
              := 1 if (duration_1 = 1) || (age_1 >= 64) else 0;
  death    :  list of teacher
              := delete(self(teacher),
                     self(teacher) if cond_2 else []);
  new      :  list of teacher
              := copy(self(teacher),
                     cond_1,
                     [age_1        :: uniform(1,25,30),
                      cond_1       :: 0,
                      cond_2       :: 0,
                      sex          :: 1 if
                                          prob(1,position.prob1_1)
                                    else 0,
                      duration_1 :: normal(2,15,5)
                                    if sex else
                                    normal(2,30,5)
                     ]);
};
```

This MIMOSE program introduces five new built-in functions: copy,
delete, self, friend and updateref. They are needed here because we
have dynamical populations (school staffs) from (into) which individual
elements (teachers) may be removed (inserted).

- friend returns a reference list, which is a list of all (in this case)
  teacher instances whose position attributes refer to the calling
  instance; thus in our case it is a list of all teachers currently employed
  at this school.
- updateref updates the current reference list with a new reference list
  – which is necessary when new instances have been inserted or old
  ones have been removed.
- copy and delete do just what their names say: delete removes all
  instances listed in its second argument (which is non-empty only if – in
  this case – cond_2 is true) from its first argument, and copy generates

a new instance if its second argument is true, using its first argument as a template and its third argument as an initialization of the attributes of the new instance (this third argument may be an empty list, if the new instance is to be a true copy of the template, or an incomplete list may be given if some attributes are to be taken from the template and others are to be initialized anew). New teachers' ages are initialized to a uniformly distributed number from 25 to 30; they are not dismissed for two periods (their dismissal conditions (cond_1 and cond_2) are set to 0 for the two previous periods); and their job duration is set to a normal variable with mean 15 periods (years) for women (30 years for men) and standard deviation 5. This is not done in the simulation run initialization, but in the first simulation step (if count = 1) or at the time of job entry (last entry in the third argument of copy), so changes to the duration mean and standard deviation can be made within the same piece of code (the expression could also have been 'hidden' in a user-defined function).

- self returns a one-element list which contains a reference from an instance to itself.

Initialization in this example is a little more intricate than in our first example and is shown below.

```
%system := 1;
system.schooltypes := makeref(system,schooltype);

%schooltype := 3;
schooltype.schools :=
makegroupref(schooltype,[1,1,1],school,[45,45,60]);

%school := 150;
school.lteacher_1 := makegroupref(school,makelist(150,1),
                            teacher,makelist(150,30));
school.sexRatioList_1 := makeinst(150,[]);
school.sexRatio_1 := makeinst(150,uniform(3,0.0,1.0));
school.prob1_1 := makeinst(150,uniform(3,0.0,1.0));

%teacher := 4500;
teacher.sex := makegroupinst(makeinst(1350,1 if prob(6,0.88) else 0),
                        makeinst(1350,1 if prob(7,0.22) else 0),
                        makeinst(1800,1 if prob(8,0.08) else
0));
teacher.age_1 := makeinst(4500,uniform(2,25,65));
teacher.duration_1 := makeinst(4500,0);
teacher.cond_1 := makeinst(4500,0);
teacher.cond_2 := makeinst(4500,0);
```

```
teacher.position := makegroupref(teacher,makelist(150,30),
                                 school,makelist(150,1));
nu := 0.1;
kappa := 0.5;
```

This model runs with 4500 teachers in 150 schools of three school types. The numbers of instances of each type are initialized in the lines beginning with the % sign.

- The `schooltype.schools` expression assigns the first 45 schools to school type 1, the next 45 to type 2 and the last 60 to type 3.
- In the same manner, the `school.1teacher_1` expression assigns 30 teachers to each school (this is because the `makelist` function returns a list of 150 1s and 30s respectively).
- The `teacher.sex` line initializes the first 1350 teachers (in school type 1: girls' schools) to be female (1) with probability 0.88, the next 1350 teachers (in school type 2: mixed) to be female with probability 0.22, and the last 1800 teachers (in school type 3: boys' schools) to be female with probability 0.08. These numbers approximate the empirical state for the year 1950 in the *Gymnasien* in Rhineland-Palatinate – not quite exact, but individual data for teachers nearly 50 years ago are lost or hard to come by.
- The `teacher.age_1` expression initializes the teachers' ages to a uniform random integer number between 25 and 65.
- The `teacher.position` expression assigns each teacher his or her school (the first 30 teachers are assigned to school 1, the next 30 belong to school 2, and so on).

The result of a simulation run is shown in Figure 6.9 on page 122. Figure 6.8 gives probability and frequency density functions for the model, but Figure 6.9 gives only a few time series for some individual schools – which, nevertheless, give the same impression of the modelled process as a whole. For this figure, the MIMOSE code was extended by a few lines, which model the administration's behaviour in the following manner:

- In every year, make all schools count how many teachers will retire (cond = 1), and make them calculate how many women would replace them if nu were 1 (since `prob1` contains nu as a multiplier, in the end we divide by last year's nu). Thus, we insert in the `school` object description:

```
sys       : list of system;
toReplace : integer
```

```
                    := haselements(lteacher.cond,1);
        wToRepl     : real := toReplace*prob1/sys.nu_1;
```

Now wToRepl contains the number of women to employ for nu=1 for all schools.

- Add (pluslist) all the schools' reports. SR now contains the number of all teachers to be employed in all the schools of the state, while SRp contains the number of all women teachers who had to be employed if nu was equal to 1. Thus for nu=1 SRp women will be among SR new teachers all over the state. Since SRp should be one half of SR, nu has to be rescaled by the factor SR/(2.0*SRp). Adjust nu accordingly. Thus, we insert in the school object description:

```
    schools : list of school;
    SR      : real := pluslist(schools.toReplace);
    SRp     : real := pluslist(schools.wToRepl);
    nu      : real := SR/(2.0*SRp);
```

Figure 6.9: MIMOSE results of the gender proportion in some of the 150 simulated schools (with variable nu)

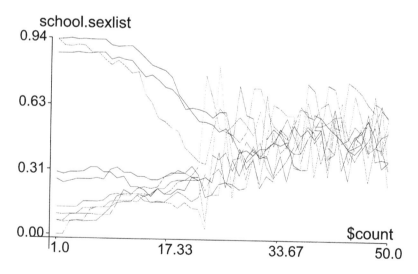

The difference between the empirical and the model graphs seems visually small and could be lowered further by means of an even finer tuning of the few parameters needed in the simulation model. The model satisfactorily explains the historical process of gender desegregation and even justifies the retrodiction that the main change in the process occurred after about 20 years of a more-or-less continuous development towards a unimodal distribution. After 1970, the overall percentage of women teachers seems to rise but then falls again in the last decade, as in the empirical data. And all this with the three simple assumptions enumerated at the beginning of this subsection.

But still there is a caveat: perhaps there are several different and equally simple models delivering graphs that for the first 40 years resemble the empirical graph to the same or even higher degrees, but which develop differently in the future. Although prediction and explanation are close relatives and methodologically very similar (Grünbaum 1962; Scriven 1969), we may have the case that 'satisfactory explanation of the past is possible even when prediction of the future is impossible' (Scriven 1969: 117 – see also the discussion in the conclusion of Chapter 2 and Troitzsch 2004b).

Simulation in this example was used to reconstruct an empirical process with the help of a simple model, and it could now be used for fine-tuning the model parameters. Estimation of the parameters, however, from the empirical data at hand, requires intricate mathematics. Thus, simulation may give at least a hint about which model might be adequate for parameter estimation. Moreover, it leads to one conclusion that might be politically important: positive discrimination takes its time.

The dove–hawk–law-abider model revisited

The dove–hawk–law-abider model discussed in Chapter 3 lends itself to a multilevel simulation: instead of modelling three subpopulations growing and shrinking, we could model one population consisting of a number of individuals who change their minds about the strategies they apply.

A MIMOSE model equivalent to the DYNAMO model reported in Chapter 3 has the following form:

```
hobbes :=
{
  hawk : real := hawk_1 + DT * (yieldh_1 - hawk_1 * yields_1);
  dove : real := dove_1 + DT * (yieldd_1 - dove_1 * yields_1);
  lawa : real := lawa_1 + DT * (yieldl_1 - lawa_1 * yields_1);

  yieldd : real
          := (dove * rdd + hawk * rdh + lawa * rdl) * dove;
  yieldh : real
```

```
              := (dove * rhd + hawk * rhh + lawa * rhl) * hawk;
   yieldl : real
              := (dove * rld + hawk * rlh + lawa * rll) * lawa;
   yields : real
              := yieldd + yieldh + yieldl;

   lHawk: list of real := append(lHawk_1,hawk);
   lDove: list of real := append(lDove_1,dove);
   lLawA: list of real := append(lLawA_1,lawa);
};
```

The MIMOSE model necessary for a multilevel version is quite straight-forward. The individuals are identified by the strategy `strategy` which they are applying. They change their strategies (0 = hawk, 1 = dove, 2 = law-abider) with population-wide probabilities that depend on the current expected revenues (`yieldh` etc.). This is why these probabilities need only be calculated at the population level. Population-wide strategy transition probabilities might seem implausible, but note that this model reflects only the traits of the macro model of Chapter 3, where population-wide strategy transition rates were also assumed.

While in the macro model subpopulations grow and shrink according to the differences between their revenue and the average revenue, we have to make one additional assumption here. The probability of a hawk applying another strategy should depend on the difference between the expected revenue resulting from the new strategy and the hawk's revenue; and the same should apply to doves and law-abiders.

The expected revenues of the particular strategies are calculated in exactly the same way as in the macro (DYNAMO) model (they are only multiplied by a small constant kappa to avoid numerical problems with the exponential function). As in the two examples above, the transition probabilities are calculated as an exponential function of the difference between the two expected revenues, multiplied by a small constant nu to make sure that probabilities never exceed 1. As in the two examples above, the constant nu can be interpreted as an overall tendency of the individuals to change their strategies, while kappa has to be interpreted as the individuals' dependence on the revenue difference (for kappa = 0, all strategy changes would have the same probability, namely nu).

Some technical remarks might be in order here.

- The random number according to which an individual makes its choice (r, a uniform random number between 0.0 and 1.0) is calculated for each individual at every time step.[3] The choice is made according to Figure 6.10: if r falls between 0.0 and p.pHawkToDove, then the dove strategy is chosen; if it falls between p.pHawkToDove and p.pHawkToDove + p.pHawkToLawA, then the law-abider strategy is chosen; and if r is greater than p.pHawkToDove + p.pHawkToLawA, then a hawk remains a hawk.

- The number of individuals applying a particular strategy is no longer calculated by a difference or differential equation – they are only counted at each simulation step (by the function haselements).
- A history is kept for each subpopulation size (lHawk, lDove and lLawA).

Figure 6.10: Random selection of a hawk's new strategy

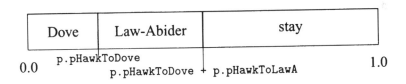

Thus, for a multilevel version we have to insert the individual transition probabilities (to be calculated at the pop level, since they are equal for all individuals) and count the individuals belonging to the respective subpopulations before they change their attitudes, and to apply the transition probabilities to the individual transitions.

This leads to the following MIMOSE program for the dove–hawk–law-abider micro model (remember that 0 means 'hawk', 1 means 'dove', and 2 or default means 'law-abider' – MIMOSE case expressions must always contain a default part):

```
individual :=
{
  r : real := uniform(1, 0.0, 1.0);
  strategy : int := case strategy_1 of
              0 : 1 if r < p.pHawkToDove_1 else
                  2 if r < p.pHawkToDove_1 + p.pHawkToLawA_1
                  else strategy_1;
              1 : 0 if r < p.pDoveToHawk_1 else
                  2 if r < p.pDoveToHawk_1 + p.pDoveToLawA_1
                  else strategy_1;
```

---

[3]For a detailed description how random numbers are generated see Appendix C, p. 272.

```
      default : 0 if r < p.pLawAToHawk_1 else
                1 if r < p.pLawAToHawk_1 + p.pLawAToDove_1
                else strategy_1;
              end;
   p : list of pop;
}
pop :=
{
   indiv : list of individual;
   hawk : int := haselements(indiv.strategy, 0);
   dove : int := haselements(indiv.strategy, 1);
   lawa : int := haselements(indiv.strategy, 2);
   yieldh : real
           := kappa*(dove*rhd + hawk*rhh + lawa*rhl)*hawk;
   yieldd : real
           := kappa*(dove*rdd + hawk*rdh + lawa*rdl)*dove;
   yieldl : real
           := kappa*(dove*rld + hawk*rlh + lawa*rll)*lawa;
   pHawkToDove : real := nu * exp(yieldd - yieldh);
   pHawkToLawA : real := nu * exp(yieldl - yieldh);
   pDoveToHawk : real := nu * exp(yieldh - yieldd);
   pDoveToLawA : real := nu * exp(yieldl - yieldd);
   pLawAToHawk : real := nu * exp(yieldh - yieldl);
   pLawAToDove : real := nu * exp(yieldd - yieldl);
   lHawk : list of int := append(lHawk_1, hawk);
   lDove : list of int := append(lDove_1, dove);
   lLawA : list of int := append(lLawA_1, lawa);
}
```

The results of this variant of our model are almost the same as the results of the macro model (at least for the parameters used here: kappa = 0.0001 and nu = 0.001) – see Figure 6.11.

As before, both hawks and doves disappear and all individuals change their strategies to be law-abiders, after a period when both 'old' The only difference is that in the multilevel variant of the model the final state where all individuals are law-abiders is reached in finite time — in the macro model the proportion of doves and hawks would always be positive (although very small) in finite time.

Thus, in this simple case, it is not the modelling technique that determines the result: both formalizations have qualitatively similar results. This need not be the case in all comparable models (cf. Troitzsch 1996: 181). Other formalizations of the transition probabilities – for example, another monotonic function instead of the exponential – might yield qualitatively different results.

Figure 6.11: Results of the dove–hawk–law-abider micro model

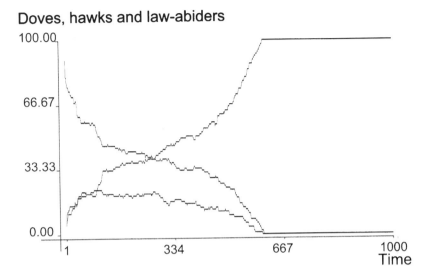

Doves, hawks and law-abiders

Commentary

So far we have seen MIMOSE as a powerful instrument for describing multilevel model (and also, in the last example, for transforming macro models into multilevel models). The MIMOSE approach allows the description of a model and its objects in a manner that does not involve the overhead necessary for initialization and analysis because these tasks are done by the MIMOSE system and user interface. The only 'overhead' task modellers have to keep in mind is providing attributes whose history should be kept, but these history attributes can always be constructed in the following manner:

```
obj := {
  attribute : ... := ...;
  history   : list of <attribute_type>
              := append(history_1, attribute);

  ...
};
```

Future releases of MIMOSE might perhaps provide the user with a mechanism by which attributes can be marked in order that their history can be kept automatically.

MIMOSE also lends itself to designing multiple experiments and running them at the same time, thus saving modellers' waiting time and allowing them to display the results of several runs in the same graph.

Moreover, it should have become clear from all three examples that refinement of a model (multiple experiments, new features such as replacing a constant by a variable attribute, or deriving a multilevel model from a macro model) can be done in a quite straightforward manner once a user has become acquainted with the functional language structure of the MIMOSE system.

In the examples discussed above, there were always interactions between objects at different levels – for example, between an object and the group or subpopulation to which it belongs. From the start, MIMOSE was designed for this type of model, although mechanisms were also provided for interactions within one level – for example, between an object and its neighbours (the curved arrows at the bottom of Figure 6.1). However, models of this type are quite clumsy to initialize, because all the neighbours have to be mentioned explicitly in the initialization. This is why MIMOSE is less appropriate for such models.

Further reading

Synergetics was founded in the early 1970s by Hermann Haken. His introduction

- Haken, H. (1978) *Synergetics: An Introduction*, Springer Series in Synergetics, vol. 1. 2nd enlarged edn. Springer-Verlag, Berlin

was first published in 1977 and is now in its third (German) edition. It deals with self-organization in multicomponent systems in physics, chemistry, biology, and – in a few pages – sociology. The first attempt at modelling social systems with the methodological tools of synergetics was made by

- Weidlich, W. and Haag, G. (1983) *Concepts and Models of a Quantitative Sociology. The Dynamics of Interacting Populations*. Springer Series in Synergetics, vol. 14. Springer-Verlag, Berlin

from which the first example of this chapter was taken. Both volumes are devoted to the mathematical analysis of multicomponent systems. The book by

- Helbing, D. (1994) *Quantitative Sociodynamics. Stochastic Methods and Models of Social Interaction Processes*. Kluwer, Dordrecht presents a number of examples of opinion formation processes and combines the synergetic perspective with game theory. This book, too, is mathematically oriented.

For the emerging role of sociophysics see for instance

- Deffuant, G., *et al.* (2003) Simple is beautiful and necessary. *Journal of Artificial Societies and Social Simulation* http://www.soc.surrey.ac.uk/JASSS/6/1/6.html.

Sociobiology has also made wide use of synergetic techniques, especially in

- Wilson, E. O. and Lumsden, C. (1981) *Genes, Mind, and Culture. The Coevolutionary Process*. Harvard University Press, Cambridge, MA.

Wilson and Lumsden introduce the concept of gene-culture translation between the level of the individual and the 'macroculture'. Their 'assimilation functions', set by 'epigenetic rules', are mathematically the same as our individual transition probabilities (μ), and their 'ethnographic curves' are the same as our macro probabilities of finding a population in a given state (p).

MIMOSE as a simulation tool for the analysis of multicomponent systems was first introduced in Michael Möhring's PhD thesis (Möhring 1990). A number of applications can be found in Part 2 of

- Troitzsch, K. G. *et al.* (eds) (1996) *Social Science Microsimulation*, pp. 105–154. Springer-Verlag, Berlin.

A German journal, *Ethik und Sozialwissenschaften*, devoted one of its recent issues to the discussion of the applicability of synergetics to the social sciences: see

- Haken, H. (1996) Synergetik und Sozialwissenschaften, *Ethik und Sozialwissenschaften. Streitforum für Erwägungskultur* 7; 587–594.

which is the main article in the issue, as well as the critical discussion on pp. 595–657 (by 33 authors), and the rejoinder on pp. 658–75.

Chapter 7

Cellular automata

Imagine a rectangular grid of light bulbs, such as those you can see displaying scrolling messages in shops and airports. Each light bulb can be either on or off. Suppose that the state of a light bulb depended only on the state of the other light bulbs immediately around it, according to some simple rules. Such an array of bulbs would be a cellular automaton (CA). This chapter will show that simulations with complex behaviour can be built using cellular automata, and that such simulations can model social dynamics where the focus is on the emergence of properties from local interactions.

We start by defining what a CA is and then consider some standard examples, mainly developed within the physical sciences. These can be adapted to model phenomena such as the spread of gossip and the formation of cliques. This leads us to a more detailed consideration of some social science models, on ethnic segregation, relations between political states and attitude change. Finally, we show how cellular automata models can be programmed.

A CA has the following features:

1. It consists of a number of identical cells (often several thousand or even millions) arranged in a regular grid. The cells can be placed in a long line (a one-dimensional CA), in a rectangular array or even occasionally in a three-dimensional cube. In social simulations, cells may represent individuals or collective actors such as countries.
2. Each cell can be in one of a few states – for example, 'on' or 'off', or 'alive' or 'dead'. We shall encounter examples in which the states represent attitudes (such as supporting one of several political parties), individual characteristics (such as racial origin) or actions (such as

cooperating or not cooperating with others).

3. Time advances through the simulation in steps. At each time step, the state of each cell may change.

4. The state of a cell after any time step is determined by a set of rules which specify how that state depends on the previous state of that cell and the states of the cell's immediate neighbours. The same rules are used to update the state of every cell in the grid. The model is therefore homogeneous with respect to the rules.

5. Because the rules only make reference to the states of other cells in a cell's neighbourhood, cellular automata are best used to model situations where the interactions are local. For example, if gossip spreads by word of mouth and individuals only talk to their immediate neighbours, the interaction is local and can be modelled with a CA.

To summarize, cellular automata model a world in which space is represented as a uniform grid, time advances by steps, and the 'laws' of the world are represented by a uniform set of rules which compute each cell's state from its own previous state and those of its close neighbours.

Cellular automata have been used as models in many areas of physical science, biology and mathematics, as well as social science. As we shall see, they are good at investigating the outcomes at the macro scale of millions of simple micro-scale events. One of the simplest examples of cellular automata, and certainly the best-known, is Conway's Game of Life (Berlekamp *et al.* 1982).

The Game of Life

In the Game of Life, a cell can only survive if there are either two or three other living cells in its immediate neighbourhood, that is, among the eight cells surrounding it (see Figure 7.1). Without these companions, it dies, either from overcrowding if it has too many living neighbours, or from loneliness if it has too few. A dead cell will burst into life provided that there are exactly three living neighbours. Thus, for the Game of Life, there are just two rules:

1. A living cell remains alive if it has two or three living neighbours, otherwise it dies.

2. A dead cell remains dead unless it has three living neighbours, and it then becomes alive.

Figure 7.1: The black cells are the neighbours of the central cell

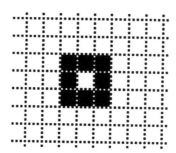

Figure 7.2: An example of the evolution of a pattern using the rules of the Game of Life

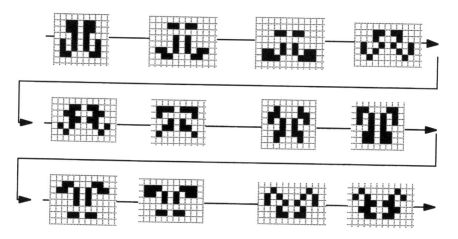

Surprisingly, with just these two rules, many ever-changing patterns of live and dead cells can be generated. Figure 7.2 shows the evolution of a small pattern of cells over 12 time steps. To form an impression of how the Game of Life works in practice, let us follow the rules by hand for the first step, shown enlarged in Figure 7.3.

The black cells are 'alive' and the white ones are 'dead' (see Figure 7.3). The cell at b3 has three live neighbours, so it continues to live in the next time step. The same is true of cells b4, b6 and b7. Cell c3 has four live neighbours (b3, b4, c4 and d4), so it dies from overcrowding. So do c4, c6 and c7. Cells d4 and d6 each have three neighbours and survive. Cells e2 and

Figure 7.3: The initial arangement of cells

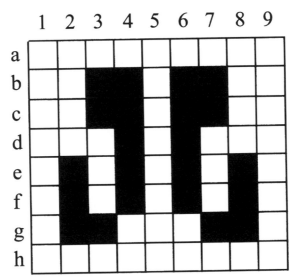

e8 die because they only have one living neighbour each, but e4 and e6, with two living neighbours, continue. Cell f1, although dead at present, has three live neighbours at e2, f2 and g2, and it starts to live. Cell f2 survives with three living neighbours, and so do g2 (two neighbours alive) and g3 (three neighbours alive). Gathering all this together gives us the second pattern in the sequence shown in Figure 7.2.

It is clear that simulating a CA is a job for a computer. Carrying out the process by hand is very tedious and one is very likely to make mistakes (although Schelling, whose work on segregation in the 1970s is discussed below, did everything with pencil and paper, while Conway is reputed to have worked out his Game of Life using dinner plates on a tiled kitchen floor!).

The eighth pattern in Figure 7.2 is the same as the first, but inverted. If the sequence is continued, the fifteenth pattern will be seen to be the same as the first pattern, and thereafter the sequence repeats every 14 steps. There are a large number of patterns with repeating and other interesting properties and much effort has been spent on identifying these. For example, there are patterns that regularly 'shoot' off groups of live cells, which then march off across the grid (Berlekamp *et al.* 1982).

Other cellular automata models

The Game of Life is only one of a family of cellular automata models. All are based on the idea of cells located in a grid, but they vary in the rules used to update the cells' states and in their definition of which cells are neighbours. The Game of Life uses the eight cells surrounding a cell as the neighbourhood that influences its state. These eight cells, the ones to the north, north-east, east, south-east, south, south-west, west and north-west, are known as its *Moore neighbourhood*, after an early CA pioneer (Figure 7.4).

Figure 7.4: Cell neighbourhoods

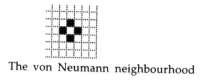

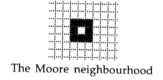

The von Neumann neighbourhood   The Moore neighbourhood

The parity model

A model of some significance for modelling physical systems is the parity model. This model uses just four cells, those to the north, east, south and west, as the neighbourhood (the *von Neumann neighbourhood*, shown in Figure 7.4). The parity model has just one rule for updating a cell's state: the cell becomes 'alive' or 'dead' depending on whether the sum of the number of live cells, counting itself and the cells in its von Neumann neighbourhood, is odd or even. Figure 7.5 shows the effect of running this model for 124 steps from a starting configuration of a single filled square block of five by five live cells. As the simulation continues, the pattern expands. After a few more steps it returns to a simple arrangement of five blocks, the original one plus four copies, one at each corner of the starting block. After further steps, a richly textured pattern is created once again, until after many more steps, it reverts to blocks, this time consisting of 25 copies of the original. The regularity of these patterns is due to the properties of the parity rule. For example, the rule is 'linear': if two starting patterns are run in separate grids for a number of time steps and the resulting patterns are superimposed, this will be the same pattern one finds if the starting patterns are run together on the same grid.

Figure 7.5: The pattern produced by applying the parity rule to a square block of live cells after 124 time steps

As simulated time goes on, the parity pattern enlarges. Eventually it will reach the edge of the grid. We then have to decide what to do with cells that are on the edge. Which cell is the west neighbour of a cell at the left-hand edge of the grid? Rather than devise special rules for this situation, the usual choice is to treat the far right row of cells as the west neighbour of the far left row and vice versa, and the top row of cells as the south neighbours of the bottom row. Geometrically, this is equivalent to treating the grid as a two-dimensional projection of a torus (a doughnut-shaped surface). The grid now no longer has any edges which need to be treated specially, just as a doughnut has no edges.

One-dimensional models

The grids we have used so far have been two-dimensional. It is also possible to have grids with one or three dimensions. In one-dimensional models, the cells are arranged along a line (which has its left-hand end joined in a circle to its right-hand end in order to avoid edge effects). There are only 32 different rules for a one-dimensional CA because there are only that many combinations of alive and dead states for the cell and its two neighbours, one to the left and one to the right.[1] Wolfram (1986) devised a classification scheme for the rules of one-dimensional automata.

Figure 7.6: The pattern produced after 120 steps by rule 22 starting from a single live cell at the top centre

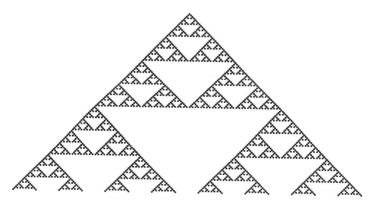

For example, Figure 7.6 shows the patterns that emerge from a single seed cell in the middle of the line, using a rule that Wolfram classifies as rule 22. This rule states that a cell becomes alive if and only if one of four situations applies: the cell and its left neighbour are alive, but the right neighbour is dead; it and its right neighbour are dead, but the left neighbour is alive; the left neighbour is dead, but the cell and its right neighbour are alive; or the cell and its left neighbour are dead, but the right neighbour is alive. Figure 7.6 shows the changing pattern of live cells after successive time steps, starting at time 0 at the top and moving down to step 120 at the bottom. Further time steps yield a steadily expanding but regular pattern of triangles as the influence of the initial live cell spreads to its left and right.

Models of interaction

These examples have shown that cellular automata can generate pretty patterns, but for us their interest lies in the extent to which they can be used

---

[1] The state of the three cells can be represented as a binary number with three bits, e.g. 101. There are 256 such three bit numbers, each with a different combination of 1s and 0s. However, some are just a mirror image of another (e.g 110 and 011) and therefore give the same patterns, and only 32 of the remainder lead to states that are not all dead or all alive.

to model social phenomena. We shall begin by examining two very simple models that can be used to draw some possibly surprising conclusions before describing a more complex simulation which illustrates a theory of the way in which national alliances might arise.

THE GOSSIP MODEL

Most commonly, individuals are modelled as cells and the interaction between people is modelled using the cell's rules. For instance, one can model the spread of knowledge or innovations or attitudes in this way. Consider, for example, the spread of an item of salacious gossip from a single originator to an interested audience. Each person learns of the gossip from a neighbour who has already heard the news, and may then pass it on to his or her neighbour (but if they don't happen to see their neighbour that day, they will not have a chance to spread the news). Once someone hears the gossip once, he or she remembers it and does not need to hear it again.

This scenario can be modelled with a CA. Each cell in the model has two states: ignorance about the item of gossip (the equivalent of what in the previous discussion we have called a 'dead' cell) or knowing the gossip (the equivalent of being 'alive'). We will colour white a cell that does not know the gossip and black one that does. A cell can only change state from white to black when one of its four von Neumann neighbours knows the gossip (and so is coloured black) and passes it on. There is a constant chance that within any time unit a white cell will pick up the gossip from a neighbouring black cell and turn black. Once a cell has heard the gossip, it is never forgotten, so in the model, a black cell never reverts to being white. Thus the rules that drive the cell state changes are as follows:

1. If the cell is white, and it has one or more black neighbours, consider each black neighbour in turn. For each black neighbour, change to black with some specific probability, otherwise remain white.
2. If the cell is black, the cell remains black.

The rules we have mentioned previously have all been deterministic. That is, given the same situation, the outcomes of the rule will always be the same. However, the gossip model is stochastic: there is only a chance that a cell will hear the gossip from a neighbour. We can simulate this stochastic element with a random number generator (see Appendix C). Suppose the generator produces a random stream of integer numbers between 0 and 99. A 50 per cent probability of passing on gossip can be simulated by implementing the first rule as follows:

1. If the cell is white, then for each neighbour that is black, obtain a number from the random number generator. If this number is less than 50, change state from white to black.

Figure 7.7: The spread of gossip: (a) with a 50 per cent probability of passing on the news; (b) with a 5 per cent probability; (c) with a 1 per cent probability

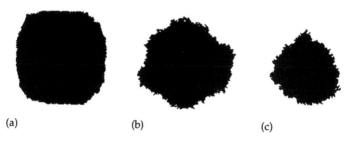

(a)   (b)   (c)

Figure 7.7(a) shows the simulation starting from a single source, using a 50 per cent probability of passing on gossip. The gossip spreads roughly equally in all directions. Because there is only a probability of passing on the news, the area of black cells is not a perfect circle but deviations from a circular shape tend to be smoothed out over time.

With this model, we can easily investigate the effect of different probabilities of communicating the gossip by making an appropriate change to the rules. Figure 7.7(b) shows the result of using a 5 per cent probability (the first rule is rewritten so that a cell only changes to black if the random number is less than 5, rather than 50). Surprisingly, the change makes rather little difference. The shape of the black cells is a little more ragged and of course the news travels more slowly because the chance of transmission is much lower (Figure 7.7(b) required about 250 time steps, compared with 50 steps for Figure 7.7(a)). However, even with this rather low probability of transmission, gossip stills spreads. We can go lower still: Figure 7.7(c) shows the outcome of a 1 per cent probability of transmission. The shape of the black cells remains similar to the previous two simulations, although the rate of transmission is even slower (the figure shows the situation after 600 time steps). The model demonstrates that the spread of gossip (or of other 'news' such as technological innovations or even of infections transmitted by contact) through local, person-to-person interactions is not seriously impeded by a low probability of transmission on any particular occasion, although low probabilities will result in slow diffusion.

The model has assumed that once individuals have heard the news, they never forget it. Black cells remain black for ever. This assumption may be correct for some target situations, such as the spread of technological know-how. But it is probably unrealistic for gossip itself. What happens if we build a chance of forgetting into the model? This can be done by altering the second rule to:

2. If a cell is black, it changes to white with a fixed small probability.

Figure 7.8: The spread of gossip when individuals have a 10 per cent chance of transmitting the news and a 5 per cent chance of forgetting it

Setting the probability of transmitting the gossip to 10 per cent and the probability of forgetting the gossip to 5 per cent gives the result shown in Figure 7.8. The small white holes represent the cells that have 'forgotten' the gossip. However, these white areas do not spread because a cell that has forgotten the news is still surrounded by other black cells, which have a high chance of retransmitting the news to the newly white cell, thus quickly turning it black again. In short, provided that the probability of transmission from all the neighbour cells is greater than the chance of forgetting, the pattern of a growing roughly circular patch of cells which have heard the news is stable in the face of variations in the assumptions we make about transmission and forgetting.

THE MAJORITY MODEL

In the gossip model, a cell turned black if it heard the gossip from any of its neighbours. This therefore was a model of person-to-person interaction. Now let us consider a model in which a cell changes state according to the joint states of all of its neighbours. For example, people might adopt a fashion only if the majority of their friends have already adopted it. Once again, the simulation will consist of a CA with cells each of which have two states: white and black. The simplest model has just a single rule:

1. The new cell state is the state of the majority of the cell's Moore neighbours, or the cell's previous state if the neighbours are equally divided between white and black.

There are eight Moore neighbours. Thus the rule says that a cell is white if there are five or more white cells surrounding it, black if there are five or more black cells around it, or remains in its previous state if there are four white and four black.

Figure 7.9: (a) A random distribution of white and black cells; (b) after many time steps using the majority rule

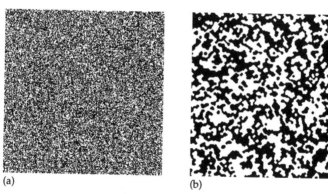

(a)   (b)

Starting from a random distribution of white and black cells, the result of running this rule is a patchwork of small white and black blocks (Figure 7.9(b)). Cells surrounded by cells of the other colour change to the colour of the majority, so that isolated cells coalesce to form blocks of one colour. Cells that happen to have half white and half black cells as their neighbours stay unchanged and form stable boundaries to these blocks. Once the cells have achieved this speckled pattern, there is no longer any opportunity for change.

The situation is very different, however, with a small alteration to the rule. Suppose that some people are sometimes more susceptible to the dictates of fashion than others. Some white cells will change to black if they have as few as four black neighbours, whereas others will only change if they have at least six black neighbours. Similarly for the black cells. The likelihood of being either susceptible or resistant to the fashion is distributed randomly in the model, so that overall, there are the same number at each time step of those who require six neighbours of the other colour to change and of those who require only four to change. In short, in this modification of the model, we no longer have every cell the same, but some varying amount of individual difference.

Figure 7.10: The majority model, with random individual variation: (a) after 5 steps; (b) after 19 steps; and (c) after 482 steps

Although the modification from the original model appears to be minor, the effect is dramatic. Instead of the blocks of black and white remaining 'frozen' once they have formed, the small randomly changing individual differences are enough to ease the coagulations into gradually larger patches of a shared colour. The sequence in Figure 7.10 shows this happening. Figure 7.10(a), after five time steps, closely resembles Figure 7.9, obtained with the strict majority rule. But after 19 steps the blocks begin to join up

(Figure 7.10(b)) and by step 482, the white and black cells have formed into large clusters (Figure 7.10(c)). It is often the case in cellular automata models that deterministic models behave in different ways at the macro level compared with variants with some degree of randomness built in.

In this subsection, we have discussed two applications of cellular automata to the modelling of simple social phenomena. The 'gossip' model was based on a rule that involved the 'infection' of a cell by at least one of its neighbours. The majority rule involved counting the number of neighbours that were of one colour. In each case we saw the emergence of macro-level patterns from the operation of these simple rules. As we noted in Chapter 1, it is nearly impossible to predict the form of these macro-level patterns just by considering the rules operating at the micro-level individual cell.

In both examples it is easy to think of the grid in rather literal, geographical terms, with people occupying each cell on an actual surface. However, the analogy between the model and the target population does not have to be, and usually will not be, as direct as this. The grid can be mapped on to many different kinds of social relationship. For example, the interactions on which the gossip model depends could be by telephone, over the Internet or in any other way in which individuals communicate with particular others.

An example: Axelrod's tribute model

The cells of a CA can also be used to represent entities other than individuals. An interesting example is Axelrod's (1995) investigation of how new political actors, such as alliances and empires, can emerge from smaller entities such as nation states. Axelrod observes that throughout history, new empires have formed in which a central authority has subordinated previously independent states, exerting control over them and asserting the right to collective action. Equally often, such entities have split into fractions that become able to exert their own authority and are recognized as states in their own right. The United States formed itself into a new actor, recognized by other nations, when it established a federal government over the 13 component states in the eighteenth century. The European Union is struggling to achieve something similar today. Meanwhile, the Soviet empire first annexed many of the semi-independent states of eastern Europe and Asia and then split up again. Similar stories can be told about the Roman and Chinese empires.

The essential features of these changes are that they are 'endogenous', that is, the formation and dissolution of empires and alliances have taken place without any external guiding hand; and in most if not all examples, there has been an element of coercion involved. It is the process of formation of aggregate actors that is the focus of Axelrod's model. The relationships between states is modelled as a 'tribute' system in which actors are able to demand payment of wealth, with the threat of war if payment is not made. The wealth that the stronger actor obtains from the weaker is used to extract further resources from other actors. Alliances in which groups of states band together to strengthen their hand are also possible.

To simplify the dynamics of the model, the actors are confined to a one-dimensional world, and are laid out along the circumference of a circle (so that every actor has neighbours on both sides). Actors are only able to inter-act (demand tribute from or form alliances with) their immediate neighbours to the left and to the right. The model is a form of one-dimensional CA, but with rather more complicated rules than previous examples.

At every time step, a randomly chosen selection of actors is activated. Each may demand a tribute from either of its neighbours. The target of the demand can either pay the tribute or decide to resist and fight. If the target elects to fight, the battle drains resources from both sides: each loses a quarter of the other side's accumulated wealth (or proportionately less if either side does not have that much). Thus the wealthier side inflicts more damage than the poorer side. This, then, constitutes a state change rule for this CA: the state of a cell is measured by its wealth, the tribute rule determining how that wealth changes at each step. In addition, there is a rule which provides every cell with the same small additional amount of wealth each time step to replenish the overall stock of money.

As a side-effect of the interactions between them, actors develop 'com-mitments' to each other. Commitments between pairs of actors increase as a result of three types of relationship: subservience, when one actor pays tribute to another, protection, when one actor receives tribute from the other, and friendship, when the two actors fight on the same side against a third party. On the other hand, commitment decreases when two actors fight on opposite sides. The commitments between actors have consequences for the choices they make about paying tribute or fighting. If two actors fight, adja-cent actors will join in on the side to which they have greater commitment and contribute wealth in proportion to their commitments. Thus alliances can form in which adjacent actors have commitments to each other and pool their wealth. The target from which an alliance may try to extract tribute can be either of its neighbours (or neighbouring alliances) – see Figure 7.11.

Figure 7.12 shows the results of one run over 1000 time steps ('years'). The top part of the chart shows the wealth of each actor, year by year. Three actors, 2, 4 and 10, clearly dominated this history, each having steadily

Figure 7.11: A typical scenario in Axelrod's tribute model

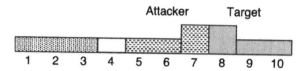

increased its wealth during the course of the millennium. Actor 9 began well, but its fortunes slumped after about 400 years. Different initial distributions of wealth to the actors and different selections of active actors in each time step result in different histories, some including dramatic collapses in wealth of even the richest participants as a result of the outbreak of damaging fights between them (a 'world war').

Figure 7.12: The outcome of running Axelrod's model for 1000 time steps

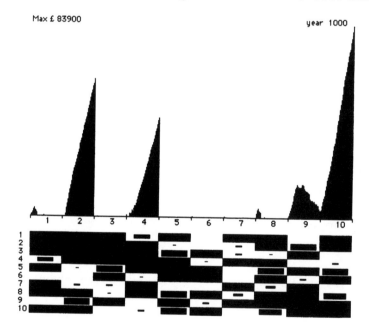

The lower part of Figure 7.12 shows the pattern of commitments between actors at the end of the 1000-year run. The relative size of the black block within each rectangle indicates the strength of the commitment between the row and column actors. Each of the three rich actors is at the centre of a

strong alliance in which their allies are heavily committed to each other and to the central actor.

The simulation shows that a simple model of interacting states can demonstrate the emergence of clusters that can act as alliances, with all the actors in a cluster operating as one. Axelrod defines a cluster as a set of adjacent states committed to each other at a level of at least 50 per cent. Members of these clusters work together, as shown by the fact that members never gang up to fight the strongest member and fights between weaker members of the cluster are rare. Moreover, the weaker members (that is, the poorer members) only rarely start fights of their own against external actors. When they do, the strongest actor tends to get dragged in, sometimes leading to the eventual collapse of the cluster (an analogue of the 'imperial overstretch' that has brought down several real empires). It does seem as though the strong protect the weak in the model. Moreover, the other actors could be seen as taking into account the total wealth of the whole cluster when contemplating a fight. This suggests that the clusters really can be regarded as new actors, in the same way as the United States is a political actor in its own right, not just the aggregation of its constituent states.

Axelrod observes that the value of this simulation does not depend on the degree of correspondence between his simulated actors and real nation states. Indeed, as another characteristic of his model is that each time it is run it produces a different sequence of events, with different clusters being formed, it would be difficult to see how one could create a model that behaved in just the way that the actual history of political development occurred. Rather, the value of the model is in clarifying and specifying new questions that political scientists might want to explore. He notes (Axelrod 1995: 37) that the construction of the model raised such questions as 'What are the minimal conditions for a new actor to emerge?', 'What tends to promote such emergence?', 'How is the dynamics affected by the number of elementary actors?' and 'What can lead to the collapse of an aggregate actor?' which had not previously been considered and which, if explored with the model, might lead to new ways of thinking about comparable questions in the real world.

Extensions to the basic model

The basic cellular automata described in the previous sections can be extended in a number of useful ways. So far, the models have actors fixed in particular locations, one actor per cell. An extension that is valuable for models that involve migration is to allow the actors to move over the grid. This means that we now have to distinguish the actors from the cells in which they happen to be placed, and we also have to consider whether more than one actor can occupy a cell at any particular moment. A second extension allows actors to be influenced by more than their immediate neighbours; state changes in such models might depend on the aggregate effect of the states of all other actors in the model, or some proportion of them.

Migration models

In a migration model, actors are not confined to a particular cell but can move around. Rules, similar to state change rules, determine when and to where they move. An interesting application of a migration model is found in Schelling's (1971) study of ethnic segregation in the United States. Schelling supposed that people had a 'threshold of tolerance' of other ethnic groups, such that they were content with where they lived provided that at least a proportion of their neighbours were of the same ethnic group as themselves. If, for instance, the threshold of tolerance was 40 per cent, people were content to stay provided that at least four in ten of their neighbours were from the same ethnic group. If this were not so, they would try to move to another neighbourhood in which at least 40 per cent were of their own group.

The conventional assumption is that ethnic segregation in the USA is at least partly due to the fact that whites are prejudiced and have a tolerance threshold of over 50 per cent. They therefore moved out of urban neighbourhoods that had a majority of blacks, leaving the neighbourhood with a still higher proportion of black people and thus accelerating the tendency towards complete segregation. This phenomenon has come to be known as 'urban flight'. Schelling's point was that tolerance thresholds much lower than 50 per cent could lead to the same result. Even a threshold as low as 30 per cent could result in almost complete segregation. Thus although people might be quite content with being in the minority in a neighbourhood, so long as they demanded that some small proportion of their neighbours were of the same ethnic group as themselves, segregation could emerge.

We can build a CA migration model to demonstrate this result. A cell on the grid can be in any of three states: occupied by a 'white' actor; occupied by a 'black' actor; or empty. The process driving the simulation is to select a cell on the grid at random. Then if the cell is occupied by an actor, the actor is examined to see whether it is 'content', that is, whether the number of Moore neighbours of the same colour is at least equal to its tolerance threshold. If the actor is not 'content', a nearby cell is found that is both unoccupied and has neighbours such that the actor would be content there. This is done by looking around the actor's cell until either a suitable cell is found or every cell on the grid has been tried. If a suitable cell is located, the actor moves there, vacating its previous cell. The simulation then chooses another cell at random to process and continues in this way until every actor is content.

Figure 7.13: The effect of a 38 per cent threshold tolerance with Schelling's model: random starting configuration on the left and final configuration on the right

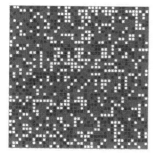 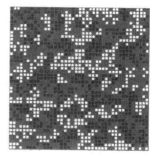

Figure 7.13 shows what happens for a threshold tolerance of 38 per cent (at least three of a cell's eight neighbours must be the same colour). On the left is the starting configuration, with black and white actors distributed over the grey grid at random. On the right is the final configuration, in which all the actors are 'content' with their positions and their neighbours. Comparing the starting and final configurations, one can see a marked degree of clustering in the latter. With higher values of the tolerance threshold, the clusters are even clearer. While this kind of model relates most obviously to ethnic segregation, it can also be applied to relationships between any number of recognizably distinct classes: not just blacks and whites, but rich and poor; and not only to spatial segregation, but also to differentiation into groups and cliques.

The example has shown the use of a migration model in which each cell can contain only one actor, as befits a simulation of people living in neighbourhoods. It is also possible to have more than one actor in a cell, but then the usual spatial metaphor of cellular automata models is lost. In the segregation model, a migrating actor searches for a suitable vacant cell at random, eventually if necessary searching the whole grid. In other cases, a more restrictive rule might be preferable. For example, Hegselmann (1996) describes a model used to study the evolution of support networks in which migration is constrained to a 'migration window' consisting of the 11×11 square of cells surrounding the migrating actor.

Extended neighbourhoods

We have considered models in which actors' changes of state have depended on the states of other actors within the local neighbourhood, defined as either the four cells above and below, left and right (the von Neumann neighbourhood) or all eight surrounding cells (the Moore neighbourhood). To distinguish this set of cells from others, such as the locality within which a migrating actor may move, we shall call the area within which cells can affect the state of the central cell, the 'interaction' neighbourhood (after Hegselmann 1996). In some models it may be useful to define the interaction neighbourhood as much more extensive than just the four or eight immediate neighbours, and in some cases the interaction neighbourhood can include all the cells in the grid. In the latter models, the state of every actor affects every other actor. To preserve some degree of locality, however, such models often use an inverse power law, meaning that while all actors influence any given actor to some extent, the degree to which they do so decreases according to the distance between the influencing and the influenced actors.

An example of such a model can be found in work by Latané and his colleagues. In the 1970s and early 1980s, Latané proposed a theory of what he called 'social impact' (Latané 1981). This theory is concerned with explaining the degree of influence that people have on the attitudes and beliefs of others. The theory states that

> the impact of other people on a given individual is a multiplicative function of the 'strength' of members of the group (how credible or persuasive they are), their 'immediacy' (a decreasing function of their social distance from the individual) and their number. (Latané 1996: 65)

This theory has been extensively tested in a number of situations and received empirical support. However, as phrased, it concerns only the impacts on a given individual. In a group, individuals will be influenced by other members of the group, but will also in turn influence the other members. This reciprocal influencing is more complicated to analyze but has been simulated in a model called SITSIM (Latané 1996).

In the simplest model, a large number of actors are distributed over a grid, one actor per cell. All actors have one of two opinions, assigned randomly at the start of the simulation: following our earlier examples, we shall label these opinions 'white' and 'black' respectively (they could be opinions for or against abortion, for or against a political party and so on). Those other actors with the same opinion as a given individual we shall call its 'supporters', and those of the other opinion 'opposers'. To each actor is also randomly assigned a 'strength' with which an opinion is held. Latané uses an inverse square law of distance, so that the social impact of one supporter j on an individual a is proportional to its strength of opinion (S_j) and inversely proportional to the square of its distance from the individual (d_{aj}). The total impact from all the N supporters on an individual a is equal to the square root of the sum of all the supporters' impacts squared, or as a formula:

$$i_{as} = \sqrt{\sum_{j=1}^{N} \left(\frac{S_j}{d_{aj}^2} \right)^2}$$

The impact of the opposers is calculated similarly, with the summation performed over all the opposing actors. Finally, the actor changes state to join the opposers if the total impact from the opposers, i_{ao}, is greater than the total impact from the supporters, i_{as}. This is the state change rule equivalent to those in other cellular automata models. It does not differ in principle from standard cellular automata model state change rules except that it includes contributions from actors all over the grid. Even an actor many cells distant makes a small contribution to the total impact because of the inverse square in the formula.

The behaviour of systems of this kind in which there are multiple reciprocal interactions can be very difficult to predict in advance of examining a simulation. In fact, the usual behaviour is that opinions polarize and clusters appear. Both these features are shown in Figure 7.14. On the left is the initial, random starting situation, set up so that half the actors are white and the rest black. After the simulation has run to stability, the number of actors with a 'white' opinion has decreased slightly and they have formed into three clusters (remembering that the grid is a torus, with the neighbours of the cells on the left edge of the diagram being the cells on the right edge). Another interesting characteristic of the simulation is that, although one of the groups generally increases in number at the expense of the other, the minority never completely disappears.

This clustering behaviour is found even when the parameters of the simulation are varied within wide limits. For instance, clusters form whatever the proportions of white and black actors at the start, unless the minority

Figure 7.14: Typical outcome (right) of the SITSIM model, from a starting configuration (left) of 50 per cent white actors. The white actors have formed three clusters by the end of the run

is initially very small. It is also consistent for different random starting configurations and variations in the social impact formula (for example, the distance law does not need to be an inverse square law; it could be a cubic law, although it does need to be at least equal to the dimensionality of the grid).

If the model is extended so that each actor has several disjoint binary attributes, each of which is independently subject to social impact, correlations develop between the clusters for each attribute. For example, attribute A might be whether you vote for the Left or the Right, and attribute B whether you prefer wine or beer. Let us assume that an individual's political preference does not affect his or her favourite drink, and vice versa. However, although these attributes are independent at the individual level, the clusters that form will be correlated. That is, an actor who is in a socialist cluster might be more likely to be found in a beer drinking cluster, and conservatives more likely to be wine drinkers (or, depending on how the random numbers play out, vice versa). Rockloff and Latané (1996) give the example of Texans who speak with a drawl and wear cowboy boots. Speaking with a drawl does not cause one to wear cowboy boots, nor does the choice of boots affect the way one speaks, yet in Texas these two attributes are correlated.

The SITSIM model has enabled the investigation of the implications of social impact theory when it is applied recursively (that is, with actors affecting each other), something that would have been difficult or impossible to do analytically, but is quite easy to simulate. The simulation has shown that one does get quite robust emergent effects, such as clustering and correlation between independent attributes. Following on from their simulation work, Latané and his colleagues devised a number of experiments with groups of people that aimed to show whether the findings from the simulation could be reproduced in human groups and have found some striking parallels (Rockloff and Latané 1996).

Software

Unlike some previous approaches to simulation discussed in this book, there are no widely available packages for running most cellular automata models. The exceptions to this are programs constructed to run variations of the Game of Life, but while the Game of Life has some interest as a dynamical system, its applications to social simulation are limited. In order to experiment with cellular automata you need to do some programming. Fortunately, however, there are now a number of specialized products that will make this task relatively easy, certainly much easier than using an ordinary programming language such as Basic or C. In this chapter, we shall demonstrate how one might construct a cellular automata model with software called NetLogo, which has been developed for learning how to program simulations. It includes a comprehensive graphical interface and a programming language which is easy to learn. It is also available for free to run on most personal computers (Windows, Macintosh and Unix).

NetLogo can be downloaded from the World Wide Web at http:// ccl.sesp.northwestern.edu/netlogo/. If you can, it is a good idea to install NetLogo and follow along with the examples.[2] NetLogo is a distant descendant of the Logo programming language that was created by Seymour Papert and colleagues in the 1960s as a tool for schoolchildren (Papert 1980; Resnick 1994). It still retains some aspects of its heritage; for example, there are 'turtles' and they move around on 'patches'. Its programming language uses a very simple syntax that is supposed to resemble English. Nevertheless, the language is powerful and is very well suited to the kinds of simulations described in this and the following chapters.

NetLogo comes with a detailed tutorial and reference section, accessed through the Help menu. Here, we shall only provide a brief overview to show what kind of programs can be created and to help you follow through the example programs later in the chapter.

---

[2]The examples in this book were written using NetLogo version 2.0.2

Getting started

When NetLogo starts, it shows the interface pane, with a large black rectangle that holds the grid of cells (Figure 7.15). There are four tabs along the top which you use to switch to the corresponding pane: *Interface*, the one shown in Figure 7.15, *Information*, which generally displays an explanation of the simulation and how it works, *Procedures*, which holds the program code, and *Errors*, which displays error messages.

Figure 7.15: The NetLogo interface window

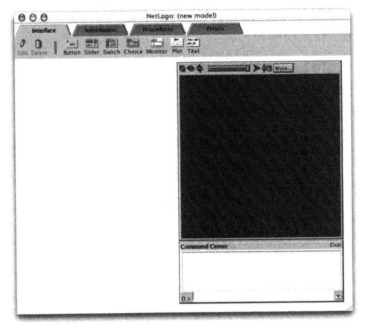

We start by loading a simulation that is provided as a demonstration within the NetLogo package. It is called Rumor Mill (Wilensky 1998) and is an implementation of the Gossip model discussed on page 137. To load it, choose the Models Library in the File menu, and find Rumor Mill among the Social science models. When it has loaded, the Interface pane shows a number of buttons, sliders and graphs (Figure 7.16). Click on the button labelled 'setup-one'. The grid will turn blue (blue is the colour of cells that have not yet heard the rumour) except for one cell in the middle, which is red to show that it does know the rumour. Now click on the button labelled 'go'.

The red area of cells will gradually expand away from the centre, showing the rumour spreading to the other cells. The graphs below the grid show that the number of cells who have heard the rumour first grows at an increasing rate and then, when most of the cells have heard it, the rate reduces.

Figure 7.16: The Rumour Mill interface

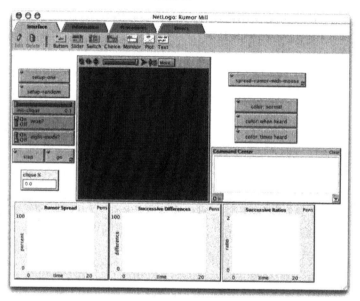

If you now click on the Information tab, there are instructions on what the other buttons and sliders do and suggestions about various experiments that you can carry out. The program code is shown on the Procedures pane. This pane consists of a large scrolling window in which you can edit your program. Keywords, comments and constants are distinguished from the rest of the code by their colour, which is applied automatically (red for numbers, blue for keywords and grey for comments and so on).

The program consists of three main sections. At the top, some variables are defined. There are setup procedures that are used to initialize the cells. And there are some procedures used to update the cells at each step, and to control the graphs and other user interface elements.

In NetLogo, cells are called 'patches'. The variables used in the simulation are declared thus:

```
globals [
   time            ;; how many clock ticks have passed
```

```
   color-mode      ;; 0=normal, 1=when heard, 2=times heard
   clique          ;; how many patches have heard the rumor
]

patches-own [
   times-heard     ;; tracks times the rumor has been heard
   first-heard     ;; clock tick when first heard the rumor
   just-heard?     ;; tracks whether rumor heard this round
]
```

Three variables, time, color-mode and clique, are declared to be 'global', meaning that they can be accessed from anywhere in the program. time will store the time in steps since the simulation started, color-mode changes according to how the cells are to be displayed on the grid, and clique counts how many cells have heard the rumour. Everything after a ';' on a line is a comment and is ignored by NetLogo. Three further variables are declared as 'patches-own', that is, variables that are owned by each cell. For example, each cell has its own variable to store the number of times it has heard the rumour.

Following this, there is a section of code that is executed when the user click on the 'setup-one' or 'setup-random' buttons on the Interface pane:

```
to setup [seed-one?]
   ca
   set time 0
   set color-mode 0
   set clique 0
   ask patches
     [ set first-heard -1
       set times-heard 0
       set just-heard? false
       recolor ]
   ifelse seed-one?
     [ seed-one ]
     [ seed-random ]
   update
   do-plots
end

to seed-one
   ;; tell the center patch the rumor
   ask patch 0 0
```

```
      [ hear-rumor ]
end


to seed-random
   ;; seed with random number of rumor sources
   ask patches with [times-heard = 0]
      [ if (random-float 100.0) < init-clique
            [ hear-rumor ] ]
end
```

The code from to setup to end is an example of a 'procedure', a set of commands that execute as a unit. Clicking the 'setup-one' button calls the setup procedure with the variable seed-one? set to true. ca stands for 'clear all' and resets everything to its initial state, thus removing the remains of any previous run. The three global variables are initialized to zero and then, using the ask command, a set of commands is sent to each cell (patch) for them to execute. These initialize the patch's own variables and set the colour of all the patches to blue (using the recolor procedure, which is further down the program).

ifelse is Netlogo's conditional, corresponding to if ... then ... else in other languages. The condition to be tested is placed immediately after ifelse (here it is the value of the variable seed-one?, which has been passed to the procedure when it was called). If the condition is true, the commands in the first pair of square brackets are executed, and if it is false, the commands in the second pair. If the user pressed the 'setup-one' button, seed-one? will be true, and so the command seed-one will be executed. seed-one is the name of another procedure, defined just a few lines below. to seed-one asks the patch in the centre of the grid (at coordinates 0, 0 – the coordinate system is centred on the grid) to hear the rumour (hear-rumor is another procedure in the program, defined at the end of the code). To finish the setup, the grid is updated (at this point the centre cell turns red to show that it has heard the rumour) and the graphs are initialized.

If you had pressed the 'setup-random' button instead of the 'setup-one' button, the setup procedure would have been called with seed-one? set to false. The ifelse command would have executed the seed-random procedure instead of seed-one. seed-random asks all those patches that have not heard the rumour (i.e. have not already been seeded) to hear the rumour, if a random number between 0 and 100.0 happens to be less than the value of the global variable init-clique. The value of this global variable is set by the user, using a slider on the Interface panel. The effect is that a random selection of roughly `init-clique` per cent of the cells are given the rumour during this initialization.

The third part of the code (below) controls what happens when the user clicks the 'go' button. The button calls the go procedure, which starts by checking whether all the cells have yet heard the rumour (a translation of the first command in the procedure could be: *if there are no patches which have heard the rumour zero times, stop*). The `time` variable is incremented and then all the patches that have already heard the rumour are asked to spread it to their neighbours. Once this has been done, each cell's state is updated and the plots that show the number of cells which have heard the rumour are drawn for this time step. The 'go' button calls the go procedure again and again until the initial stop condition becomes true.

```
to go
  if not any? patches with [times-heard = 0] [ stop ]
  set time (time + 1)
  ask patches
    [ if times-heard > 0
        [ spread-rumor ] ]
  update
  do-plots
end

to spread-rumor  ;; patch procedure
  locals [neighbor]
  ifelse eight-mode?
    [ set neighbor random-one-of neighbors ]
    [ set neighbor random-one-of neighbors4 ]
  if wrap? or not wrapped-neighbor? neighbor
    [ set just-heard?-of neighbor true ]
end

;; the neighbors and neighbors4 primitives always wrap,
;; so if WRAP? is false we need to reject "neighbors" that
;; are only neighbors because of wrapping
to-report wrapped-neighbor? [neighbor]  ;; patch procedure
  report (abs (pxcor - pxcor-of neighbor) > 1) or
         (abs (pycor - pycor-of neighbor) > 1)
end

to hear-rumor  ;; patch procedure
  if first-heard = -1
```

```
      [ set first-heard time
        set just-heard? true ]
    set times-heard times-heard + 1
    recolor
  end


  to update
    ask patches with [just-heard?]
      [ set just-heard? false
        hear-rumor ]
  end
```

The spread-rumor procedure starts by declaring a local variable, neighbor. This variable only exists while the procedure is being executed. Next, a variable that is set by a switch on the user interface (the one labelled 'eight-mode') is used to decide whether to set the value of the local variable, neighbor, to a randomly chosen one of the eight neighbouring cells (the Moore neighbourhood) or the four cells in the von Neumann neighbourhood. Finally, the procedure tells the selected neighbour that it has heard the rumour by setting the neighbour's just-heard? variable to true. There is a complication with this: the NetLogo grid is a torus, with the left column of cells adjoining the right column. However, a switch on the interface allows the user to turn this off, so that the edge cells have no neighbours. The condition, if wrap? or not wrapped-neighbor? neighbor and the following procedure, to-report wrapped-neighbor? handle this. (A to-report procedure is one that returns a value. Ordinary procedures, which start with to, do not return anything.)

This cellular automaton works in two phases: first, the rumour is spread and the just-heard variable of all the receiving cells is set to true by spread-rumor; then, in the second phase, all cells that have a true just-heard variable are registered as having heard the rumour (by incrementing times-heard). The reason for using this two phase approach is important in understanding how this program and many other cellular automata work. Each cell executes its procedures autonomously and at its own speed. If the program had been written to update the receiving cells immediately they heard the rumour, they could then in turn spread the rumour to other cells, but the latter may already have executed all their code and be unable to receive the rumour. The results would be unpredictable. With the two phase approach, all the rumour spreading is done before all the rumour hearing.

update is the procedure that handles the second phase, resetting the just-heard variable and calling the hear-rumor procedure to record that the cell has received the rumour from a neighbour.

The remaining procedures deal with colouring the cells on the grid according to whether they have heard the rumour and with controlling the plotting of the graphs, and we shall not comment in detail on them. Instead, we shall work through two other examples, showing how one might create new simulations. The first is for the majority model (see page 139) and the second, more complicated example replicates the SITSIM model introduced on page 148.

The majority model

The majority model is a cellular automaton in which each cell's state copies the state of the majority of its eight Moore neighbours. The program will start by randomly setting the cells to either 'on', represented by a black cell, or 'off', represented by a white cell. We can do this with the following setup procedure:

```
to setup
    ask patches [
        ifelse random 2 = 0
            [ off ]
            [ on ]
    ]
    set steps 0
end
```

random 2 generates either a zero or a one, so the ifelse condition has an equal chance of executing either the off or the on procedure. on and off are procedures that will change the state of a cell, which we have yet to write. The variable steps will record how many steps the simulation has run. It needs to be defined as a global variable, accessible to other procedures and to the user interface (shortly, we shall create a 'monitor' for this variable on the user interface to show how many steps the simulation has run).

```
globals [
    steps
    ]
```

Next, we can start coding the go procedure that is activated when the user clicks on the 'go' button. This needs to ask each patch to count how many of its Moore neighbours are 'on'. As with the previous model, we shall use a two-phase approach, getting all the cells to record the state of their neighbourhoods first, and then in the second phase getting the patches to update their own state. The first phase is easily accomplished if we assume that each patch will have a variable on? that records its state, either 'on' or 'off' :

```
ask patches [
    set on-neighbors count neighbors with [on?]
]
```

For the second phase, each patch needs to see whether there are a majority of 'on' cells surrounding it (more than four of the eight) and if so, turn itself 'on'. If there is no majority of 'on' cells, there may be a majority of 'off' cells (the number of 'on' cells is less than four). In this situation, the cell must turn itself 'off'. If there are exactly four 'on' and four 'off' cells in the neighbourhood, the cell's state will remain unchanged. This can be achieved with:

```
ask patches [
    ifelse on-neighbors > 4
        [ on ]
        [if on-neighbors < 4 [ off ]]
]
```

Putting these together with a command to increment the step counter, we get the following go procedure:

```
to go
    ask patches [
        set on-neighbors count neighbors with [on?]
    ]
    ask patches [
        ifelse on-neighbors > 4
            [ on ]
            [if on-neighbors < 4 [ off ]]
    ]
    set steps steps + 1
end
```

The only coding that remains is to define the procedures to change the state of a cell, on and off. These set the on? variable and change the colour of the patch on the grid (pcolor is a built-in variable that holds the current colour of the patch):

```
to on
    set on? true
    set pcolor black
end

to off
    set on? false
    set pcolor white
end
```

The complete program is:

```
globals [
    steps
    ]

patches-own [
    on?
    on-neighbors
    ]

to setup
    ask patches [
        ifelse random 2 = 0
            [ off ]
            [ on ]
    ]
    set steps 0
end

to go
    ask patches [
        set on-neighbors count neighbors with [on?]
    ]
    ask patches [
        ifelse on-neighbors > 4
            [ on ]
            [if on-neighbors < 4 [ off ]]
    ]
    set steps steps + 1
```

```
end

to on
    set on? true
    set pcolor black
end

to off
    set on? false
    set pcolor white
end
```

The final step is to design a user interface with a 'setup' button, a 'go' button and a monitor for the number of steps (see Figures 7.17 and 7.18).

Figure 7.17: The majority model after the 'setup' button has been pressed

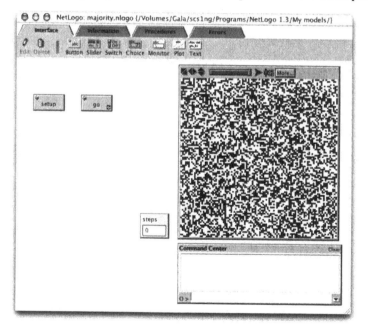

There are improvements that could be made to this code. First, it runs for ever, or until the user clicks the 'go' button a second time to stop it. It would be useful to add a test to see whether any cell had changed colour. Second, we could add code to implement the majority model with random individual

Figure 7.18: The majority model at the end of a run

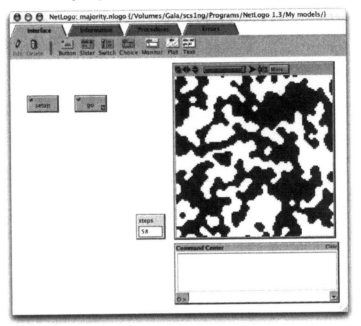

variation (see Figure 7.10). This would involve changing the second part of the 'go' procedure to:

```
ask patches [
    ifelse on-neighbors > 4
        [ on ]
        [ ifelse on-neighbors < 4
            [ off ]
            [ if individualDiff [
                ifelse (random 2) = 0
                    [ on ]
                    [ off ]
                ]
            ]
        ]
]
```

and adding a switch to set the variable `individualDiff` on the user interface. In the initial version, when there are four 'on' neighbours, no action was taken (neither the `on-neighbors > 4` nor the `on-neighbors < 4` conditions were satisfied). In the new code, when there are four 'on' neighbours, the individualDiff variable is tested and if it is true, the patch is set to 'on' or 'off'.

A second example: the SITSIM model

To begin replicating the SITSIM model, we need to write its setup procedure. First, it is a good idea to clear away any remains of a previous run, with ca or clear-all. Then we should initialize all the patches, using the ask-patches command.

Each patch should decide whether it should start as white or black. The overall proportion of white to black patches will be set by the user with a slider, which sets the value of a variable that we shall call initial-white. The easiest way of getting about the right number of white and black patches is to use the random number generator to create random numbers in the range from zero up to 100, and then make the patch white if the random number is less than initial-white. We also need to assign the patch's 'Strength' of opinion, again using a random number generator. Assembling all this, we get:

```
to setup
    clear-all
    ask patches [
        ifelse (random 100 < initial-white)
            [set pcolor white]
            [set pcolor black]
        set strength random 100
        ]
```

The user will need to see the changing number of white and black cells. A small procedure would be helpful for this (it is always a good plan to separate small units of code that do one job into their own procedures):

```
to countColors
    set whites count patches with [pcolor = white]
    set blacks count patches with [pcolor = black]
end
```

This procedure sets the variables whites and blacks to the number of patches that are white and black respectively (pcolor is a built-in variable that holds the current colour of the patch). If we had needed to find the value of just one variable using this procedure it would have been best to write it as a reporter, returning the value to the caller, but in this case we need to return two values: the numbers of whites and blacks. The most convenient way of doing this is to define whites and blacks as global variables, so that they can be accessed from elsewhere in the program. Hence, we need to add a suitable declaration at the top of the code:

```
globals [
    whites          ;; number of white cells
    blacks          ;; number of black cells
]
```

One place where these global variables will be useful is in constructing 'monitors' on the user interface that will display the current counts.

We also need to note that each patch will have its own variable to record its strength of opinion:

```
patches-own [
    strength ;; of influence, set to an
             ;;              unchanging random value
]
```

countColors can now be appended to the setup code, which in its entirety is:

```
to setup
    clear-all
    ask patches [
        ifelse (random 100 < initial-white)
            [set pcolor white]
            [set pcolor black]
        set strength random 100
        ]
    countColors
end
```

The next step is to define the go procedure. This will be called when the user clicks the 'go' button and needs to run one step of the simulation, asking each patch to see whether the impact on it of others' opinions is such as to make it change its own opinion. So we need another ask patches command:

```
to go
    ask patches [ beInfluenced ]
    countColors
end
```

Once the patches have been influenced, we shall see how many whites and blacks there are, using countColors again.

The user's 'go' button will keep calling the go procedure again and again indefinitely. To ensure that eventually the program stops when the cells are no longer changing, we shall add a test. We set a variable, changed?, to false before asking the patches to run the beInfluenced procedure, and arrange that if any patch changes its colour, it sets changed? to true. Then, after all the patches have finished, we will test the changed? variable and stop if it is still false. The go procedure becomes:

```
to go
    ;; assume that no cell will change its colour
    set changed? false
    ask patches [ beInfluenced ]
    countColors
    ;; stop if no cell has changed its colour
    if (not changed?) [stop]
end
```

We must also remember to declare that changed? is a global variable since it will be accessed by the patches' code when they are changing colour.

```
globals [
    changed?         ;; has any cell changed its colour?
    ]
```

Next, we need to write the beInfluenced procedure. The SITSIM model is an example of a cellular automata in which all other cells influence the state of each cell. A patch's colour changes if the total impact from 'opposing' cells is greater than the impact from 'supporting' cells. So a first sketch of beInfluenced would be:

```
to beInfluenced
    set impactFromWhite sqrt sum values-from patches
        with [pcolor = white] [impact myself]
    set impactFromBlack sqrt sum values-from patches
        with [pcolor = black] [impact myself]
```

```
;; if this cell is white and the impact from blacks is
;; greater than that from whites, change the cell
;; colour to black, and vice versa for black cells
if pcolor = white and impactFromBlack > impactFromWhite
    [set pcolor black
     set changed? true]
if pcolor = black and impactFromWhite > impactFromBlack
    [set pcolor white
     set changed? true]
end
```

The first two lines sum the impacts of the patches that are white and black respectively. impact is a reporter procedure that we have yet to write; this will work out the impact of a patch on the patch being influenced ('myself'). The first line could be translated as: set the variable impactFromWhite to the square root of the sum of the impact of a patch on myself for all patches whose colour is white. Once we have these total impacts, we can see whether this patch's colour is to change. This is the purpose of the last six lines. Notice that if the colour does change, we also set the changed? variable to true, to ensure that the simulation will run for at least one more cycle.

To complete this procedure, we need to declare that the variables, impactFromWhite and impactFromBlack, are local variables. They should be local because they are specific to this patch and used only in this procedure. To do this, the line

```
locals [impactFromWhite impactFromBlack]
```

must be added at the beginning of the procedure.

We have yet to work out what the impact of one patch on another is. The formula (page 149) says that the impact is equal to the square of the other patch's strength divided by the square of the distance between this and the other patch. We can write this as a simple reporter procedure:

```
to-report impact [otherCell]
    ;; report the impact of otherCell on myself
    report square (strength / (square distance otherCell))
end
```

distance calculates the straight-line or Euclidian distance between the patch and another patch. The procedure to find the square of a number is simple:

Figure 7.19: The SITSIM model after the 'setup' button has been pressed

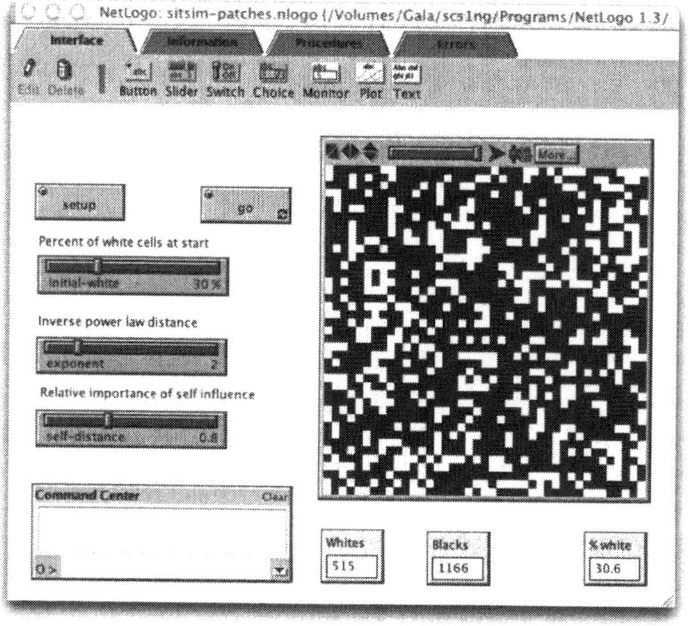

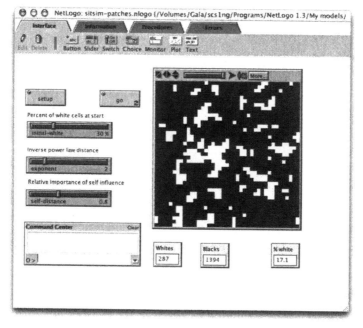

Figure 7.20: The SITSIM model at the end of a run

```
to-report square [x]
   report x * x
end
```

There are a couple of complications that need to be considered. First, the procedure will fail when otherCell happens to be identical to the patch that is executing the procedure, because in this case, the distance will be zero, and so the procedure would be trying to divide strength by zero. The SITSIM model tells us that in this case the distance to be used is the 'self-distance', a parameter that the user can set using a slider. Second, it would be interesting to allow the user to change the power to which the distance is raised with another slider (thus varying the effective range of the influence of other patches). For this, we can use the ^ operator, which means 'raise to the power of'.

```
to-report impact [otherCell]
   ;; report the impact of otherCell on myself
   locals [d]
   ifelse (self = otherCell)
       [ set d self-distance]
       [ set d distance otherCell ]
   report square (strength / d ^ exponent)))
end
```

That completes the code for this model. In addition, we need to add some buttons and sliders for the user interface. The resulting model is shown in Figures 7.19 and 7.20.

Commentary

The examples have shown that, using a package like NetLogo, it is not difficult to program simple cellular automata to achieve clear and visually impressive patterns. While we have room in this book to show only fairly small programs, NetLogo will accommodate much larger and more complex ones. Its main drawback is slow speed: a cellular automata for a grid of 100×100 cells will involve 10,000 evaluations of the cells' states for every step of the simulation and even with today's fast computers, this can take some significant time. Compared with some other systems, NetLogo is relatively slow because it is based on an interpreted language. The same program in C or C++ would probably run an order of magnitude faster, but would take two orders of magnitude longer to write and would be much harder to debug. The ultimate in speed-ups can be obtained using parallel hardware (see, for example, the description of the hardware designed by Toffoli and Margolus 1987).

All the models we have seen in this chapter have been very abstract. Obviously, the majority model does not represent all that can be said about the spread of political opinion, for example. Nevertheless, even these very abstract models do have some value. The majority model, for instance, showed graphically the importance of individual variation not just on the distribution of individual characteristics, but also on the 'shape' of wider patterns, a point that is hard to make convincingly in other ways. However, the tendency in recent work has been to create increasingly more complex models, in which the rules driving the cells are a lot more complicated than the ones we have seen in this chapter.

One topic area that has taken forward the cellular automata approach with promising results is the investigation of the dynamics of political opinion change. For example, Deffuant *et al.* (2003) study a model similar in many respects to the majority model, but give the cells the possibility of having an opinion on a continuous scale, not just 'black' or 'white'. They also introduce the idea of 'uncertainty': some people may be convinced that they are correct, whereas others may be rather uncertain about their opinions. They investigate the effect of giving some cells very positive or negative opinions with low uncertainty, in order to model political extremists. They then study the circumstances in which the extremists are influential, either persuading the whole of the population to move to one extreme, or dividing the population into two roughly equal, opposed camps.

While these models use more complicated rules than the models covered in this chapter, the basic structure is the same: a spatial grid of cells each of which interacts with its neighbours. A different strand of work has generalized cellular automata in another direction, freeing the actors from their cells and giving them the possibility of being autonomous and goal-directed. These models are best classified as multi-agent models, the subject of the next chapter.

Further reading

The best general introductions to the use of cellular automata in the social sciences are

- Hegselmann, R. (1996) Cellular automata in the social sciences: perspectives, restrictions and artefacts. In R. Hegselmann *et al.* (eds), *Modelling and Simulation in the Social Sciences from the Philosophy of Science Point of View*, pp. 209–234. Kluwer, Dordrecht.
- Hegselmann, R. (1996) Understanding social dynamics: the cellular automata approach. In K. G. Troitzsch *et al.* (eds), *Social Science Microsimulation*, pp. 282-306. Springer-Verlag, Berlin.

A book which develops the ideas in this chapter and provides examples and programs for using cellular automata in the social sciences is

- Gaylord, R. J. and D'Andria, L. J. (1998) *Simulating Society: A Mathematica Toolkit for Modelling Socioeconomic Behavior*. TELOS Springer-Verlag, Berlin.

Wolfram was one of the pioneers of cellular automata and has recently published a work of monumental size and ambition which argues that cellular automata are fundamental to understanding the universe.

- Wolfram, S. (2002) *A New Kind of Science*. Wolfram Media, Champaign, IL.

Another work of similar size is

- Ilachinski, A. (2001) *Cellular Automata. A Discrete Universe*. World Scientific, Singapore, New Jersey, London, Hong Kong

which is a textbook for everyone who is interested in cellular automata. It deals with almost all possible features and applications of cellular automata from physics to artificial life (in Chapter 11, pp. 557–602) and also mentions 'mobile CAs' – those for modelling migration processes.

Another more technical, but much older discussion of attempts to understand CA models analytically, with a complete description of Wolfram's notation for classifying one-dimensional rules, is

- Wolfram, S. (ed.) (1986) *Theory and Applications of Cellular Automata*. World Scientific, Singapore.

An accessible introduction to cellular automata in science in general and a description of special hardware built to run cellular automata very quickly may be found in

- Toffoli, T. and Margolus, N. (1987) *Cellular Automata Machines*. MIT Press, Cambridge, MA.

One of the first collections of papers on cellular automata was

- Farmer, D. *et al.* (eds) (1984) *Cellular Automata: Proceedings of an Interdisciplinary Workshop.* Los Alamos, New Mexico, 7–11 March, 1983. North Holland, Amsterdam.

Chapter 8

Multi-agent models

In the previous chapter we saw how to build simulations in which very simple automata interacted on a grid so that patterns of behaviour at the global scale emerged. In this chapter we explore how one might develop automata for social simulation which are somewhat more complex in their internal processing and consequently in their behaviour. Such automata are conventionally called *agents*, and there is now a growing literature on how they can be designed, built and used.

While there is no generally agreed definition of what an 'agent' is, the term is usually used to describe self-contained programs that can control their own actions based on their perceptions of their operating environment (Huhns and Singh 1998). Agent programming is rapidly becoming important outside the field of social simulation. For example, agents have been built to watch out for information as it becomes available over the Internet, informing the user if it finds relevant sources (Maes 1994). The agent is instructed about the topics thought to be interesting and it then continuously monitors known sources for items fitting this profile. Other agents have been built to help with electronic network management, business workflow and to guide people to use software more effectively (the agent monitors keystrokes and mouse movements and provides suggestions for faster ways of doing tasks).

The aim of agent design is to create programs that interact 'intelligently' with their environment. Agent software has been much influenced by work in artificial intelligence (AI), especially a subfield of AI called distributed artificial intelligence (DAI) (Bond and Gasser 1988; Chaib-draa *et al.* 1992).

DAI is concerned with the properties of and the design of networks of interacting agents – for example, how one might design a group of agents, each with different expertise, to cooperate to solve a problem. Because of DAI's interest in building networks of 'intelligent' agents and investigating their properties, there is much in this field relevant to social simulation. At the same time, those interested in DAI are increasingly influenced by ideas from the social sciences (Conte *et al.* 1997). This chapter reviews some of the basic ideas of DAI and explains how models involving many agents (so-called multi-agent models) can be used for the simulation of societies. We start with a brief description of the characteristics of agents and how these are typically implemented, before examining some of the research which has used agents. The later sections of the chapter describes a very simple multi-agent model built using NetLogo and a rather more complex model about crowd behaviour.

Agents and agency

Applied to people, the concept of agency is usually used to convey the purposive nature of human activity. It is thus related to concepts such as intentionality, free will, and the power to achieve one's goals. When applied to agents as computer programs, the scope of agency is generally rather weaker. Wooldridge and Jennings (1995) note that computer agents typically have the following properties:

- *autonomy* – agents operate without others having direct control of their actions and internal state;
- *social ability* – agents interact with other agents through some kind of 'language' (a computer language, rather than natural language);
- *reactivity* – agents are able to perceive their environment (which may be the physical world, a virtual world of electronic networks, or a simulated world including other agents) and respond to it;
- *proactivity* – as well as reacting to their environment, agents are also able to take the initiative, engaging in goal-directed behaviour.

In addition, agents are often attributed a degree of intentionality. That is, their behaviour is interpreted in terms of a metaphorical vocabulary of belief, desires, motives, and even emotions, concepts that are more usually applied to people rather than to computer programs. For example, we might say that an agent built to collect relevant items from a supply of news articles was 'trying' to find something appropriate for the user, 'wanted' to get the most relevant article, and 'believed' that articles on a related topic would also be interesting. The habit of attributing intentionality to software agents in this way is liable to cause a great deal of philosophical confusion to the unwary (Shoham 1990). For our purposes, it is only necessary to view the ascription of intentionality to agents as a matter of modelling: a computer agent does not have intentionality, but is constructed to simulate some (much simplified) aspects of human intentions.

With this in mind, we can now list some of the attributes that we may want to model with agents.

Knowledge and belief

Agents will need to base their actions on what they know about their environment (including other agents). Some of the information they have may be incorrect, as a result of faulty perception, faulty inference or incomplete knowledge. We call such possibly erroneous information the agents' *beliefs* to distinguish them from true knowledge.

Inference

Given a set of beliefs, agents may be able to infer further information from them. For example, believing that agent B has recently 'eaten' some 'food', agent A could infer that the place to find food is near where agent B was located. Of course, this inference may be wrong (perhaps agent B consumed all the food).

Social models

Some agents may be capable of learning about the interrelationships between other agents in their world – for example, that agent A has recently interacted with agent B. On the basis of such snippets of data, agents may be able to put together a picture of the social relationships in their environment – that is, a 'social model'. Agents may also have models of other aspects of their world, for example, they may develop a model of the 'geography' of their environment. Note that these agents' models are quite different from the simulation model that the researcher builds; agent models are built by the agents themselves while the simulation runs.

Knowledge representation

In order to construct its models, an agent needs some way to represent its beliefs. Techniques for doing this have been studied by AI researchers under the heading of 'knowledge representation'. One generally useful approach is to use predicate logic to store declarative statements, such as 'There is food at location 143', and formulae such as 'If an agent is eating at location X, there is food at location X', where X is a variable to be filled in depending on what the agent 'sees' around it. Another approach, which can be used alone or in conjunction with logic, is based on semantic networks in which objects and their attributes are related together, often as a hierarchy. For example, an agent may know that all sources of food yield energy, and also know about several specific kinds of food, each with different energy levels and different means of extracting that energy. These facts would be related in a tree-like structure, with the most general facts about food at its root and more specific facts about different types of food at its branches.

Goals

Since agents are built to be autonomous and purposive, if they are to engage in action they need to be driven by a need to satisfy some internal goal such as survival. Surviving may in turn require the satisfaction of subsidiary goals, such as acquiring energy and avoiding lethal dangers. The problem for the designer is how to get agents to define their own subgoals relevant to the situation at hand. There can also be difficulties in deciding how to manage several goals which may be of differing importance and relevance and which may possibly conflict. The solution to these problems is often the responsibility of a 'planner' module built into the agent.

Planning

An agent needs to have some way of determining what behaviour is likely to lead to the satisfaction of its goals. This may be very straightforward: an agent may be programmed to move away if it finds itself adjacent to a stronger and aggressive attacker, for example. Such simple condition–action rules, taking the form 'if you find yourself in this state, then do that', can be very powerful when several are used in combination (see, for example, the discussions in Steels and Brooks 1995), but often it is desirable for agents to do some more complex planning. Planning involves working backwards from a desired goal state, inferring what action would lead to that goal, what state would be required before that action can be carried out, what action is needed to arrive at that state, and so on, until one gets back to the current situation of the agent. The process is rather similar to working out a travel itinerary when one knows where one needs to be at some future time, but there are a number of possible routes, some good, some bad, to get there. AI researchers have built some very sophisticated planners, but it has been argued that the kind of planning they perform is not a realistic model of human planning and, indeed, that most human action is driven by routine reaction to the particularities of a situation rather than by elaborately calculated plans (Agre and Chapman 1987; Suchman 1987; Brooks 1990).

Language

All multi-agent models include some form of interaction between agents, or, at a minimum, between individual agents and the environment in which they exist. The interaction might involve the passing of information from one agent to another, the negotiation of contracts (Smith and Davis 1981), or even one agent threatening another with 'death' (compare, for example, the communication between political agents in Axelrod's simulation described in the previous chapter). In some models the interaction may convey only factual or non-intentional meaning. A good example is found in Drogoul's multi-agent model of ants' nests (described in more detail below) where simulated ants emit 'stimuli' into the environment as a side-effect of their activities. These stimuli spread out from the emitting ant according to an inverse square law of intensity and are detected by other ants, whose behaviour is thereby affected. Although the ants interact with each other by this means, the stimuli are not spread with any intention of conveying meaning.

In contrast, people speak with the intention of communicating with other people (apart from some special cases such as involuntary exclamations). Such communications need to be modelled by specifying a 'language' for communication. There have been some attempts to develop specialized computer languages for communciation between agents (the best-known example is KQML; Mayfield *et al.* 1996), but these have been designed for their conciseness, simplicity, ease of implementation and similar characteristics rather than as simulations of social interaction. While there is a considerable literature on the topic (Gazdar and Mellish 1989; Hurford *et al.* 1998a; Cangelosi and Parisi 2001), modelling human language remains an area of considerable difficulty and debate. Much of the literature assumes as given what is in fact problematic – for example, that agents start with a common language and that there is perfect correspondence between the words in an agent's vocabulary and their reference in the world – but see the description of Hutchins and Hazlehurst (1995) in Chapter 10. One way of avoiding some of these difficulties is to assume that messages pass directly between agents, 'brain to brain'. Depending on the object of the simulation, this may or may not be a permissible simplification.

Emotions

Although people have emotions such as happiness, sadness, grief and anger, there has been little research within AI on how these can best be modelled and there are still some basic questions about emotions that remain to be clarified (Oatley 1992). Unresolved issues include whether emotional states are entities or are emergent features of other cognitive and subconscious states, and the relationship between emotions and goals. For example, if one succeeds in achieving a goal, does that cause happiness, or is happiness a goal in its own right?

One school of thought views emotions as a form of control signalling: for example, if you are sad because you have not succeeded in reaching a goal, the sadness impels you to look for a change in your goals so as to become happier. The emotional state motivates a change in goal (Ortony *et al.* 1988). An alternative theory sees emotions as essentially epiphenomenal, happiness being an indication to oneself that one has had success in managing within one's environment, and sadness the realization that one's plans are not working out (Wright 1996). None of these theories emphasizes the social consequences of emotion, such as the expectation that those who hold certain social roles will engage in 'emotional labour' by providing solace, encouragement and so on (Hochschild 1983).

This brief survey of those characteristics of autonomous agents that we might want to model has shown that there remain many significant unsolved problems and that it would be unrealistic to expect multi-agent models to be able to simulate the great majority of human psychological and social phenomena to any level of detail. As with other forms of simulation discussed in this book, we should aim to extract the features of the target that are of most theoretical significance and concentrate on modelling those, disregarding the many features which are fundamental aspects of humans but which are not central to the matter under investigation.

Agent architecture

The traditional AI approach to building agents with cognitive abilities is known as the symbolic paradigm. This is based on the 'physical-symbol system hypothesis' (Newell and Simon 1976), which asserts that a system that manipulates symbols according to symbolically coded sets of instructions is capable of generating intelligent action. Thus traditional AI involves building programs which work with symbols. For example, an agent might receive the symbol 'Hallo' as a message from another agent, and respond appropriately. In this case, the agent would need to recognize the in-coming symbol and be able to generate the reply, probably by using pattern matching and a rule which states that a response along the lines of 'Can I help you?' is to be sent whenever a 'Hallo' is received.

However, the symbolic paradigm has generated a host of difficult problems which look insoluble in general, although they may be avoided or minimized in specific applications. These problems can be summarized as: fragility (a system may work well in specific context, but it may not cope successfully with even minor variations); complexity (some problems, such as the planning task mentioned above, require algorithms of considerable complexity); and difficulty in solving some problems that people seem to manage easily (such as representing 'commonsense' knowledge). A variety of techniques and algorithms have been developed over the 50 years since the birth of AI to overcome these difficulties. The ones that are important for multi-agent simulation are production systems, object orientation, language parsing and generation, and machine learning techniques. The first two of these will be reviewed in this section. An introduction to computational linguistics and the understanding and production of 'natural' languages can be found in Jurafsky and Martin (2000). Learning will be considered further in the next chapter, where we will review a variety of approaches to learning and evolution, including the use of methods that break away from the physical-system hypothesis in favour of non-symbolic approaches to machine intelligence.

Production systems

Most agents in multi-agent models are built using some kind of rule system, of which the simplest is a 'production system'. A production system has three components: a set of rules, a working memory and a rule interpreter. The rules each consist of two parts: a condition part, which specifies when the rule is to fire; and an action part, which states what is to happen when the rule fires. For example, a robot agent might include the rule 'if (a) your arm is raised and (b) the goal is to pick up an object and (c) an object is on the table, then lower your arm'. This would be one of perhaps hundreds of such rules. Whether the condition part of a rule is in fact satisfied at any moment is determined by looking in the agent's working memory which stores facts such as the location of the arm, the robot's current goal and its knowledge of the state of the environment. The job of the rule interpreter is to consider each rule in turn, check whether the conditions of the rule are met and then, if necessary, carry out the action.

The main advantage of a production system is that the designer does not have to decide beforehand in which order the rules are to fire. In contrast with the more determined order of execution one gets with an ordinary program or a flow chart, the agent can to some extent react appropriately to the situation it finds itself in. Which rules fire and when they do so depends on the contents of working memory and thus on the past experiences of the agent and the state of its environment.

The designer needs to decide what the interpreter should do when the condition parts of more than one rule are satisfied. The possibilities are: to fire just the first rule whose condition is satisfied; to fire all the rules that can be fired; or to use some other 'conflict resolution' procedure to choose which to fire. The last is particularly important if the rulebase includes rules specific to particular situations and also more general rules that apply to many situations, including those covered by the more specific rules. For example, in addition to the rule about lowering the arm to pick up an object, there might be a more specific rule to cover the situation when the object to be picked up is taller than the robot and the arm is therefore to be raised, not lowered. In these circumstances, we would want to fire the specific rule, but not the general rule, although the condition parts of both are met.

When a rule has been fired by carrying out its action part, the rule interpreter cycles round and looks again at all the rules to find which to fire next. The action that the agent carried out might have changed the contents of its memory, so the rules which fire on the second cycle may not be the same as the ones which fired first time round. For example, the robot might have lowered its arm because the rule cited above fired. If the agent's memory now records that the arm is in the lowered position, one of the conditions of that rule will no longer be satisfied, but some other rule including the condition 'the arm is in a lowered position' may be able to fire. It is usual for rules to specify actions that either directly affect the agent's memory or affect the environment in a way which the agent can perceive. If a rule does not have either of these consequences, it will be fired on every cycle until the effect of some other rule makes its condition part no longer true.

Object orientation

A natural way of programming agents is to use an 'object-oriented' programming language. In this context, 'objects' are program structures that hold both data and procedures for operating on those data. In object-oriented programming, the data are stored in 'slots' within the object and the procedures are called 'methods'. In most object-oriented languages, objects are created from templates called 'classes' that specify the composition of the object, the data it can hold and the methods it uses. All the objects derived from the same class are similar in terms of the methods and slots they possess, although the data values of different objects may differ. The classes themselves are arranged in a hierarchy, with subordinate classes inheriting the methods and slots of superior classes but adding additional ones or replacing some of the superior's slots and methods with more specialized substitutes. For example, consider a simulation of pedestrian flow through a shopping precinct (cf. Molnár 1996). There may be a class representing the structure and procedures of a simulated pedestrian. The class would define slots in which to store, for instance, the location of the pedestrian agent and its current direction, and a method that specifies how to walk, as well as several others. This basic agent class might have two subclasses, one for pedestrians walking alone, and one for pedestrians who are part of a group. Both would inherit the slots describing location and direction from the basic pedestrian class, but the latter would add a further slot to the structure to store a list of the other pedestrians in its group. The class for group members would also specialize the general method for walking to take into account the motion of the other group members – for example, to reduce the walking speed if the agent is moving too far ahead of the rest.

Once a set of classes has been defined, individual agents are generated by creating instances from them ('instantiation'). The advantage of the object-oriented approach is that the slots can represent the internal states of the agent (including its working memory and the rules, if it has been designed as a production system), while the methods can implement the rule interpreter. By specifying the rules at the class level, all agents instantiated from that class can share the same rules, while the contents of their memories can differ between agents. In addition, the object-oriented approach leads naturally to a useful encapsulation, with each agent clearly distinguishable within the program. The fit between object orientation and multi-agent modelling is so close that nearly all multi-agent simulations are written using object-oriented programming languages. Examples of such languages are C++ (Stroustrup 1993), Objective C (NeXT Corporation 1993), Lisp (Graham 1996), Smalltalk (Goldberg 1989) and Java (Arnold and Gosling 1998).

Modelling the environment

In all multi-agent simulations, the agents are located in an environment. What constitutes an environment depends on what is being modelled, but if the agents are individual people, rather than organizations, one of the main functions of the environment will be to provide a spatial context. Each agent will be located in a simulated space, in much the same way as cellular automata are located on a grid. In many models, the agents are able to move around the environment. Although such a spatial world is the most common environment, others are possible. For instance, the agents may move through a network of nodes and links (this might be useful if, for instance, the simulation was concerned with markets and trading, with the network modelling trading links).

Once agents are positioned within an environment, they will need 'sensors' to perceive their local neighbourhood and some means with which to affect the environment. Usually, communication between agents is routed through the environment, which forwards messages on to the appropriate recipient. In this case, agents will also need to be able to 'hear' messages coming from the environment and to send messages to the environment for onward transmission.

The designer will also need to decide about the order in which the agents in the simulation are given computing time. Ideally, all agents ought to operate in parallel. However, because most simulations run on sequential rather than parallel computers, the desired parallel operation must itself be simulated, usually by running the program code for each agent in a round robin fashion, or by choosing the next agent to run at random. Unfortunately, the order in which agents are run can have a major effect on the course of the simulation unless suitable precautions are taken. For example, if agent A sends a message to agent B, but B is run before A, agent B will not get the message from A until the next round, by which time the message may no longer be relevant. Computer scientists have investigated such problems under the heading of 'concurrency' and there are a number of well-understood, although complicated techniques for dealing with them (Fisher and Wooldridge 1995). However, the relatively simple solution of buffering messages within the environment is often all that is needed. During each time step, messages from agents are collected and stored in the environment. At the beginning of the next time step, all the stored messages are delivered to their recipients. Alternatively, some of the ideas of discrete event modelling (see Chapter 5) can be used to order events explicitly.

Building multi-agent simulations

In this section, we shall explain the form of a multi-agent simulation at a practical, implementation level, by developing a small demonstration program written in NetLogo (for a brief introduction to NetLogo, see Chapter 7). This will show the basic elements of a multi-agent simulation in only a few pages of code.

NetLogo is a good medium for building multi-agent models because it is object-oriented (the 'turtles' are objects in this sense), because the turtles can easily be programmed to have 'autonomy' (in the limited sense mentioned at the beginning of this chapter) and because it provides a good range of graphical methods of entering parameter input and displaying outputs.

We start with a toy model in which there are agents that each have a shopping list, and a number of shops, each of which sells a product that might be bought by the agents. The agent shoppers have to go to all the shops that sell the products they want, and buy what is on their shopping list, but first they have to find these shops. In the first and simplest version of the model, the agents stumble blindly around trying to find the shops. We shall then make the agents more complicated, observing the effect of their additional 'intelligence' on how long it takes for them to complete their shopping trips.

The model involves two kinds or classes of objects: the agents themselves and the shops. NetLogo allows one to specify different classes of object as 'breeds' (think of breeds of turtle or dog). So we shall have an agents breed and a shops breed. Each has its own slots to hold the data that the object needs to keep. In this model, each agent needs to know what is still to be bought on its shopping list (if the list becomes empty, the agent has completed its shopping) and each shop needs to know which product it sells. The following NetLogo commands establish these breeds.

```
breeds [ agents shops ]
agents-own [ shopping-list memory ]
shops-own [ product ]
globals [ tick products junk ]
```

The global statement defines two variables that can be accessed by any object. They will store the simulated time (tick) and the complete set of all products available in this artificial world (products), both of these being attributes of the model's environment.

As usual, we define a setup procedure to initialize the objects, invoked from the interface by the user when he or she presses the Setup button. For our model, we need to create some agents, place them randomly on the NetLogo world, and give each of them a shopping list of products to buy. The ten agents look like small stick men on the display (a 'person' shape) – see Figure 8.1. Each shopping list is constructed by creating a list (with n-values of ten randomly selected products (some of which may be duplicates) from the list of all products previously stored in the global variable, products.

Figure 8.1: The shoppers' world

The 12 shops, one per product, are represented as black squares, each selling a different product (for simplicity, each shop only sells one product) and are also distributed around the display at random.

At the end of the setup procedure, there are ten agents, each with a shopping list of ten products to buy, and 12 shops, one for each of the 12 available products. All these are randomly scattered over the landscape.

```
to setup
  locals [ product-number ]
  clear-all

; background: make all the patches white
  ask patches [ set pcolor white ]

; products
  set products ["beans" "chocolate" "soap" "bread"
                "toothpaste" "milk"  "apples" "cake" "oranges"
                "butter" " peas" "beer"]

; shoppers
  set-default-shape agents "person"
  create-custom-agents 10 [
    ; locate the agent at a random position
    setxy (random screen-size-x) - screen-edge-x
          (random screen-size-y) - screen-edge-y
    ; set the colour etc. of the shape on the screen
    set color pink  set heading 0  set size 3
    ; give it a list of products to buy
    set shopping-list n-values 10
      [ item (random (length products)) products]
    set memory []
    ]

; shops
  set-default-shape shops "box"
  set product-number 0
  create-custom-shops 12 [
    setxy (random screen-size-x) - screen-edge-x
          (random screen-size-y) - screen-edge-y
    set color black set heading 0 set size 2
    set product item product-number products
    set product-number product-number + 1
    ]
```

Figure 8.1 shows what the simulation looks like at the start, after the Setup button has been pressed.

When the objects have been initialized, the user can press the Go button, which repeatedly calls the go procedure:

```
to go
  ask agents [ act ]
  if count agents with [ not empty? shopping-list ] = 0
      [ stop ]
  set tick tick + 1
end


to act
  if not empty? shopping-list [ shop ]
end
```

The go procedure asks each agent to act, that is, to search for a shop, and then checks to see whether the simulation should finish because all the shoppers have bought everything on their lists. tick counts the number of rounds of simulation, so that we can see how long it takes for all the agents to complete their task.

```
to shop
  if any? shops-here [ buy-if-needed ]
  move-randomly
end

to buy-if-needed
  locals [ shop-to-buy-from ]
  set shop-to-buy-from random-one-of shops-here
  if member? product-of shop-to-buy-from shopping-list [
      set shopping-list remove product-of shop-to-buy-from
                              shopping-list
      ]
end
```

For agents, acting means shopping, provided that there are items still needing to be bought. And for these simple agents, shopping consists of seeing whether there are any shops in the same patch as their current location, and if so, buying from one of them, and then making a random move. shops-here reports the shops on the same patch as the agent. There may be more than one shop on that patch, so they randomly choose one of them. Then the agent looks to see whether the product sold by that shop is on its shopping list, and if so, the agent removes the product from its shopping list (it has 'bought' it).

```
to move-randomly
  set heading (random 360)
  move
end

to move
  forward 1
end
```

Moving randomly consists of setting the agent's heading (i.e. the direction in which it will move) to a random angle and then moving one unit in what is now the forward direction. The result is that the agents engage in what is often called a 'random walk' over the grid. While they are likely to bump into all the shops eventually, it may take many ticks for them all to visit all the shops they need to empty their shopping lists.

Because of the random nature of the agents' moves, the time taken for the simulation to complete will vary, but running it a hundred times gives an average tick value of 14,310 (standard deviation 4150) at the end of a run, when all the agents have bought all they need. The agents are very inefficient at finding the shops they want because they are so stupid.

As the next stage in the development of the model, let us add the ability for the agents to perceive their environment. They will 'see' any shops that are in their Moore neighbourhood and head towards one of them if there are no shops in their current patch.

Most of the code remains unchanged, but the following modifications and additions are needed:

```
to shop
  locals [ closest-shop-i-know ]
  remember products-on-sale-around-here
  if any? shops-here [ buy-if-needed ]
  set closest-shop-i-know scan-memory
  ifelse closest-shop-i-know != "None"
      [ move-towards closest-shop-i-know ]
      [ move-randomly ]
end

to-report products-on-sale-around-here
  report values-from (shops-on neighbors)  [ (list product xcor yco
end

to remember [ shop-locations ]
```

```
set memory remove-duplicates sentence memory shop-locations
end
```

The shop procedure becomes more complicated because the agent has to look around to see which shops are nearby and then has to remember what it sees. When moving, it first searches its memory for the closest shop to its current location and then heads in that direction.

The agent needs to remember three things about the shops that it sees: the product the shop sells, the x-coordinate of the shop's location, and the y-coordinate of the location. So, the procedure products-on-sale-around-here is designed to return a list of those three things for each shop that is on any of the patches which are neighbours of the patch the agent is on (shops-on neighbors). To remember these data involves appending the new shop locations to the existing ones held in memory (the curiously named sentence procedure joins two lists together) and discarding any duplicates, in case the same shop is seen twice.

Then, when the agent wants to move, instead of moving randomly, it will scan its memory to find the location of a shop it already knows about. The scan of its memory is done in two stages. First, the memory records are filtered to extract only those that relate to shops selling products that are on the agent's shopping-list. If there are no known shops that sell products that the agent wants, the procedure returns "None" (see the code fragment below). Otherwise, the agent sorts the records about shop locations according to the distance between it and each shop, and returns the first record in the sorted list, the one for the shop that is nearest the agent.

```
to-report scan-memory
  locals [ shops-to-visit ]
  set shops-to-visit
    filter [ member? (first ?) shopping-list ] memory
  ifelse empty? shops-to-visit [ report "None" ]
    [ report first (sort-by [
        distancexy (last butlast ?1) (last ?1) <
                distancexy (last butlast ?2) (last ?2)
      ] shops-to-visit) ]
end
```

In these procedures, the memory record about each shop is held as a three part list. The first element in the list is the name of the product, the second the x-coordinate of the shop, and the third is the y-coordinate. These elements can be retrieved using the NetLogo procedures, first (which returns the first item in a list, in this case the product), last (which returns the last item in the list, the y-coordinate) and butlast, which returns the whole list except the last element. Thus the last butlast of a list returns the second but last item. The other unfamiliar symbols in the code above are ?1 and ?2. The sorting procedure, sort-by, does a comparison of each element in the list to be sorted with every other item, to see in what order they should be placed in the sorted list. The comparisons are done two elements at a time by the expression inside square brackets, substituting the one element for ?1 and the other for ?2. For example,

```
distancexy (last butlast ?1) (last ?1) <
        distancexy (last butlast ?2) (last ?2)
```

compares the distance between the agent and the spot defined by the x and y coordinates extracted from one memory record ((last butlast ?1) (last ?1)) with the distance between the agent and the spot defined by another record ((last butlast ?2) (last ?2)).

```
to move-towards [ shop-location ]
  if not (xcor = (last butlast shop-location) and
       ycor = (last shop-location))
    [ set heading towardsxy
                  (last butlast shop-location)
                  (last shop-location)
      move ]
end
```

When a memory record has been selected and returned to the shop procedure, the agent then moves towards the location of that shop using move-towards. This procedure (above) checks that the agent is not coincidentally already where it wants to be. If it is, it doesn't need to move. If not, it sets its heading towards the shop's location and moves one unit in that direction.

We assumed that giving the agents the ability to memorize the locations of the shops that they had moved past would speed up their shopping. Is this true? Testing the augmented code by averaging 100 runs shows that it does: the average number of ticks before all the agents have completed their shopping drops from about 14,000 to 6983 (standard deviation: 2007) or to about half.

The agents are now slightly less stupid than the randomly moving ones we started with. While they are obviously very simple, they now do have the ability to perceive their environment and react to it. They do not, however, have any perception of other agents; each operates individually and without regard for the others. Let us continue the development of this model by allowing the agents to exchange information about the shops that they have previously encountered.

These more advanced agents have the additional ability to 'talk' to other agents they come across in their travels. They can talk to other agents on the same patch as they are, and in doing so, they exchange their knowledge about shop locations: agent A gets all the knowledge of agent B to add to its own, and B gets all the knowledge of A. Of course, this is not a faithful model of humans talking: fortunately, we do not do a 'brain dump' of everything we know onto other people in the way that these agents do! But this simple model could be the basis for experimentation about factors such as the effect of exchanging only some knowledge and what is the effect of introducing errors in the transmission of knowledge.

To implement this addition, a line is added to the act procedure to make the agents talk if there are other agents on the same patch as this one. Talking consists of selecting one of the other agents on the patch to talk to, and then copying its memory into the agent's memory, and vice versa.

```
to act
  if any? other-agents-here [ talk ]
  if not empty? shopping-list [ shop ]
end

to talk
  locals [ partner ]
  set partner random-one-of other-agents-here
  remember memory-of partner
  ask partner [ remember memory ]
end
```

Knowledge about shop locations gathered by one agent can now be spread among the population. We have already discovered that knowing about the locations of shops reduces the number of ticks required to fulfil the agents' shopping lists, but how much difference will the social exchange of knowledge that we have now implemented make? Without the talk procedure, the agents took an average of 7000 ticks to finish; with the addition of talking, the time taken falls dramatically to about 2000 ticks (standard deviation: 777).

This sequence of successively more complex agents shows how one can construct increasingly more 'intelligent' agents by building on previous capabilities. There is not space here to develop these agents further, even though so far they remain very unsophisticated. For example, it would be possible to restrict the exchange of knowledge to those agents which were thought to be 'friends' according to some definition of friendship. Another possibility would be to build a more realistic method of exchanging information – in the code above there is only a direct and error-free symbolic exchange from one agent to the other.

Nevertheless, even this very simple example of multi-agent modelling has some of the features mentioned at the beginning of this chapter. The agents control their own actions and internal state (they have autonomy). The agents are able to interact with other agents (they have social ability). The agents can perceive the (simulated) environment and respond to it (they have reactivity). Finally, they are able to engage in goal-directed behaviour (proactivity).

It would not be difficult to add code to test the effect of mistaken beliefs. For example, shops could have a limited supply of the product they sell, and so might eventually run out. However, agents would not be aware of this and would still therefore move to them, expecting to be able to buy. Agents' beliefs that the shops could help them with their shopping lists would become less accurate over time. The information about shops constitutes a crude form of a model of the environment which the agents construct as they wander over the landscape. Other information could easily be added, such as the locations of the other agents. At present, agents' beliefs about shop locations are kept in an unstructured form as a list. If more complex beliefs were to be retained, one might consider constructing a semantic network or another type of knowledge representation. The agents have just one simple goal – to complete their shopping – and no planning abilities, and both these aspects of the agents' design could be augmented.

The extent to which the agents in this simple example have the attributes and capabilities of human agents is of course extremely limited. The challenge for the builder of a multi-agent simulation is to develop them sufficiently so that useful and illuminating simulations of human societies can be constructed. In the next section, we shall summarize three typical examples of multi-agent models.

Examples of multi-agent modelling

In this section we will review several multi-agent models, beginning with one in which the agents are only slightly more complex than the cellular automata discussed in the previous chapter, and moving through other examples which implement significantly more sophisticated and 'intelligent' agents. As we do so, we shall see that the more complex models allow for experimentation with features more obviously associated with human societies, such as the emergence of non-uniform distributions of wealth and the impacts of shared beliefs.

Sugarscape

Sugarscape (Epstein and Axtell 1996) is a good example of a multi-agent model which, although the agents are rather simple, yields a range of interesting results about the emergence of social networks, trade and markets, and cultural differentiation and evolution. Sugarscape models an artificial society in which agents move over a 50 × 50 cell grid. Each cell has a gradually renewable quantity of 'sugar' that the agent located at that cell can eat. However, the amount of sugar at each location varies spatially and according to how much of the sugar has already been eaten (most Sugarscape experiments are conducted on a landscape in which there are two 'peaks' of high sugar values in opposite quadrants of the grid). Agents have to consume sugar in order to survive. If they harvest more sugar than they need immediately, they can save it and eat it later or, in more complex variants of the model, can trade it with other agents.

Agents can look to the north, south, east and west of their current locations (but not diagonally) and can see a distance that varies randomly according to the agents' 'genetic endowment', so that some agents can see many cells away while others can only see adjacent cells. Agents move in search of sugar according to the rule: look for the unoccupied cell that has the highest available sugar level within the limits of one's vision, and move there. Agents not only differ in the distance they can see, but also in their 'metabolic rate', the rate at which they use sugar. If their sugar level ever drops to zero, they die. New agents replace the dead ones with a random initial allocation of sugar. Thus there is an element of the 'survival of the fittest' in the model, because those agents that are relatively unsuited to the environment because they have high metabolic rates, poor vision, or are located in places where there is little sugar for harvesting, die relatively quickly of starvation. However, even successful agents die after they have achieved their maximum lifespan, set according to a uniform random distribution.

Epstein and Axtell present a series of elaborations of this basic model in order to illustrate a variety of features of societies. The basic model shows that even if agents start with an approximately symmetrical distribution of wealth (the amount of sugar each agent has stored), a strongly skewed wealth distribution soon develops. This is because a few relatively well-endowed agents are able to accumulate more and more sugar, while the majority only barely survive or die.

Such simple agents exhibit few of the features of agents described earlier. The only features they do have are goal orientation (their goals are to survive and accumulate wealth) and being rule-driven. The agents in Sugarscape become more interesting when the model is augmented to simulate inter-agent trade. For this, an additional commodity is introduced: 'spice'. Spice, like sugar, is distributed over the landscape and is a requirement for agents' survival. An agent's metabolic rates for sugar and spice are independent of each other, so that some agents may consume sugar at a high rate, but little spice, while for others the reverse is true. Moreover, agents can barter sugar for spice, if they are short of one, have an excess of the other and can find another agent prepared to trade. This scenario can be used for a number of investigations of economic equilibrium, price setting, the operation of markets and so on.

First, however, a number of additions to the capabilities of the agents have to be made. Agents need to have a way of comparing their needs for the two commodities: a welfare function. This function is used to calculate which of the cells available for an agent to move to is best for it. Agents also need ways of valuing sugar and spice when it comes to making or receiving offers to barter, negotiating a price and determining the quantity of each commodity to exchange. Each of these factors is determined by rules common to all agents.

Epstein and Axtell draw several conclusions from observing the trading in this extended model. All barters occur in a local context, negotiated between pairs of agents without any central authority or 'auctioneer'. Nevertheless, prices do converge to an equilibrium level as predicted by neo-classical economic theory, although this equilibrium is a statistical rather than a deterministic one and some individual trades occur at prices that deviate from the equilibrium price. Furthermore, the aggregate quantities traded are less than the market-clearing quantities predicted by economic theory. Another interesting consequence of introducing trade into the model is that the distribution of wealth among the agents becomes even more skewed and unequal.

MANTA

While Sugarscape is firmly allied to the cellular automata approach, although using a non-homogeneous grid for its landscape and agents that have some limited cognitive abilities, the next example is closer to the idea of distributed artificial intelligence. It is one of the few examples described in this book that does not model a human society, but it is nevertheless interesting for the way in which it employs a variety of kinds of agent, including agents which are used to simulate the environment of other agents. The example is MANTA, an acronym for Modelling an Anthill Activity, and the simulation is of the birth of an ant colony (Drogoul and Ferber 1994; Drogoul *et al.* 1995).

The queen ant of the tropical ant species *Ectatomma ruidum* is the mother of all the ants in her colony. During the very first days of the colony, the queen ant is alone or with very few other ants, yet has to care for and, in particular, feed the whole brood. That the process is difficult in nature is shown by the fact that even in laboratory conditions, 86 per cent of new ant colonies perish and the queen ants die before ten worker ants have been born. The process of generating an ant colony and the ant society within it from just the queen ant is called *sociogenesis*, and the authors of MANTA aimed to simulate this process with an artificial ant society.

The ants in MANTA are modelled as agents able to move around a simulated ants' nest environment (Figure 8.2). Ants carry out tasks to maintain the colony, a task being a preset plan of activity built from a suite of primitives, such as picking up objects, eating and looking after the brood. The tasks are triggered by stimuli from the environment or from sources internal to the ant, such as its goals. As mentioned previously, the ants do not interact with each other in the normal sense of the word. Instead they drop stimuli into the environment (analogous to leaving trails of chemical substances in a physical environment) and these stimuli diffuse away along a gradient field. Some of the stimuli are deposited intentionally (for example, to repulse other ants), and some are deposited unintentionally in the course of performing tasks. Other ants detect the stimuli and may react to them, triggering some new task.

An ant can only engage in one task at a time. Which task is performed depends on that task's weight, threshold and activity level. The weight indicates the relative importance to the ant of that task compared with others. Repeatedly carrying out a task raises the task's weight, as the ant is considered to become more specialized in carrying it out. The threshold decreases continuously so long as the task is not carried out. When the task is performed, the threshold increases again. In this way, the threshold indicates

Figure 8.2: View of the simulated ant colony in MANTA (reproduced from Drogoul and Ferber 1994)

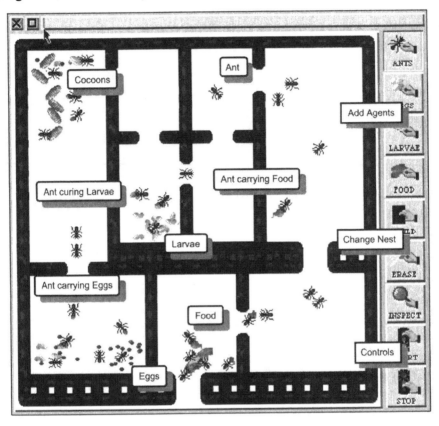

the ant's 'motivation' to carry out a task. When the task is started, the activity level is set to be proportional to the task's threshold and the activity level then decreases continuously so long as the task continues to be performed. The ant switches to a new task when the product of the threshold and the weight of the new task is greater than the activity level of the current task.

In MANTA, the use of agents is not restricted to modelling the ants. The environment is also represented by means of agents. There are food agents, humidity agents and light agents, as well as 'dead ant' agents. All these environmental agents have just one task: to emit stimuli. For example, food emits a stimulus which attracts hungry ants.

Thus in MANTA, although the agents have goals and a repertoire of actions, there is no attempt to model cognitive or even symbolic processing. Instead, the agents are reactive, acting only according to the contextually specific stimuli in which they are immersed. The way in which they behave depends on the type of agent they are. Each type (egg, larva, cocoon or ant) reacts in a different way to a given stimulus. The agents are also simple in that they have no social model (indeed, they have no direct knowledge of other ants) and no planning or knowledge representation capacity.

The simplicity of the agents' design is appropriate for the modelling of ants, whose cognitive capacity is obviously very limited. This is shown by the fact that the simulation is able to reproduce some of the observed features of natural sociogenesis. A typical experiment starts with some 'humidity agents' near the left-hand wall of the artificial nest (Figure 8.2) and a light agent outside the nest. Food agents are provided and replenished as necessary. A single queen agent is placed in the nest and the simulation allowed to run. The queen produces eggs that mature into larvae, cocoons and eventually worker ants. Once 20 worker ants have been bred, the experiment is treated as successful. More often, the queen dies from starvation before this point has been reached. Observations can be made of the conditions that encourage success and in Drogoul *et al.* (1995) experiments which examine the effect of having more than one queen ant in the nest are reported.

The Evolution of Organized Society (EOS)

In the next example, we move from simulations such as Sugarscape and MANTA which have used rather simple agents, to one based on agents with much more complex capabilities for knowledge representation and inference. The Evolution of Organized Society (EOS) project set out to explore theories which account for the growth of social complexity among the human population in the Upper Palaeolithic period (around 30,000 to 15,000 years ago) in south-western France (Doran *et al.* 1994). At that time, there is believed to have been a change from relatively small (family-sized) and autonomous groups of hunter-gatherers to much larger groups, associated with the development of the well-known cave art, the creation of more elaborate artefacts and evidence of trade. Archaeologists consider these to be indicators of the development of social complexity, including the emergence of status and roles within the society, and, in particular, leadership and authority relationships (Mellars 1985; Gamble 1991). They have hypothesized that this change resulted from environmental pressures that tended to concentrate food resources in particular places and at particular times of the year. These resource concentrations led to localized high population densities and a problem in coordinating activities and avoiding cognitive overload (for example, resulting from trying to deal individually with a large number of people). The solution to these problems was to stratify the society and to assign individuals to roles, thus increasing the complexity of the society.

The EOS model was intended to simulate such environmental conditions and thereby investigate their consequences for the pattern of interactions between agents. The simulation consists of a landscape with a population of mobile agents and a scattering of resources which provide 'energy' for the agents. The agents themselves are production systems which include rules to implement agent-to-agent communication. The agents are able to build models of their environment (including the other agents) and to do some rudimentary planning.

The essential aspect which EOS investigated was the formation of relationships between agents: either of hierarchy (leader–follower relations) or alliances (groups of agents in a reciprocal relationship with each other) (Doran and Palmer 1995). The assumption was that if the conditions that promoted the formation of such relationships could be determined, this would indicate the factors that led to social complexity. In particular, Doran considered whether spatial concentration tended to encourage the formation of hierarchies.

Agents in the EOS simulation could either acquire resources alone, working individually, or they could construct 'plans' involving other agents in order to secure the resources collectively. These plans identified the resources to target, the agents which should take part, and the expected payoff and its distribution among those involved. Having constructed such a plan, an agent would then negotiate carrying it out with other agents. Since initially all agents made plans, they were all likely to have several plans to choose from, their own plan and those formulated by other agents, and they selected the one with the greatest expected payoff.

In situations of plentiful resources, or resources very thinly distributed, agents are likely to find that working alone had a greater payoff. But where agents and resources are spatially concentrated, and especially when some resources need several agents working together to harvest them, more complex plans involving several agents will be more profitable. As time passes, some agents will repeatedly adopt the plans proposed to them by particular other agents, and these agents will come to see themselves as followers, led by the agents whose plans they participate in.

Numerous experiments varying the parameters of this rather complex model have been undertaken by Doran and Palmer (1995) and Doran *et al.* (1994). As expected, agents had a much higher chance of surviving starvation and were found to form extensive hierarchies when they and the resources were concentrated together. However, even when they were close together, if there were not sufficient resources to maintain the agent population, agents died, upsetting the hierarchies and leading to relative disorganization. It was also found that if the hierarchies, once established, were persistent, the agents' chances of survival were worse than if the leader–follower relations were relatively temporary. Further experiments have explored the effect of introducing misperceptions: inaccurate social models have the effect of reducing hierarchy formation (Doran 1998).

The EOS experiments illustrate how one can build a multi-agent simulation in which the agents include simplified models of human cognition: they can perceive their environment and other agents, formulate beliefs about their world, plan, decide on courses of action, and observe the consequences of their actions. However, building such agents is a substantial exercise, involving some difficult problems of design and programming. In addition, practical problems have to be solved to ensure that such complex simulations are in fact working as intended (see the discussion of verification and validation in Chapter 2) and to run sufficient experiments to assess the effects of each of the many parameters included in such models. The next chapter reviews some suggestions for making the design of multi-agent models easier.

Further reading

Multi-agent modelling is still new and there are few textbooks about the construction of multi-agent systems. One recent example is:

- Ferber, J. (1998) *Multi-agent Systems*. Addison-Wesley, Reading, MA.

Epstein and Axtell show clearly and simply what can be achieved using quite simple multi-agent models in:

- Epstein, J. M. and Axtell, R. (1996) *Growing Artificial Societies – Social Science from the Bottom Up*. MIT Press, Cambridge, MA.

Unfortunately, the book does not include any examples of code, but the algorithms are described explicitly and could be implemented fairly easily using a multi-agent framework or toolkit. Many of Epstein and Axtell's examples have subsequently been implemented using other programming systems (e.g. Swarm, RePast, NetLogo).

- Minar, N., *et al.* (1996) The Swarm simulation system: a toolkit for building multi-agent simulations (`http://www.santefe.edu/projects/swarm/`).
- RePast :: An Agent Based Modelling Toolkit for Java (`http://repast.sourceforge.net/`).

JESS is a production rule engine and scripting environment written in Java by Ernest Friedman-Hill. It is available freely from `http://herzberg.ca.sandia.gov/jess/`.

Many of the fundamental ideas used in multi-agent modelling (for example, production systems, knowledge representation, semantic networks) have been borrowed from artificial intelligence. The standard text on artificial intelligence, and still one of the best, is:

- Winston, P. H. (1992) *Artificial Intelligence.* Addison-Wesley, Reading, MA.

Another good text on AI that takes an agent perspective is

- Nilsson, Nils J. (1998) *Artificial Intelligence: A New Synthesis.* Morgan Kaufmann, San Francisco, CA.

Chapter 9

Developing multi-agent systems

The previous chapter introduced the idea of multi-agent systems and offered some examples of simulations based on this approach. This chapter goes into more detail about designing and building multi-agent systems, outlining a design process that will help with moving from an initial idea to a working system. We shall review some techniques for describing, testing and validating multi-agent systems and conclude by considering how multi-agent simulations can be integrated into research and policy development. Chapter 2 introduced some of these methodological issues, but this chapter will go into more detail and apply them to multi-agent simulations.

The chapter will be illustrated by reference to a quite typical small-scale multi-agent model published in the Journal of Artificial Societies and Social Simulation (Jager *et al.* 2001). The article reports on a study of conflict in crowds made up of two groups, such as when the supporters of opposing football teams meet in the street. As the authors remark, the outcome can vary from the peaceful mingling of the two groups to the occurrence of fights and riots. The model allows the authors to experiment with different sizes of groups, made up of different proportions of 'hardcore' agents, 'hangers-on' and 'bystanders'. Eighty simulation runs were conducted with a variety of group sizes and compositions and the article concludes that fights are most common in large groups with a relatively large proportion of hardcore members when the groups are quite different sizes (see Figure 9.1).

Figure 9.1: An example for the two-party crowd model (dots in light and dark grey), with some participants fighting (black dots). From a re-implementation of Jager *et al.* (2001) in NetLogo. 300 participants of one party and 100 of the other; 5 per cent hardcore

Making a start

The research question and the model that is to be designed is sometimes clear from the start. More often, one has an idea of the topic, but not anything more precise. It is essential that a general interest in a topic is refined down to a specific question before the model design begins. If this is not done, the design task can either seem impossibly difficult or your model can become too encompassing to be helpful. It is useful to think about narrowing down a research question in terms of a moving through a set of layers (see Punch

2000 for a helpful treatment). An area of research, such as group processes, contains many topics, for example, the behaviour of two party crowds. More specific is a general research question, usually phrased in terms of theoretical concepts and the relationship between these. The research question asked in Jager *et al.*'s paper is, what is the relationship between the characteristics of a two-party crowd and the occurrence of fights among the participants? The general research question will generate a small number of specific research questions, such as what is the relationship between the proportion of 'hardcore' members of a crowd and the chances of there being fights? The specific research questions should be at a level of detail such that their concepts can be used as the main elements of the model. Finally, there are data questions that the model will answer with proportions or percentages: for example, how much difference does it make to the likelihood of fighting if the hardcore percentage is 1 or 5 per cent?

The social world is very complicated, a fact that modellers are well aware of, especially when they begin to define the scope of a model. As noted in Chapter 2, the art of modelling is to simplify as much as possible, but not to oversimplify to the point where the interesting characteristics of the phenomenon are lost (Lave and March 1993). Often, an effective strategy is to start from a very simple model, which is easy to specify and implement. When one understands this simple model and its dynamics, it can be extended to encompass more features and more complexity.

The simplest model of a crowd is probably a system in which the agents, all identical and scattered over a square grid, randomly drift from one cell to the next. Such a model can be constructed in just a few lines of NetLogo. The behaviour will not be interesting - if the agents start at random locations and move randomly, the pattern of agents on the grid will remain random – but it will serve well as the baseline from which more interesting behaviours can be added. The baseline model can be designed to be the equivalent of a null hypothesis in statistical analysis: a model which is not expected to show the phenomenon in question. Then if an addition to the baseline model is made, and the model behaves differently, one can be sure that it is the addition which is having the effect.

Jager *et al.*'s model includes three developments of this baseline model: a set of agent behaviours that vary according to the number of other agents in the locality; a division of the agents into two 'parties' which are potentially in conflict with each other; and a division of the agents into three types: hardcore, hangers-on and bystanders. Each of these developments affect the patterns that are obtained from the simulation in interesting ways. However, there are many other extensions that could be made to the model (for example, adding obstructions to the uniform grid over which the agents move) and each of them could have unanticipated interactions with other extensions. To reduce the complexity of all these possibilities, it is best to start simple and then gradually add features one by one.

This strategy also has the advantage that it helps to focus attention on the research question or questions that are to be answered. A modeller should always have at the forefront of their attention why they are building the model and what they are seeking to obtain from it. It is a good idea to write down at the beginning one or two questions that the modelling aims to answer. This could be as a summary objective, together with a few sub-objectives. The authors of the Jager *et al.*'s paper state that their concern was with the characteristics of large groups that encouraged fighting among their members. Hence their question was, what are the effects of group size, group symmetry and group composition on the likelihood of outbreaks of fighting in two-party crowds? A clear statement like this of the research question can be very helpful in guiding the development of a multi-agent model.

If the baseline model is simple enough, the first prototype implementation can sometimes be a 'pencil and paper' model, in which the designer (or the designer and a few colleagues) play out the simulation 'by hand' through a few rounds. This simulation of a simulation can quickly reveal gaps and ambiguities in the design, without the need to do any coding.

From theory to model

Designing a model is easier if there is already a body of theory to draw on. At an early stage, therefore, one should look around for existing theory, in just the same way as with more traditional social science methodologies. Theories that are about processes of change and that consider the dynamics of social phenomena are of course likely to be more helpful than theories about equilibria or static relationships, but any theory is better than none. What the theory provides is an entry to the existing research literature, hints about what factors are likely to be important in the model, and some indications about comparable phenomena. For example, Jager *et al.* explain in the introduction to their paper that early theories assumed that people's personalities are different in crowd situations as compared with their normal personality, but later writers agree that this is not so. What is different is that normal cultural rules, norms and organizational forms cease to be applicable in crowds, and people fall back on simpler behavioural rules that can be understood by all without instructions or much cultural knowledge.

This theoretical orientation informs their choice that the participants will be modelled using a set of three rather simple behavioural rules, which they call the restricted view rule, the approach-avoidance rule and the mood rule.

The role of theory can thus be to direct attention to the relevant features that need to be modelled (such as Jager *et al.*'s behavioural rules), but it can also be more fundamental to the modelling work. Malerba *et al.* (1999) coined the term 'history-friendly' to describe a model that is intended to encapsulate an existing theory, previously only formulated as text. Reporting a study of the long-term evolution of the computer industry, they write:

> We have taken a body of verbal appreciative theorizing, developed a formal representation of that theory, and found that the formal version of that theory is consistent and capable of generating the stylized facts the appreciative theory purports to explain. Going through this analytic exercise has significantly sharpened our theoretical understanding of the key factors behind salient aspects of the evolution of the computer industry.
> (Malerba *et al.* 1999: 3)

Another function of theory can be to identify clearly the assumptions on which the model is built. These assumptions need to be as clearly articulated as possible if the model is to be capable of generating useful information. For example, in the crowd model, Jager *et al.* assume that there are three types of participant, hardcore, hangers-on and bystanders, and that the proportions of each of these types is about 1:2:97, that is the great majority of the crowd are bystanders. The article discusses the effect of varying these proportions, for example, of increasing the hardcore component to 5 per cent, and compares the proportions with evidence from observation of actual crowds.

The design process

Once the research questions, the theoretical approach and the assumptions have been clearly specified, it is time to begin to design the simulation. There is a sequence of issues that need to be considered for almost all simulations, and it is helpful to deal with these systematically and in order. Nevertheless, design is more of an art than a science and there is no 'right' or 'wrong' design so long as the model is useful in addressing the research question. Although designing models may seem hard the first time, it becomes easier with practice and experience.

The first step is the definition of the types of objects to be included in the simulation. Most of these objects will be agents, representing individuals or organizations, but there may also be objects representing inanimate features that the agents use, such as food or obstacles. The various types of object should be arranged in a class hierarchy, with a generic object at the top, then agents and other objects as sub-types, and if necessary, the agent type divided into further sub-types.

These classes can be arranged in a 'tree' structure, as in Figure 9.2. This diagram shows the class hierarchy for the simulation of crowds. The diagram is simple because in this simulation there are only three types of agent and no inanimate objects. If we had wanted to extend the model to include, for example obstacles which participants would have to move around, this would have meant an additional class, as shown.

Figure 9.2: Class hierarchy for the Two-Party Crowd model

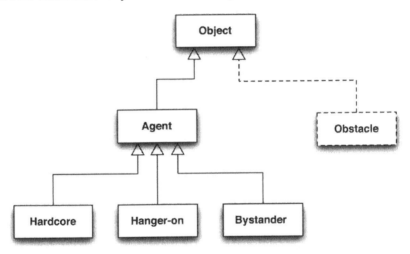

Notice that we have defined a class of Agent, as a type of generic object, and that each of the types of crowd member is a sub-type of this Agent. This means that we shall be able to arrange for much of the coding to be located in the Agent class and that each type of participant is just a small modification - a 'specialization' - of the basic Agent type. Arranging it in this way makes it much easier to see what differs between the crowd members, and what is the same.

The diagram shows classes or types of object. Each actual object in the simulation will be an example of one of these types (an 'instance' of the class). All instances of a class are identical in terms of the code that creates and runs them, but each instance can be in a different state, or have different attributes.

Once the objects have been decided, one can consider the attributes of each object. An attribute is a characteristic or feature of the object, and is either something that helps to distinguish the object from others in the model, or is something that varies from one time in the simulation to another. For example, in the crowd simulation, the level of aggression is an attribute of the agents that varies over time. Hardcore agents scan their surroundings more frequently than hangers-on, and so scan frequency is a good choice for another attribute of an agent. Attributes function like variables in a mathematical model, and most of the things that vary will need to be treated as attributes in the simulation.

Consider each object in turn, and what features it has that differ from other objects. Properties such as size, colour or speed might be relevant attributes in some models. State variables such as wealth, energy and number of friends might also be attributes. An attribute might consist of a single one of a set of values (for example the colour attribute might be one of red, green, blue or white); a number, such as the energy level of the agent; or a list of values, such as the list of the names of all the other agents that an agent has previously encountered. Sub-types inherit the attributes of their types, so that, for instance, if all objects have a location, so do all sub-types of Object, such as Agents and Obstacles.

When the attributes for each class of object have been decided, they can be shown on the class diagram, as in Figure 9.3. This way of representing classes and attributes is taken from a design language called the Unified Modelling Language (UML) (Booch *et al.* 2000) and is commonly used in object-oriented software design. In the example, the attributes for partici-pants in the crowd are shown in the Agent box. In this example, the sub-types of agent – hardcore, hanger-on and bystander – have only one attribute in addition to the ones that they inherit by virtue of being types of Agent, but in other models, sub-types will commonly have attributes that they alone possess, to represent features particular to that type.

There will be some features that can either be implemented as attributes or as sub-classes. For example, we could define distinct sub-classes for the three types of crowd participant, as suggested above, or there could be one type of agent with an attribute called, for example, 'participant-type' and taking one of the values, 'hardcore', hanger-on' or 'bystander'. Do which ever seem to be more natural, provided that there are not too many sub-classes (while it is reasonable to have three sub-classes of Agent, one for each type of participant, it would be awkward if there were a hundred types

Figure 9.3: Class hierarchy with attributes

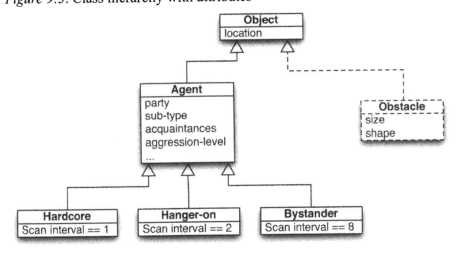

of participant and a sub-class for each, while it would not be a problem to have an attribute with a hundred possible values).

The next stage is to specify the environment in which the objects are located. Often, the environment is a spatial one, and each object has a location within it (in that case, the objects need to have attributes that indicate where they are at the current time). But there are other possibilities, such as having the agents in a network linked by relations of friendship or trade with other agents. Sometimes it may be convenient to represent the environment as another object, albeit a special one, and specify its attributes. One of the attributes will be the current simulated time. Another may be a message buffer which temporarily holds messages sent by agents to other agents via the environment before they are delivered.

In the course of defining the classes, attributes and environment, you will probably find yourself going back and forth, adding or refining each of them in an iterative process until the whole set seems consistent. When this is done, at least to a first approximation, you have a static design for the model. The next step is to add some dynamics, that is, to work out what happens when the model is executed.

Adding dynamics

It is usually easiest to start by considering the interactions of each class of agent with the environment. An agent will act on the environment in one or more ways. For example, the participants in the crowd simulation move from location to location. You should list all these interactions, and also create a list of the ways in which the environment acts on the agent. For example, the environment prevents crowd members from moving into a location that is already occupied by another agent.

Once these lists of the actions of the agents and the environments have been created, we can move on to consider when the actions happen. Against the list of agent actions on the environment, indicate the conditions under which these actions should occur. This table of conditions and actions will lead naturally to defining a set of condition-action rules. Each rule should be associated with a unique state of the agent (a unique set of attribute values and inputs from the environment).

After the interactions with the environment have been decided, the same job can be done for interactions between agents. In the crowd simulation, there are two types of interaction: the agents can approach other agents that they know, and they can fight agents of the other party. As before, these actions need to be associated with the conditions under which the actions are taken; for example, in the crowd simulation, agents will fight only when they have an 'aggression motivation' higher than 25 units and they are adjacent to their victim.

It is likely that, in working through these lists, it will be realized that additional attributes are needed for the agents or the environment or both, so the design process will need to return to the initial stages, perhaps several times. When a consistent set of classes, attributes and rules has been created, it can be helpful to summarize the dynamics in a sequence diagram, another type of UML diagram. A sequence diagram has a vertical line for each type or class of agent, and horizontal arrows representing messages or actions that go from the sender object to the receiver object. The sequence of messages is shown by the vertical order of the arrows, with the top arrow representing the first message and later messages shown below. Figure 9.4 is an example. The diagram shows two types of agent having a fight which lasts for 100 time steps. This diagram is rather simple because there are only two objects and two messages shown, but in more complex models, sequence diagrams can become quite elaborate (see Figures 2 and 3 of Etienne *et al.* 2003 for an example).

It can also be useful to employ statechart and activity diagrams to

Figure 9.4: Sequence diagram

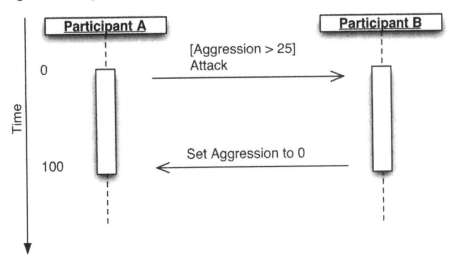

Figure 9.5: Activity diagram showing the behavioural rule for crowd participants (after Jager *et al.* 2001)

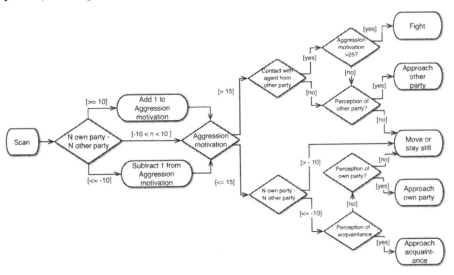

summarize the behaviour of agents (Fowler and Scott 1999). A statechart diagram shows each distinct state of an agent and what is involved in moving from one state to another. An activity diagram shows how decisions are made by an agent. Figure 9.5 shows the behavioural model of a crowd agent as an activity diagram (adapted from Jager *et al.* 2001).

Cognitive models

Figure 9.5 could be thought of as a rather simple cognitive model of an agent. It describes how the agent reacts when presented with stimuli from the environment. However, as a cognitive model it suffers from being divorced from psychologists' understanding of how human cognition works. If the research question warrants it, cognitive models that are relatively well-supported by psychological data can be used either directly in a simulation, or as the inspiration for psychologically informed agent rules. One of the first cognitive models was Soar (Laird *et al.* 1987), and it continues to be developed to this day (for a recent overview, see Wray and Jones 2005). Soar is a production rule system, meaning that it includes condition-action rules, such as those discussed in the previous chapter, although it can also handle more powerful rules that include variables (using predicate, rather than propositional logic). Soar also has a working memory, but in contrast to the simple production rule architecture introduced in Chapter 8, this memory is partitioned into 'states', corresponding to the different problems that the agent has been solving. The condition of more than one production rule may be matched at any one time, and Soar has a system of preference procedures to prioritize which rule is to fire among all those whose conditions match. Soar runs repeatedly through a 'decision cycle' in which it first obtains perception inputs from the environment, computes the set of rules that could fire, applies the preference procedures to select one rule to fire, and then fires that rule by carrying out the action it specifies. Finally, any output to the environment is performed. This cycle is repeated indefinitely. (This is a simplified account of a more complex mechanism; for details see Rosenbloom *et al.* 1993.)

ACT-R is another cognitive model (or 'architecture') with similar aims to Soar: to simulate and understand human behaviour (Anderson and Lebiere 1998). It is a modular system, with distinct modules that deal with memory, perceptual inputs from the environment, buffers that manage the interfaces between modules, and a pattern matcher that determines which rules are able to fire. Like Soar, ACT-R includes a production system, but it also has a sub-symbolic level that controls the activities of the symbolic modules. For example, the sub-symbolic system is used to weight rules in order to decide which one of several candidates should fire, taking the place of Soar symbolic preference procedures. At the symbolic level, information in working memory and production rules are divided into chunks and can be retrieved according to their sub-symbolic 'activation'. The activation of a chunk is influenced by factors such as how frequently it is accessed, how long it has been since it was last accessed, and how closely linked into other active information it is. This allows ACT-R to be used to model learning and forgetting.

The advantage of these architectures is that they build on decades of cognitive science research on human performance. Using one of them therefore increases the chance that the behaviour of one's agent corresponds to the behaviour of a human given the same situation, history and perceptions. Both SOAR and ACT-R are available as implementations that can be downloaded over the Internet and used much like a programming language to build models. However, this comes at a cost. The amount of knowledge that needs to be built into a cognitive model in order for it to operate at all may be out of proportion to the value obtained from using it. Because of their complexity, these cognitive models require a lot of preliminary work to learn how to operate them, generally run slowly, and are rather difficult to integrate with other simulation tools (for example, SOAR is a stand-alone program, whereas ACT-R is a library written in the programming language Lisp; the rest of one's multi-agent simulation will also therefore need either to be written in or be able to interface with Lisp). Rather than using the programs directly, it is also possible to implement some elements of their cognitive architectures in one's own models, in whatever level of detail seems appropriate to the research question.

The user interface

At this stage in the design process, most of the internal aspects of the model will have been defined, although normally there will still be a great deal of refinement needed. The final step is to design the user interface. Depending on the toolkit being used, the components of this interface will be sliders, switches, buttons and dials for the input of parameters, and various graphs and displays for the output, to show the progress of the simulation. Initially, for simplicity it is best to use a minimum of input controls. As understanding of the model improves, and additional control parameters are identified, further controls can be added. Similarly, with the output displays, it is best to start simple and gradually add more as the need for them becomes evident. Of course, every model needs a control to start it, and a display to show that the simulation is proceeding as expected (for example, a counter to show the number of steps completed). At the early stages, there may also be a need for output displays that are primarily there for debugging and for building confidence that the model is executing as expected. Later, if these displays are not required to answer the research question, they can be removed again.

For their article on clustering in two-party crowds, Jager *et al.* used three displays: a view of the square grid over which the agents moved (see Figure 9.1); a plot of a clustering index against simulated time and a plot of the number of fights started at each time step. It is likely, however, that in the work that led up to the writing of the article, several other plots would have been examined. It is the requirement to build plots quickly and without much extra effort that makes the use of toolkits for multi-agent modelling so necessary. For example, an advantage of NetLogo, the package described in the previous two chapters, is that a fully labelled line plot showing how some parameter changes over time can be added with only two lines of program code.

Unit tests

Even before the coding of a model is started, it is worth considering how the simulation will be tested. A technique that is gaining in popularity is 'unit testing'. The idea is that small pieces of code that exercise the program are written in parallel with the implementation of the model. Every time the program is modified, all the unit tests are re-run to show that the change has not introduced bugs into existing code. Also, as the model is extended, more unit tests are written, the aim being to have a test of everything. The idea of unit tests comes from an approach to programming called XP (for eXtreme programming, Beck 1999), a software engineering methodology that is particularly effective for the kind of iterative, developmental prototyping approach that is common in most simulation research. When there are many unit tests to carry out, it becomes tedious to start them all individually and a test harness that will automate the process is needed. This will also have to be designed, possibly as part of the design of the model itself, although there are also software packages that make the job easier (see, for example, the open source Eclipse toolset, http://www.eclipse.org/).

When the model is working as expected, it will probably be necessary to carry out sensitivity analyses (see Chapter 2) involving multiple runs of the simulation while varying the input parameters and recording the outputs. Doing such runs manually is also tedious and prone to error, so a second reason for having a test harness is to automate analysis. You should be able to set the starting and ending points of an input range and then sweep through the interval, rerunning the model and recording the results for each different value. To enable this to be done, the model may have to have two interfaces: a graphical one so that the researcher can see what is happening and an alternative test- or file-based interface which interacts with the testing framework (for example NetLogo has a facility called the 'BehaviorSpace').

Debugging

It is very likely that all the output you will see from your first run of your model is due, not to the intended behaviour of the agents, but to the effect of bugs in your code! Experience shows that it is almost impossible to create simulations that are initially free of bugs and, while there are ways of reducing bugs (for example, the unit test approach mentioned above), you should allow at least as much time for chasing bugs as for building the model. The most important strategy for finding bugs is to create test cases for which the output is known or predictable, and to run these after every change until all the test cases yield the expected results. Even this will not necessarily remove all bugs and modellers should always be aware of the possibility that their results are merely artefacts generated by their programs.

Another kind of test is to compare the results from the model with data from the target (that is, from the 'real world' being modelled). While such comparisons are highly desirable, it is not often that they can be achieved. Often, the target is itself neither well understood nor easy to access (that this is so is one reason for building a simulation, rather than observing the target directly). In addition, the behaviour of both the target and the model may be stochastic (influenced by random events) and very sensitive to the conditions or parameters at the start (Goldspink 2002). If the latter is the case, even a perfect model could be expected to differ in its behaviour from the behaviour of the target. It may be possible to run the model many times to obtain a stable statistical distribution of the output, but normally it is not possible to 'run the real world' many times. As a result, the best one can do is to test that there is a reasonable likelihood that the observed behaviour of the target could be drawn from the distribution of outputs from the model – which is rather a weak test.

The most thorough way of verifying a model (of ensuring that the output does reflect the underlying model and is not a consequence of bugs - see Chapter 2) is to re-implement the model using a different programming language and, ideally, a different implementer. Hales *et al.* (2003) comment:

> It is now clear that MABS [multi-agent based simulation] has more in common, methodologically, with the natural sciences and engineering disciplines than deductive logics or mathemat-

ics – it is closer to an experimental science than a formal one. With this in mind, it is important that simulations be replicated before they are accepted as correct. That is results from simulations cannot be proved but only inductively analyzed. This indicates that the same kinds of methods used within other inductive sciences will be applicable. In its simplest form a result that is reproduced many times by different modellers, re-implemented on several platforms in different places, should be more reliable. Although never attaining the status of a proof we can become more confident over time as to the veracity of the results. (Hales *et al.* 2003: 1.4)

Some experiments in re-implementing multi-agent models have been carried out, a process sometimes called 'docking', with interesting results: in a few cases, it has been found impossible to replicate even published models (see Axelrod 1997b and Hales *et al.* 2003 for examples). In preparation for writing this chapter, the Jager *et al.* model (which was originally written in the programming language C++) was re-implemented in NetLogo. Because the paper describing the simulation was well written, the re-implementation could be done without recourse to the authors, except for a few matters requiring clarification. The re-implementation yielded the same patterns of clustering and fighting as reported in the original article.

Having obtained a simulation that you believe to be free of bugs and accurately representing your design, it remains only to compare the simulation with the target and use the model to generate results. The process of validation and use has been described in Chapter 2 and there is little that is special to multi-agent models in this respect. To recall, it is desirable to engage in a sensitivity analysis to examine the extent to which variation in the model's parameters yield differences in the outcome. One result that may come from such analysis, or from the theoretical background to the research question, is the range of applicability of the model, that is, the circumstances in which the model corresponds to the target. For example, the two-party crowding model would not apply if the number of participants is very low (there is not then a 'crowd'). It is important when presenting results to state clearly the range of applicability of the model.

Using multi-agent simulations

Many agent-based simulations are built in order to develop and test social theories, others have a more practical objective: to help a group of people understand their world in order to control and change it. For example, social simulation is now being used to develop policy for the management of water resources, suggest advice to online companies about marketing products on the Internet, understand the implications of major bank strategic policies, manage rural ecosystems and learn how better to respond to epidemics. The connection between these otherwise disparate topics is that in each case there is a group of 'stakeholders' who are interested in the simulation because they hope to learn from the results and thus improve their effectiveness.

Rather than merely presenting the results of simulation research to potential users at the end of a project, it is becoming increasingly common for the stakeholders to become involved at all stages, from the formulation of the initial research question to the synthesis of the research conclusions. There are several advantages to having stakeholders closely involved. First, one can be more confident that the research question being tackled is in fact one whose answer is going to be relevant to the users. In the traditional mode, it is all to easy for projects to study issues which are of interest to the researcher, but of little relevance to the audience for the research. Bringing in the stakeholders at an early stage helps to make this less likely. Second, stakeholders are more likely to feel some obligation to respond to the research findings if they have been closely involved in the project. The research report is less likely to be filed and forgotten. Third, stakeholders are often a rich source of knowledge about the phenomenon being modelled. Fourth, their involvement in the research is itself likely to raise their interest in and level of knowledge about the issues. These advantages of 'participatory modelling' (Hare *et al.* 2003) can outweigh the disadvantages, which include the added complication and expense of involving stakeholders, the need to maintain stakeholders' motivation during the project, and the possibilities of bias resulting from the particular viewpoints of stakeholders.

Agent-based simulation is well suited to participatory research (Ramanath and Gilbert 2004). The idea of autonomous agents carrying out activities and communicating with each other is easy to grasp for people who are not familiar with modelling. Another advantage is that it is sometimes possible to design the model so that the stakeholders themselves can act as agents. For example, it may be possible to run the model, not as a computer simulation, but as a board game, with users playing roles and following the rules that otherwise would have been programmed into the agents (see Hare *et al.* 2002). Alternatively, one or more of the 'agents' in a computational simulation can be played by a person who selects which actions to carry out at each step, the computer running the other agents in the ordinary way. The benefit of this is that the person can get a deep knowledge of what is involved in playing the role. For example, this is the approach adopted in a project that was designed to help the stakeholders involved in providing domestic water to the city of Zurich. The 'Zurich Water Game' (Gilbert *et al.* 2002) was a multi-agent simulation in which some of the agents could be switched to being controlled by the game players. The game ran over the Internet, with a central server generating the environment and simulating all the agents that were not being directly controlled by the players. Using the game, players could explore the consequences of their own decisions on other players' strategies, and the feedback effects of those strategies on their own opportunities and strategies.

Conclusion

In this chapter, we have described a process for designing multi-agent models. It will be of most help to you if you have an idea of the topic that you are interested in but not yet a clear research question or a model design. Experience has shown that moving from a research interest to a model design is probably the hardest part of building multi-agent models and it is therefore useful to set about the task in a systematic way. On the other hand, it is possible to design good models without following any of the suggestions made in this chapter, which should be treated only as useful heuristics.

In the next chapter, we move to examining simulation models that are capable of adapting and learning from their experience. The design issues remain the same as with the simpler multi-agent models we have been considering in this chapter, but have the added complication that the behaviours of the agents may change during the course of the run.

Further reading

The process of designing multi-agent models is also described in

- Axelrod, R. (1997) Advancing the art of simulation in the social sciences. *Complexity*, 3(2):16–22.

- Gilbert, N., and Terna, P. (2000). How to build and use agent-based models in social science. *Mind and Society*, 1(1): 57–72.

The value of cognitive architectures in social simulation and some examples are reviewed in:

- Sun, Ron (ed.) (2005) *Cognition and Multi-Agent Interaction: From Cognitive Modeling to Social Simulation.* Cambridge University Press, Cambridge.

Soar can be found at http://sourceforge.net/projects/soar and ACT-R at http://act-r.psy.cmu.edu/software/.

Chapter 10

Learning and evolutionary models

In previous chapters we encountered a wide range of types of model, but all share the characteristic that they remain unchanged during the course of the simulation. In this chapter, we consider models that incorporate learning: as the simulation runs parameters change, or even the form of the model itself changes, in response to its environment. These models are based on work in machine learning and optimization, both very active areas of research. This chapter cannot cover all the current approaches and we shall concentrate on two that are influential in current social simulation: the use of artificial neural networks and models based on evolutionary programming.

Both are loosely based on analogies from biology. The brain is composed of cells called neurons, which communicate by means of a dense web of interconnections conveying electrochemical impulses. Each neuron obtains inputs from a number of other neurons, and if it receives an excitatory input of sufficient strength, it 'fires' and outputs a pulse to other neurons. The human brain is estimated to contain around 100 million neurons. Learning takes place when two neurons fire at the same time, strengthening the connection between the two and reinforcing that particular pathway. Artificial neural network models are based on a drastic simplification of these biological findings about the brain. Although an artificial neural network typically consists of less than 50 'units', each analogous to a neuron, rather than the 100 million of a human brain, it is capable of learning that when presented with a stimulus it should output an appropriate signal.

The other analogy used to construct learning models is the process of evolution by natural selection. Imagine a large population of rabbits that breed, producing baby rabbits, and then die. The rabbits exist in a moderately unfriendly environment and have to face predators, limited food supplies and disease, so that not all baby rabbits survive to breeding age. Suppose that rabbits with large ears are 'fitter' within this environment and therefore are more likely to reproduce than those with smaller ears. Pairs of rabbits mate and produce offspring based on the combination of the parents' genes. Gradually, as the population reproduces itself, there will be a tendency towards rabbit ears becoming larger, because big-eared rabbits are the more likely to breed and produce correspondingly big-eared offspring. The population taken as a whole can be considered to be 'learning' how to adapt to an environment that favours big-eared rabbits, although no individual rabbit has any knowledge of this fact.

Genetic algorithms (GAs) have been developed that mimic this process of natural selection (Holland 1975). They are particularly useful for finding optimal solutions to complex problems. For example, a wholesaler might want to plan the route of a delivery van so that it visits a number of shops. The order in which the van goes to the shops is not important but the route must minimize the total distance travelled. This is an example of the well-known class of 'travelling salesman problems', which have been shown to have no general analytical solution. However, one efficient method of finding a good route is to simulate multiple copies of the delivery van (each corresponding to one agent in a large population), and give each van a route generated at random. The fitness of each of these routes is assessed according to how far the delivery van has to travel: the 'fitter' routes are those that are shorter. Then new routes are 'bred' from the previous routes by mixing, so that the 'offspring' route has some parts taken from one parent's route and some parts taken from the other. The pairs of parents are chosen in a way that favours shorter routes over longer ones. In this way, successive generations include better and better routes as selection discards long routes and favours progressively shorter ones (for an extended discussion, see Michalewicz 1996: Chapter 10).

Genetic algorithms are a sub-field of an area called 'evolutionary computation'. As we shall see in the second half of this chapter, evolutionary computation can be used to model changes within societies, provided that there is some analogue to the reproduction of individual members with offspring inheriting genetic material from their parents. The 'reproduction' does not have to be sexual: one can also model the reproduction of ideas and norms. Genetic algorithms can also be used as a 'black box' optimization technique, in which the evolutionary details are irrelevant, for example to simulate agents' adaptation to their environment. Before considering such models in detail, we shall review the use of artificial neural networks for social simulation.

Artificial neural networks

An artificial neural network consists of three or more layers of 'units' arranged so that every unit in one layer is connected to every unit in the adjacent layers (Figure 10.1). Every connection has a numerical weight associated with it. One layer of units is known as the *input* layer, and this receives stimuli from the environment (by convention this layer is drawn on the left-hand edge of the network). On the right-hand edge is the *output* layer, which emits the response of the network. In the middle are one or more *hidden* layers. In operation, a pattern of stimuli is applied to the input units, each unit receiving a particular signal. The hidden units take the signals they receive from the units in the preceding layer, process them and generate an output signal which is passed to the succeeding layer.

Figure 10.1: An artificial neural network

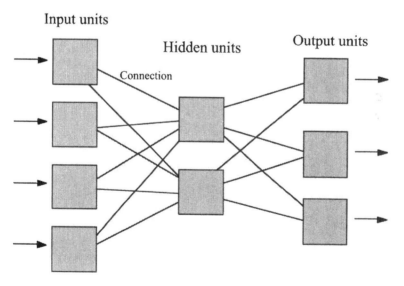

The strength of the output from a unit is called its *activation*. The activations of the input layer's units are set directly by the stimulus, and the activations of the output layer units are decoded to provide the network's response. For all but the input layer units, activation depends on the strength of the inputs a unit receives, the weights associated with each of its input connections and a mathematical function (the *activation function*) which is used to calculate the resulting activation from all the unit's weights and inputs.

The activation function processes the inputs by multiplying the magnitude of each of the input signals arriving along a connection by the corresponding weight for that connection and summing the results of these multiplications. The sum is then rescaled using a nonlinear transformation so that it has a value between zero and one. Most often, the transformation used is the sigmoid or logistic function (Figure 10.2). The result is then passed on to the next layer.

Figure 10.2: A sigmoid curve ($y = \frac{1}{1+e^{-x}}$)

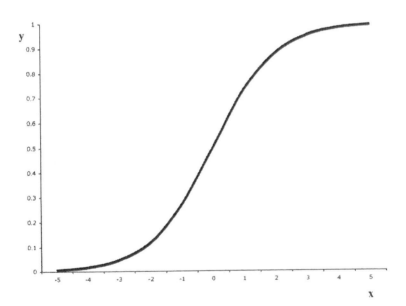

Consider a three-layer network trained to recognize handwritten digits. In order to convert a handwritten '9', for example, into something the network can process, one would need to devise a coding scheme in order to transform pen marks into numbers for presentation to the input layer. This is known as the *encoding* problem and we shall consider it in more detail in a later section. For the moment, assume that a square grid of 6 × 6 cells is overlaid on the image of the digit and a value of one is recorded for every cell which contains some ink and zero for every cell which does not. This yields a pattern of 36 ones and zeros which forms the input. We use a network with 36 units in the input layer, four in the hidden layer and ten in the output layer, and feed a one or zero to each input unit. Those units that have an input of one will fire and each will feed its activation to all the units in the hidden layer. Each unit in the hidden layer will absorb the signals it receives from the input layer, transform them according to the weights associated with each of its input connections and generate an activation which is sent to the output layer units. With a well-trained network, just one output unit will be activated as a result of the inputs it receives from the hidden layer and this output will correspond to the number 9. Presenting the digit 8 to the input layer should result in a different output unit being activated, and so on for each possible digit. The network is thus able to recognize handwritten characters, decoding them to yield a response on one of the ten output units, according to the input stimulus.

The description so far has assumed that the network is already *trained* so that it gives the right output for a given input. The training involves adjusting the weights on the connections between layers so that the correct output is obtained for each input. This is done by a procedure called *backpropagation* of error. It is a completely mechanical process that does not involve the network gaining any kind of 'understanding' of the inputs it receives. To train a network, one needs a large set of *training data*, examples of the patterns that the network is intended to recognize. Starting with weights randomly assigned to connections, the network is repeatedly given the training data to process, and the weights associated with each connection are adjusted until the network is able to recognize all the training examples correctly.

Training therefore consists of presenting known examples to the input layer (for example, a pattern of bits corresponding to a handwritten digit '9') and comparing the pattern of activations in the output layer with the desired pattern – which is that one and only one output unit is activated. To carry out backpropagation, the 'error' (the difference between the actual and the desired output patterns) is calculated. The weights of the connections leading into the output layer are then adjusted slightly to reduce the error. Then the weights on the connections leading to the hidden layer units are modified, according to the contribution that each unit's activation has made to the output error. This is done by multiplying each weight on a connection from a hidden unit by the magnitude of the error on the output unit to which it runs. Summing all these error quantities gives a value for the total error produced by that hidden unit. It is this sum that is used to adjust the weights of the connections leading into the hidden unit. The amount by which the connection weights are adjusted depends on four factors: the derivative of the activation function (the amount by which the output changes for a small change in input); the magnitude of the error; the learning rate (a constant which controls how fast the network learns); and a momentum (which is proportional to the size of previous weight changes). Using all these factors has proved by experience to be an effective way of adjusting weights to allow a network to learn quickly.

For the sake of simplicity this description has only considered the task of recognizing stimuli such as handwritten digits. This kind of application is the most common use of neural nets. They have also been employed for recognizing human speech, tracking trends in stock market data, recognizing representations of objects in video images and even selecting recruits using data taken from application forms. In addition to these practical applications, neural networks can also serve as potentially interesting models for social processes. In the next section we shall introduce two such models: one which explores the first steps in the development of language and one which illustrates how altruistic behaviour can be generated by apparently self-interested agents.

Using artificial neural networks for social simulation

Learning a lexicon

People communicate through a shared lexicon. By 'shared lexicon' we mean that two speakers of the same language employ the same symbols (sounds or written representations) to 'mean' the same things. For example, suppose that there are three coloured blocks on the floor and I want to tell you to pick up the blue block. In order to communicate this to you, it would be useful to have a language that included the symbol 'blue' and for both you and I to think that 'blue' referred to the colour blue (rather than, for instance, you describing the green block as 'blue' or failing to notice that there is any significant difference between the blocks). There are two basic conditions for communication using language to succeed: first, there must be sufficient symbols to make the necessary distinctions; and second, the symbol used for a particular concept must be the same for all users. As Hutchins and Hazlehurst (1995: 161) put it: 'A shared lexicon is a consensus on a set of distinctions.'

Although the idea of a shared lexicon applies most clearly to the words of a language, there are many other areas of social life where the same considerations arise. When people make status distinctions based on visible attributes such as fashion or race, these depend on the availability of symbols (for example, miniskirt and calf-length skirt) and a consensus about their significance. A number of linguists, developmental psychologists and sociologists have asked how such shared lexicons arise. The most extreme version of this problem can be stated thus: imagine a group of agents without a shared lexicon who wish to communicate. How could they develop a common language 'from nothing', without any external agency teaching them the words and their meanings? This is the problem to which Hutchins and Hazlehurst (1995) propose a solution using a model based on interacting artificial neural networks.

The networks they use are of a special type called *auto-associators*. These are networks for which the desired output pattern is exactly the same as the presented input pattern. An auto-associator network is trained on a large set of examples until its outputs precisely reproduce the training examples applied to its inputs. When trained, the pattern of activations of the hidden layer units turns out to be an efficient encoding of any regularities in the input data. In other words, the hidden units are able to distinguish the critical features which distinguish the inputs into different types. This is valuable for the development of a lexicon, because these encodings could correspond to the different symbols that would be used to describe the inputs.

Hutchins and Hazlehurst develop this idea by using one auto-associator network to model each agent in a communicating population. The networks have one input layer (consisting of 36 units), two hidden layers of four units each, and one output layer, also of 36 units. The inputs to the network are thought of as encodings of visual scenes (the input layer is the agent's 'eyes'). The second hidden layer's activations are considered to be the agent's verbal representation of the input visual scene, that is to say, the symbol it generates for each scene (Figure 10.3). This layer is therefore called the verbal input/output layer. In training the networks, each input layer is presented with 12 binary patterns of 36 bits, corresponding to encodings of 12 visual scenes (phases of the moon in their example). A trained network is able to make distinctions between these 12 scenes and reflect these in the patterns of activation in the verbal input/output layer. If we simply gave the same set of binary patterns representing the 12 scenes to a number of such networks, each would learn how to make distinctions between the scenes, but the 'verbal output' of each would be different (the precise pattern for each scene would depend on the particular random starting configuration of connection weights). The agents could all 'talk' about the scenes, but they would all be using different lexicons and could not communicate.

Figure 10.3: An agent's network (taken from Hutchins and Hazlehurst 1995)

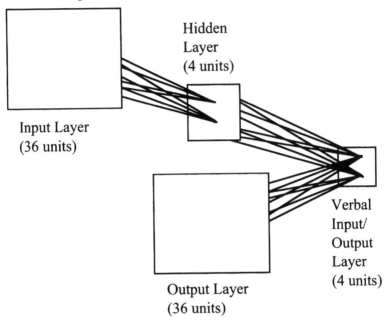

Hidden
Layer
(4 units)

Input Layer
(36 units)

Verbal
Input/
Output
Layer
(4 units)

Output Layer
(36 units)

To represent interaction between agents, Hutchins and Hazlehurst en-sured that during the training session, the 'error' used in backpropagation came not only from the usual comparison of input and output activation patterns, but also from comparing the activations at the verbal input/output layers of pairs of agents. Two agents were chosen at random and each given the same scene to 'look at'. Because the networks are auto-associators, the output of a trained network should be identical to the input pattern. The error was calculated by finding the difference between the input and output in the normal way. The difference between the agents' verbal input/output layers was also calculated and added to the normal error and this total error used for backpropagation. As a result, the networks not only tended towards generating a representation at the output layer which was more like the input stimulus, but also tended towards adopting the same shared characterization of the inputs at the verbal layer. In short, the networks learned both to make distinctions between the scenes applied as input, and to use the same 'symbols' in order to make those distinctions.

Figure 10.4 illustrates the results of the simulation graphically showing the state of four agents after 2000 interactions between pairs of agents. The graphs show the activation levels of each of the four verbal layer units

Figure 10.4: The state of four agents after having learnt the moon lexicon (from Hutchins and Hazlehurst 1995)

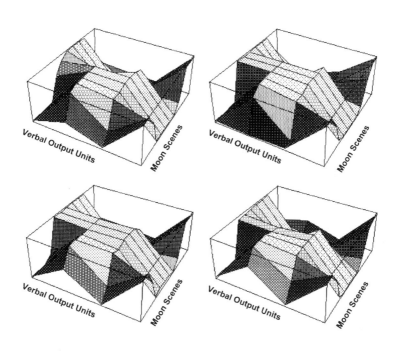

for each of the 16 moon scenes arranged in arbitrary order. The point to note about these graphs is that they are almost identical, meaning that each agent has adopted the same 'symbol' (pattern of verbal layer activations) for each of the moon scenes. However, the particular symbol adopted by the 'language community' to represent a given moon scene is entirely arbitrary (depending on the chance allocation of weights at the beginning of the training) and will differ from run to run. It seems reasonable to say that the agents have collectively developed a (very simple) language *ab initio* without any initial external linguistic resources. One might want to refine the model to see whether the agents can generate not only lexical items, but also syntax (that is, 'grammar'). This would probably involve a more complex task than the ostensive description of a small number of scenes (see Hurford *et al.* 1998b, Cangelosi and Parisi 2001 and Christiansen and Kirby 2003 for recent reviews of work on the evolution of language). One could imagine building artificial societies in which agents exchanged commands or engaged in negotiation, again developing the necessary language resources from within the interaction itself.

In Hutchins and Hazlehurst's model, the agents learned a lexicon, which emerged from their interaction. In the next example, we see how altruistic behaviour can emerge from interactions between neural networks. This second example will also set the scene for the description of genetic algorithms in the second half of this chapter.

Learning to be altruistic

Parisi *et al.* (1995) experimented with a population of 100 agents, each represented by a neural network. The agents were divided into 20 groups of five 'sisters'. At the beginning of the simulation all the sisters in a group had identical connection weights. Every agent was given the same number of pieces of food at the start of its life. During the course of each agent's fixed lifespan, it encountered other agents at random and could decide to give away or keep pieces of food. At the end of the lifespan (during which time each agent had been involved in 100 encounters), the 20 agents with the highest number of pieces of food in their possession were selected and reproduced five times each to form a new generation of groups of sisters. All the first-generation agents were then discarded.

An agent's decision about whether to give away a piece of food is controlled by its neural network. The network is very simple, consisting of two input units, three hidden units and one output unit. The input stimulus is the type of partner in the encounter: either the partner is a sister or it is not. The output indicates whether the agent will give the partner a piece of food or not. When a network is reproduced to form the next generation, the connection weights are copied from a parent to its offspring, but with small random changes ('mutations'). In a standard artificial neural network, the connection weights are changed by the backpropagation of error. Parisi's networks did not use backpropagation; instead the weights evolved through generations of agents.

The simulation was run for 50 generations. One might expect the network weights to evolve so that all the outputs represented a decision not to give away a piece of food in any encounter. In this way, agents would retain their initial allocation and possibly gain additional food from other agents. This 'egotistical' behaviour was indeed observed for agents encountering those other than their sisters. However, the agents also evolved altruistic behaviour towards their sisters, that is, they tended to give their food to sisters when they encountered them. This initially surprising behaviour is predicted by kin-selection theory (Hamilton 1964). For a food giver, the decrease in the chance of being selected for reproduction as a result of retaining less food is compensated by the increase in the chance of the food's recipient being selected for reproduction. Since the recipient is a sister (and therefore has the same pattern of weights as the donor), the effect is to maintain the family's reproduction chances.

In this model, therefore, the individual agents act on the basis of decisions controlled by a neural network. However, instead of the connection weights in the network being set by the results of an extensive training programme, the weights are evolved over successive generations. The set of weights of a 'fit' network has more chance of being reproduced in the next generation than the weight set of a less fit agent. In the simulation, a fit agent is one that has weights that favour altruistic behaviour towards the agent's kin, that is, towards networks with the same set of connection weights as the donor.

Designing neural networks

Neural networks come in all shapes and sizes and designing a good one is an art rather than a science, where 'good' means one that will learn efficiently with a reasonable set of training examples. Among the parameters that can be varied are the way in which the inputs are encoded, the number of hidden layers, the number of units in each layer, the form of the activation function, the magnitude of the learning rate and momentum constants, and the way in which the error is calculated. In this section we shall briefly discuss some of these parameters, offering advice on how a choice can be made when building network models.

Data encoding

As we saw in the lexicon-learning example where the data consisted of 'moon scenes', there is usually a need to encode the inputs into a form suitable for activating the input layer. Input data can be classified as continuous or having a very large number of possible values (examples are wealth, number of interactions with other agents); categorical (partner is or is not a sibling, one of 12 moon scenes); or having features (the data item is blue, heavy and has a sweet taste). Continuous values can be scaled to fall between zero and one and then input directly, or converted into categories by distributing them into discrete 'bins' according to their magnitude. Categories can be coded by assigning one input unit to each possible category. For example, a unit can be assigned to each cell of a visual grid, the unit receiving an activation of one if its grid cell is black and zero if it is white. Features are best coded in binary with units assigned to each binary position. For example, if a feature can be one of eight possible colours, each colour is assigned a binary number between zero and seven, and three units are activated according to the binary representation of the colour of the item under consideration.

Number of hidden layers

The number of hidden layers required depends on the complexity of the relationship between the inputs and the outputs. Most problems only require one hidden layer and if the input/output relationship is linear (able to be represented by a straight-line graph), the network does not need a hidden layer at all. It is unlikely that any practical problem will require more than two hidden layers.

Number of units in each layer

The numbers of units in the input and output layers depend on how the data are encoded. For example, if the input is coded into ten categories, there needs to be ten units in the input layer. Similarly, if five types of input are to be recognized and distinguished, the output layer will need to consist of five units. Deciding the number of hidden units is considerably more difficult. A number of rules of thumb and estimation procedures have been developed to give rough guides (see Swingler 1996: 55). For example, the number of hidden units should never exceed twice the number of input layer units. If the problem consists of feature extraction (as did the language-learning example), there should be considerably fewer hidden units than input units. Ideally, there should be one for each feature, but this number may not be known in advance.

Neural networks have the ability to recognize input that is not identical to any of the training examples, but only similar. That is why, for instance, neural networks have been used for handwriting recognition. A network can be trained to recognize the digit '9' by presenting many examples of the digit from different writers. However, it is unlikely that the next '9' presented will be identical to any of the '9's it has previously seen, even after the network has been extensively trained. Nevertheless, because neural networks are capable of a degree of generalization, it is still possible for the network to recognize the new '9' correctly.

A network should not over-generalize, however. A handwritten digit '7' should not be recognized as a '9' even though the two figures are similar. The aim is to permit a certain amount of generalization, but not so much that recognition errors are introduced. The main way in which the degree of generalization can be controlled is through the number of hidden units in the network. As the number of hidden units is increased, the accuracy of input recognition increases, but the capacity for generalization decreases. When the number of hidden units approaches the number of different input examples, the network can recognize every different example exactly, but has no ability to generalize.

Measuring 'error'

As we saw earlier, a network develops by adjusting its weights to minimize the difference between the activation levels of its output units and the target levels from the training data. The usual measure of error is a simple difference between output and target level, calculated separately for each output unit. In addition, it is often useful to assess the overall success of a network in recognizing an input. This is commonly measured by the root square error, the square root of the sum of the squared errors from each output unit.

As the network learns, the root square error should gradually decrease. Eventually, when 'enough' training examples have been presented to the network, the rate of decrease of root square error should level off: there is little further improvement in error no matter how many further training examples are provided. The set of weights should then be optimal. Unfortunately, however, it is possible that this may only be a 'local minimum', rather than the true optimum. At a local minimum, any small adjustment to the weights makes the recognition worse and the network weights remain stable. However, there may be a completely different set of weights, the 'global minimum', which has a much better performance. This global minimum cannot be found by a training procedure that depends on incrementally adjusting weights. Various techniques have been proposed to try to avoid networks settling into local minima, but the only reliable procedure is to repeat the training exercise several times using the same network and different initial sets of random weights, checking that the final set of weights is the same each time. If they are, this suggests that the same minimum is being obtained using approaches from several different directions and therefore it is likely that the minimum is indeed global.

Evolutionary computation

The biological metaphor

Artificial neural networks are models that are based loosely on a theory of how brains work. Nevertheless, as we have seen, they can be used for much more than modelling brains and can represent agents that are capable of simple learning. Evolutionary computation is also based on a biological analogy, drawing on the theory of evolution by natural selection. Just as with neural networks, one can either regard evolutionary computation as a 'black box' that aims to find optimal solutions to complex problems, or one can take the analogy with evolution more seriously and use genetic algorithms (GAs) as models of evolving social processes. We shall discuss examples of both these approaches later in this chapter. First, however, we shall briefly review the biological basis from which evolutionary computation draw its inspiration.

In nature, individual organisms compete with each other for resources, such as food, water and shelter. Individuals of the same species also compete for mates. Those individuals that are the most successful in surviving and finding mates (the 'fittest' individuals) will be the most likely to produce offspring, while relatively unsuccessful individuals will have fewer or no offspring. Each individual has a set of 'genes' (composed of DNA in the cell nucleus) which determine the form of its body and its abilities. Sexual reproduction involves combining the genes of two parents from the same species and passing the combination to the offspring. Thus the genes of the fittest individuals are spread to the next generation. The process of combining parents' genes can generate new individuals of a type not previously found in the population and these new individuals may be even fitter than either of the parents. In this way, a species evolves to become more and more suited to its environment.

Biologists use a number of special terms, in describing evolution, which have been taken over (with slight modification to their meaning) by researchers using evolutionary computation. Chromosomes in biology are chains of DNA found in the cell nucleus. They are composed of sequences of genes, each of which occupies a fixed place on the chromosome (the gene's *locus*) and provides the code for one or more related functions. The complete set of chromosomes is an organism's *genome*. The overall genetic composition of an individual is known as its *genotype*, while the characteristics of an individual expressed by its genome are known as its *phenotype*. For example, I have a Y chromosome consisting of several genes as part of my genome which causes my sex to be male, an aspect of my phenotype.

There are several important points about biological evolution that need emphasizing. First, it is the population as a whole that evolves, not the individuals. One can judge the adaptation of a species to its environment only by looking at characteristics of the population, not at any particular individual (an individual may be quite different from the general population of which it is a member). Second, evolution can only work while diversity exists in the population. Without diversity, all individuals will have the same fitness and there can be no increase in fitness from combining parents' genes. Third, while species are adapting through evolution to the environment, that environment may itself be changing, perhaps as a result of the activity of the population itself or the evolution of other species. Fourth, skills or other attributes that individuals acquire during their lifetime are not passed on to their offspring. Only genetic material is inherited (the idea that 'acquired characteristics' can be inherited is known as Lamarckism and, although not biologically realistic, could be of interest for social simulation; Reynolds 1994).

The genetic algorithm

Genetic algorithms take the essential aspects of this picture of biological evolution and represent them as computer models. They work with a population of 'individuals' each of which has some measurable degree of 'fitness'. The fittest individuals are 'reproduced' by breeding them with other fit individuals, to produce new offspring which share some features taken from each 'parent'. The parents then 'die' and the fitness of the individuals in the new generation is measured. Once again, the fittest individuals are allowed to breed and the process continues until the average fitness of the population has converged to an optimal value.

One area where GAs have been used is in modelling rational action. Social scientists and especially game theorists have investigated the conditions under which rational actors would engage in cooperation (Elster 1986;

1989). In some kinds of cooperation, while those who cooperate gain from doing so, each individual would gain more by not cooperating. For example, joining a trade union and taking industrial action to obtain a pay rise can be valuable for each union member, but any one individual may gain more from remaining outside the union, not paying the union dues but nevertheless taking the increased pay (Olson 1965). For situations such as these, there is a problem in explaining how cooperative groups arise and continue because one would expect that every rational member would defect.

The prisoner's dilemma is a standard scenario used by social scientists to investigate collaboration and cooperation. The story is that two prisoners are held in separate cells. Each prisoner is asked independently to betray the other. If only one prisoner agrees ('defects'), this prisoner is rewarded and the other is punished. If both prisoners defect, both are punished, but to a lesser extent. If both remain silent (both 'cooperate'), both receive moderate rewards. The payoffs for all four possible cases are shown in Figure 10.5 (assume that a payoff of 3 or more is a reward and a payoff of 2 or less is a punishment). The selfish choice (defection) always yields more than cooperation, no matter what the other prisoner does, but if both defect, both do badly. The dilemma is whether to cooperate or to defect. In many situations, the choice is not made once, but again and again. A trade union member, for example, will continually be faced with the option of defection. If the same participants are choosing repeatedly and they think that their opponents' previous choices are likely to influence their subsequent choices, the situation is known as an iterated prisoner's dilemma.

Figure 10.5: A prisoner's dilemma payoff matrix

		Player B	
		Cooperate	Defect
Player A	Cooperate	*Reward for mutual cooperation* A receives 3 B receives 3	*B defects and A cooperates* A receives 0 B receives 5
	Defect	*A defects and B cooperates* A receives 5 B receives 0	*Punishment for mutual defection* A receives 1 B receives 1

The iterated prisoner's dilemma can be played as a game between two players, each following their own strategy, either defecting or cooperating at each turn, and aiming to maximize their own accumulated payoff. The question for the players is what strategy should be adopted to maximize their gain. Axelrod (1987) used a GA to evolve a good strategy. Every player from a population, each with its own strategy, played the prisoner's dilemma with all other players. Those that were most successful reproduced to form the next generation, with the offspring using a strategy formed from the strategies of the parents.

Axelrod defined a player's strategy as a rule that determined its next move, cooperate (C) or defect (D), on the basis of the outcomes of its previous three games. That is, for every possible combination of 'cooperate' and 'defect' over the previous three games, the strategy dictated what the player's next move would be. There are four possible outcomes for each game (CC, CD, DC and DD), so there are $4 \times 4 \times 4 = 64$ different combinations of the previous three games, and for each combination the strategy indicates what the next move should be.

When designing a GA, the first problem to tackle is the representation to be used. For the prisoner's dilemma game, we need to represent each player's strategy as a chromosome, using a coding scheme that will permit it to be combined with another when breeding new individuals. Since a strategy can be coded as a set of 64 C or D next moves, one for each possible combination of the outcomes of previous games, a sequence of 64 bits will serve. There also needs to be information about how to start the series of games. This requires six further Cs or Ds in the strategy (one pair for each of the outcomes of the last three matches), making 70 bits in all. Each of the 70 Cs or Ds represents one gene in a chromosome 70 bits long.

Axelrod generated an initial population of 20 agents, each with a randomly generated chromosome. Every agent was then pitted against all the others. The fitness of each agent was measured in terms of its average success with the other 19 in 151 successive bouts of the prisoners' dilemma,[1] with each player following its genetically coded strategy. The more successful individuals were used to breed the next generation and the process was repeated for 50 generations.

The chromosome determining the strategy inherited by an offspring was constructed from the chromosomes of its parents using two 'genetic operators': crossover and mutation. Crossover involves taking the two parent chromosomes, breaking them both at the same randomly chosen location and rejoining the parts, one from each parent (see Figure 10.6). The procedure is a very much simplified version of one of the mechanisms involved in the

---

[1] There were 151 because this was the number used in previous experiments with hand-crafted strategies.

biological recombination of chromosomes. The effect is that the offspring inherits part of the chromosome from one parent and part from the other. Mutation then takes place by randomly changing a very small proportion of the Cs to Ds or vice versa.

Figure 10.6: Schematic diagram of the crossover genetic operator

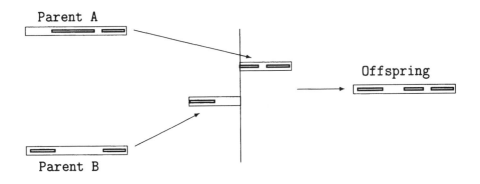

Axelrod (1987: 38) notes that the population begins by evolving away from whatever cooperation was initially displayed. The less cooperative strategies do best because there are few other players that are responsive to cooperative overtures. The decreasing level of cooperation in the population causes all the individuals to get lower scores as mutual defection becomes more and more common. After 10 or 20 generations, the trend starts to reverse as some players evolve a pattern of reciprocating when they encounter cooperation and these players do very well. The average scores of the population therefore start to increase as cooperation based on reciprocity becomes better and better established. As the reciprocators do well, they spread in the population, resulting in more and more cooperation.

Axelrod's model has been taken forward by other researchers, most notably Lomborg (1996) who used a model involving 1 million agents, each of which plays iterated prisoner's dilemma games with a random selection of other agents. The agents' strategies develop using an algorithm slightly different from the standard GA, involving agents copying ('imitating') the strategies of those other agents that they observe to be doing better than themselves. In the course of the copying, agents can occasionally innovate, through making random small changes to the other agent's strategy. In combination, imitation and innovation amount to a population learning strategy not unlike the GA. In addition, Lomborg observes that it is important to include 'noise' in the model if it is to be at all interesting for what it says about social relations. The noise comes from a small chance that agents might misperceive their fellow players' actions (for example, that another defected when in fact it cooperated). Lomborg finds that in this model, cooperative strategies are likely to develop, even with substantial amounts of 'noise' present. Rather than one strategy coming to dominate the population, however, the populations develop mixtures of strategies which are stable together, although they might not be successful alone.

Design issues

In the next subsection we shall work through a program that performs the genetic algorithm. Schematically evolutionary computation can be represented by the loop shown in Figure 10.7. For every model that uses a GA, the researcher has to make several design decisions about how the GA is to be programmed. This subsection discusses each of these decisions in turn.

Fitness measures   The genetic algorithm evolves a population to optimize some fitness measure. The measure used depends on what is being modelled. It must be possible to calculate a single numerical indicator of 'fitness' for every individual in the population. Devising a plausible fitness measure is often the hardest part of designing GAs for social simulation. If the theoretical approach being used accepts that actors maximize some externally observable and calculable 'utility', as in many theories of economic rationality, then this utility can be used directly as a fitness measure. For example, fitness might be based on agents' accumulated 'wealth' (Parisi *et al.* 1995), on their 'happiness' (Chattoe and Gilbert 1996), on the time that they survive, or on some combination of these and other individual characteristics. Whatever measure is used, for reasons of computational efficiency it needs to be possible to calculate it reasonably easily. The evaluation of individuals' fitness is usually the most demanding part of a GA program because it has to be done for every individual in every generation.

As the GA proceeds, the average fitness of the population is expected to increase because individuals with poor fitness are selectively bred out. Eventually, the rate of improvement in fitness will decline and the population should converge on the 'best' chromosome (see Figure 10.8). The route to the overall maximum may pass through one or more local maxima, as shown

Figure 10.7: The evolutionary computation algorithm

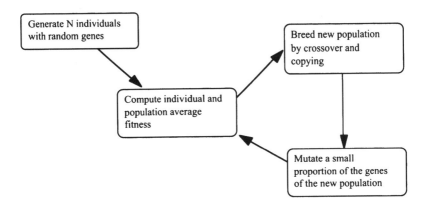

In more detail:

generate an initial population of N individuals with random genes
compute the fitness of each individual
repeat
    select the fitter individuals and put them into a 'mating pool'
    choose P pairs of individuals from the mating pool
    for each of the P pairs of individuals:
        combine the chromosomes of the parents using a crossover
            operator to produce two new individual offspring
        add the two new individuals to the new population
    copy $N - P$ individuals unchanged into the new population
    mutate a small proportion (M) of the genes of the new population
    dispose of the old population
    compute the fitness of each individual in the new population
    compute the mean fitness of the population
until the average fitness of the population is no longer increasing

in the figure, after which the fitness of the best individual decreases for short periods (for example, from generation 6 to 7).

Figure 10.8: A typical run of a genetic algorithm, showing the decreasing rate of improvement of fitness and the average fitness (thick line) approaching the fitness of the best individual (thin line)

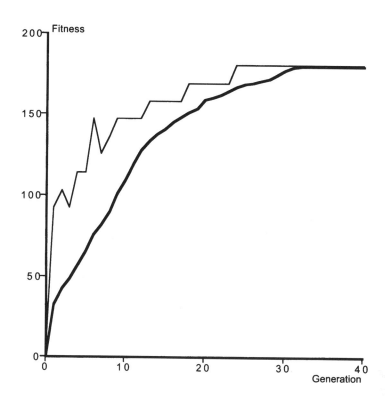

Selection mechanisms   The reason why the GA optimizes is that breeding is carried out from the fitter individuals. The choice of parents to produce offspring is somewhat more subtle than it might appear. Simply choosing the very best individual and breeding from that will not generally work successfully, because that best individual may have a fitness that is at a local rather than a global maximum. Instead, the GA ensures that there is some diversity among the population by breeding from a selection of the fitter individuals, rather than just from the fittest. Various ways of choosing those to breed have been devised (Goldberg and Deb 1991), but the commonest and simplest is called *tournament selection*. Pairs of individuals are picked at random and the one with the higher fitness (the one that 'wins the tournament') is used as one parent. The tournament selection is then repeated on a second pair of individuals to find the other parent from which to breed.

In order to maintain some of the better chromosomes unchanged across generations, it is usual to have only a proportion of the new population bred as offspring from parents. The remainder of the new generation is simply copied from the old, again using tournament selection to pick those to be copied. Typically, 60 per cent of the new population are bred from parents (the P individuals of Figure 10.7) and the remaining 40 per cent continue from the old population.

Genetic operators   The most important genetic operator is crossover, the process of taking two chromosomes, snipping them both at the same randomly chosen position, and then choosing one end from each (Figure 10.6). This is single-point crossover; it is also possible to cross at two points, by considering the chromosome to be a continuous loop and snipping it at two random places, thus creating two segments to exchange from each chromosome. Experiments on these and other variations indicate that the crossover design chosen is often not critical. What is important is that the crossover operator should preserve contiguous chunks or 'building blocks' of genes from one generation to the next.

The importance of these building blocks or segments of genes is that they represent parameter values that the algorithm has discovered work well together and which lead to improved fitness when incorporated into an individual. The GA works well as an optimizer because the crossover operator is able to preserve the blocks once they have been 'discovered'. When designing a scheme for coding a model's parameters as genes, one of the issues that needs to be borne in mind is the degree to which it encourages the formation of these 'building blocks'. This can be done by ensuring that related genes are close together in the chromosome and that the contribution of a gene to the fitness of the individual is relatively independent of the values of the other genes elsewhere in the chromosome. The extent to which the contribution to fitness of one gene depends on the values of other genes is known as *epistasis* and this should be low for the GA to work most effectively. We shall return to the design of gene coding schemes later in this chapter.

The other common genetic operator is mutation. As a population evolves, there is a tendency for some genes to become predominant until they have spread to all members. Without mutation, these genes will then be fixed for ever, because crossover alone cannot introduce new gene values. If the fixed value of the gene is not the value required at the global maximum, the GA will fail to optimize properly. Mutation is therefore important to 'loosen up' genes that would otherwise become fixed, but if the mutation rate is too high, the selection pressure on genes resulting from breeding with fitter individuals is counteracted. A common value for the mutation rate is to change one gene in every thousand.

Population size Although biological evolution typically takes place with millions of individuals in the population, GAs work surprisingly well with quite small populations. Axelrod used only 20 individuals in the study described earlier in this chapter and success has been reported with as few as ten individuals (Reeves 1993). If the population is too small, there is an increased risk of convergence to a local maximum and the rate of convergence may be reduced. A rule of thumb is that the product of the number in the population and the number of generations should exceed 100,000. In addition, the number of individuals in the population should considerably exceed the number of genes in each individual's chromosome.

Implementation

In this section the coding of a genetic algorithm will be illustrated by working through a re-implementation of the model described in Axelrod (1987) and mentioned above. In this model, agents play repeated prisoner's dilemma matches against each other, using a strategy encoded in 70 bits. The agent strategies are subjected to a genetic algorithm, with the payoff from the matches as the measure of fitness. According to Axelrod, we should expect the strategies of all the agents to co-evolve until there is almost universal cooperation.

The model can be divided into two parts. The first implements a typical GA and uses the algorithm of Figure 10.7 to improve the fitness of the agents' strategies. The second part implements the prisoner's dilemma matches between agents and reports agents' average payoffs as their fitness to the GA. The two parts can be coded more or less independently, with just a call from the GA to the fitness function as the communication between them.

First, however, we must specify the agents to use. We shall show how the model can be implemented in NetLogo (see Chapter 7) with agents represented as 'turtles'. Each turtle possesses a chromosome: a list of 70 ones and zeroes. Each turtle will also need to note its fitness and the generation in which it was created (its 'cohort'). When it engages in a match with another turtle, its choice of whether to cooperate or defect depends on the outcomes of its last three matches with the same opponent and so it needs to remember these.

This suggests the following attributes for turtles:

```
turtles-own [
    chromosome          ; a list of ones and zeroes
    fitness             ; the fitness of this turtle
    cohort              ; the generation this turtle was born in
    ; History of encounters, coded thus:
    ;  Me: Cooperate  Opponent: Cooperate   - code = 3
    ;  Me: Cooperate  Opponent: Defect      - code = 2
    ;  Me: Defect     Opponent: Cooperate   - code = 1
    ;  Me: Defect     Opponent: Defect      - code = 0
    outcome             ; the outcome of the last match
    last-outcome        ; the outcome of the previous match
    last-but-one-outcome  ; the outcome of the match before that
    ]
```

There will need to be some variables accessible throughout the program:

```
globals [
    number-of-turtles   ; the number of agents (turtles)
    chromo-length       ; the length of a chromosome (the number
                        ;    of bits)
    mutation-rate       ; average number of mutations per
                        ;    chromosome per generation
    generation          ; count of generations
    ]
```

The first three of these define the size of the problem.[2]

With these preliminaries out of the way, we can turn to the GA itself. The setup procedure initializes the global variables and creates the first generation of turtles. Each turtle is given a randomly generated chromosome. Then the turtles are added to the NetLogo graphic display and the fitness of each agent calculated (the method used to do this will be shown below).

```
to setup                        ; observer procedure.
    clear-turtles
    clear-all-plots
```

---

[2]It is a good idea to put numbers such as these into global variables and then refer to them, rather than use the numbers themselves within the program. Then if, for example, you want to experiment with a larger number of agents, only one number needs to be changed.

```
    set generation 0
    set chromo-length 70
    set number-of-turtles 20
    set mutation-rate 0.5

    create-custom-turtles number-of-turtles [
      set cohort 0
      ; make the chromosome a list of random 0s and 1s
      set chromosome n-values chromo-length [ random 2 ]
      ]
    ask turtles [
      find-fitness
      display-turtles
      ]
end
```

The go procedure follows the algorithm of Figure 10.7 closely. Sixty per cent of a new generation of the population of agents are bred by 'mating' pairs of 'parents'. The remaining 40 per cent are copied unchanged from the old to the new generation. The mating first chooses two parents, using a tournament selection coded in select-a-turtle, performs a crossover between the parents, and then generates two new turtles for the new generation.

Once all the new generation have been bred, the old generation are disposed of (with the die command), a small amount of mutation is applied and the fitness of the new generation is calculated. Finally, the generation count is incremented, the current fitness is plotted on the display and the simulation continues until generation 50 has been reached.

```
to go                             ; observer procedure.
  locals [ turtleA turtleB ]
  ; Breed  60% of the new population and mate them to
  ; produce two offspring
  repeat (0.3 * number-of-turtles) [
      set turtleA select-a-turtle
      set turtleB select-a-turtle
      ask turtleA [ cross turtleB ]
      breed-a-turtle turtleA
      breed-a-turtle turtleB
      ]
  ; Just copy 40% of the population into the
  ; new generation
  repeat (0.4 * number-of-turtles) [
```

```
        breed-a-turtle select-a-turtle
        ]
    ; Kill off the old generation
    ask turtles with [ cohort = generation ] [ die ]
    ; Mutate the new generation, display them, and
    ; find their fitness
    ask turtles [
        mutate
        display-turtles
        find-fitness
    ]
    set generation generation + 1
    plot-results
    if (generation =  50) [ stop ]
end
```

The tournament select simply chooses two turtles at random from the current generation and selects the one with the higher fitness for breeding. This biases the selection of agents for reproduction towards those with greater fitness, but also allows for variation within the population. Breeding a turtle is also straightforward: the child turtle receives a copy of its parent's chromosome.

```
to-report select-a-turtle        ; turtle procedure.
                                 ; Use a tournament selection.
                                 ; The turtle reported is the
                                 ; fitter of two chosen at
                                 ; random.
    locals [turtleA turtleB ]
    set turtleA
        random-one-of turtles with [ cohort = generation ]
    set turtleB
        random-one-of turtles with [ cohort = generation ]
    ifelse (fitness-of turtleA > fitness-of turtleB)
        [report turtleA]
        [report turtleB]
end

to breed-a-turtle [ parent ]     ; turtle procedure.
                                 ; Make new turtle and give it
                                 ; the genes of its parent
                                 ; turtle.
    create-custom-turtles 1 [
```

```
    set cohort generation + 1
    set chromosome chromosome-of parent
    ]
end
```

The crossover procedure (see Figure 10.6) takes two chromosomes, randomly selects a cut-point within the length of the chromosome and swaps the genes between the chromosomes from the start to that cut point. The mutation procedure randomly chooses a location within the chromosome and flips the gene value from 1 to 0 or vice versa.

```
to cross [ mate ]      ; turtle procedure. Exchange a chunk of my
                       ; and my mate's chromosomes by swapping
                       ; the genes from the beginning to a
                       ; randomly chosen stopping place
    locals [ place my-gene your-gene ]
    set place 0
    repeat random (chromo-length) [
        set my-gene (item place chromosome)
        set your-gene (item place chromosome-of mate)
        set chromosome
          (replace-item place chromosome your-gene)
        set chromosome-of mate
          (replace-item place chromosome-of mate my-gene)
        set place place + 1
    ]
end
```

```
to mutate                  ; turtle procedure.  Flip a bit with
                           ; a probability of 1 in 1/mutation-rate
    locals [ place old new]
    set place (random (chromo-length / mutation-rate))
    if (place < chromo-length) [
        set old (item place chromosome)
        ifelse (old = 0)
            [set new 1]
            [set new 0]
        set chromosome (replace-item place chromosome new)
    ]
end
```

That completes the code for the GA itself. All that remains is to show how the fitness of agents is calculated. This closely follows Axelrod's method. The procedure `find-fitness` is called for each turtle in turn. This organizes a game between the turtle and each other turtle, collecting the payoffs received (see Figure 10.5 for the payoff matrix) and setting the turtle's fitness to the average payoff per turtle opponent.

```
to find-fitness        ; turtle procedure.  Report my fitness.
                       ; This procedure will change according to
                       ; the problem that the Genetic Algorithm
                       ; is expected to solve.

  ; play a sequence of prisoner's dilemma encounters with
  ; every other turtle
  locals [ total-payoff ]
  set total-payoff 0
  ; note that here we are asking another turtle to play a game
  ; against me, so, confusingly, the 'other' turtle in play-game
  ; is me (this only has consequences for the arrangement of the
  ; payoff matrix)
  ask turtles with [self != myself] [
    set total-payoff total-payoff + play-game myself
    ]
  set fitness total-payoff / ( count turtles - 1)
end
```

A game consists of 151 matches with the same opponent. For each match, the turtle works out whether to cooperate or defect according to the history of the last three matches and the turtle's strategy, encoded in its chromosome. Because at the beginning of the sequence, there are no previous matches, the last six bits of the turtle's chromosome are used to indicate 'hypothetical' prior outcomes. This means that at the beginning of each game, the turtle has to fill in its history with these outcomes from its chromosome and this is done by the `setup-game` procedure, which encodes the bits from its chromosome and copies them into the three outcome variables.

```
to-report play-game [ other ]    ; turtle procedure.
                                 ; Play a game against the
                                 ; 'other' turtle

  locals [ winnings ]
  set winnings 0
  setup-game
  ask other [ setup-game ]       ; A game is a sequence of 151
                                 ; matches with the same opponent
```

```
repeat 151 [ set winnings winnings + (play-match other) ]
report winnings
end
```

```
to setup-game               ; turtle procedure. Set up the
                            ; three outcomes which
                            ; hypothetically preceded the
                            ; game using bits
                            ; from the end of the chromosome
  set last-but-one-outcome
    2 * (item (chromo-length - 6) chromosome) +
    item (chromo-length - 5) chromosome
  set last-outcome
    2 * (item (chromo-length - 4) chromosome) +
    item (chromo-length - 3) chromosome
end
```

Playing a match consists of working out the turtle's own move (Cooperate or Defect), asking the opponent to do the same, recording the outcome in the turtle's own history of the last three matches (and getting the opponent to do the same in its history) and finally working out the payoff.

```
to-report play-match [ other ]   ; turtle procedure.
                                 ; Using my strategy and the
                                 ; previous outcomes, find my
                                 ; move and the same for the
                                 ; other. Record the outcome
                                 ; and report the payoff
  locals [ my-move other-move ]
  set my-move find-move
  ask other [ set other-move find-move ]
  record-history my-move other-move
  ask other [ record-history other-move my-move ]
  report payoff my-move other-move
end
```

```
to-report payoff [ my-move other-move ]   ; turtle procedure
                                          ; Report the payoff from my
                                          ; and the other's move,
                                          ; using the payoff matrix
                                          ; 1 = cooperate 0 = defect
  locals [ payoff ]
  ifelse (my-move = 1 and other-move = 1) [ set payoff 3 ]
```

```
[ ifelse (my-move = 1 and other-move = 0) [ set payoff 5 ]
  [ ifelse (my-move = 0 and other-move = 1) [ set payoff 0 ]
    [ set payoff 1 ]
  ]
]
report payoff
end
```

Finding the right move to make is a matter of looking up the correct bit in the chromosome, indexed by the last three outcomes. The indexing is done by noting that there are four possible outcomes (Cooperate/Cooperate; Cooperate/Defect; Defect/Cooperate; and Defect/Defect) and three sequential outcomes to take into account.

```
to-report find-move           ; turtle procedure.
                              ; Use my strategy and the
                              ; last three match outcomes,
                              ; report my next move
                              ; (cooperate (1) or defect (0) )
  locals [ place ]
  set place
    (((last-but-one-outcome * 4) + last-outcome) * 4) + outcome
  report item place chromosome
end
```

Once both the turtle's own and the opponent's moves have been made, this outcome can be recorded in the turtles' histories and this is done by the record-history procedure.

```
to record-history [ my-move other-move ]  ; turtle procedure
                              ; remember the outcome from
                              ; this match
  set last-but-one-outcome last-outcome
  set last-outcome outcome
  set outcome 2 * my-move + other-move
end
```

There remains only some procedures related to displaying the agents on the NetLogo user interface.

```
to colour-turtle              ; turtle procedure. Set the
                              ; colour of the displayed turtle,
                              ; using the binary value of
```

```
                              ; the chromosome to index the
                              ; colour scale
   set color wrap-color reduce [ ?1 * 2 + ?2 ] chromosome
end


to display-turtles            ; turtle procedure. Display the
                              ; turtle on the perimeter of
                              ; a circle
      colour-turtle
      set heading who * (360 / number-of-turtles)
      fd 10
end


to plot-results               ; observer procedure.  Plot the current
                              ; mean fitness
      set-current-plot "Fitness"
      set-current-plot-pen "average"
      plot mean values-from turtles [ fitness ]
end
```

A typical run (Figure 10.9) shows the average fitness of the agents decreasing at first, as the population evolves from the random initial outcomes. However, after about 25 generations, the agents begin to co-evolve strategies that reciprocate the cooperation that they get from other agents, and these pairs of cooperating agents do very well and drive the average fitness sharply upwards. Since these agents have high fitness scores, they become the parents of the next generation. In this way, the fitness score gradually increases until it approaches 453 – the score when all agents are cooperating all the time. Some variation remains because even after all agents inherit a chromosome for a cooperative strategy, mutation ensures that there will be some defectors in the population.

Developments and variations on evolutionary computation

We have so far been considering only the classical GA, but there are also a number of important variations and extensions, some of which are more useful for social simulation than the classic form. The variations concern what is represented in the individuals' genes and the details of the process of evolution. We shall consider the issue of representation first.

Figure 10.9: A typical run of the re-implementation of Axelrod's model, plotting the average fitness of the agents by generation

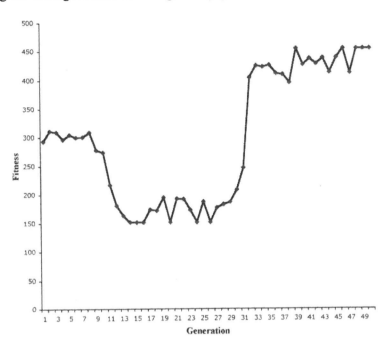

REPRESENTATION

The classical GA codes the attributes of individuals in a chromosome consisting of a sequence of bits in a binary sequence. In this, it diverges from the biological analogue, since DNA uses a fourfold coding scheme: each base can be one of four possible nucleotides – adenine, thymine, cytosine and guanine. Because any information can be coded into a binary string, attention could be confined to binary chromosomes, but two alternatives are convenient and useful: genes consisting of real numbers and genes consisting of computer programs.

Real numbers   For many problems, the parameters that are to be encoded in the chromosome are ordinary real (floating-point) numbers, rather than binary, and it is more efficient to construct chromosomes from these directly, rather than having to code them into a binary representation first. The GA works exactly as before, with the exception of the mutation operator. Standard mutation involves 'flipping a bit' from one to zero or vice versa; this is not possible if the gene consists of a real number. Instead, to implement mutation a small random number (taken from a normal distribution with zero mean and with standard deviation similar to the standard deviation of the parameter in the population) is added to a small proportion of the genes.

Programs   When agents are evolved using the classic GA, the genes encode the values of the parameters which direct the agents' activity. The program controlling each agent always remains the same, although the parameter values will vary from individual to individual. For example, in Axelrod's model, agents evolved different strategies for playing the prisoner's dilemma game, but the differences between agents consisted only of what the next move – cooperation or defection – would be. An alternative approach is to allow the agents' controlling programs to evolve directly, by encoding the program itself, not just some parameters, in the chromosome. This technique is known as genetic programming (Koza 1992; 1994).

For example, suppose that we wanted to evolve an agent that can do simple personal budgeting, that is, an agent which is capable of deciding on what it wants to buy from a regular income – food, accommodation and so on (Chattoe and Gilbert 1997). The chromosome of such an agent will encode a program which uses the agent's 'bank balance', current stocks of goods and strength of 'needs' as inputs and produces a purchasing decision as output. A program of this kind could consist of nothing more than a formula made up of variables representing the bank balance, the stock levels and the needs, linked by arithmetic operators such as addition, subtraction, multiplication and division, and a comparison operator. To work out what to buy at any moment, the agent would apply the formula, substituting current values of the variables in order to assess the amount of each commodity to buy (see Figure 10.10 for an example of such a formula).

To start the evolutionary process, each agent is given a chromosome representing a random formula: a random assortment of variables and operators, but constructed so that it is syntactically correct. While few of the agents will do a good job of budgeting with their initial formulae (most will run out of money before satisfying many of their needs and will 'starve to death'), breeding new formulae from the best in the population will eventually improve the average performance.

The main difference between genetic programming and the classical genetic algorithm is that the crossover and mutation operators used for genetic programming have to be designed to ensure that the program represented by the chromosome always remains syntactically correct. One way to achieve this is to represent the program as a tree (Figure 10.10) and perform

Figure 10.10: Tree and conventional functional representation of a formula for deciding whether to purchase a good, evolved by genetic programming

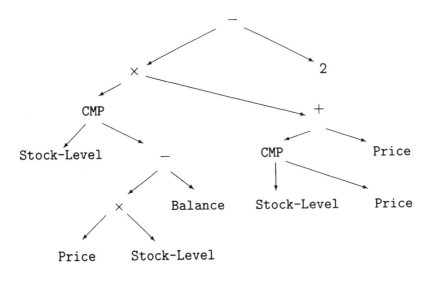

```
(- (* (CMP Stock-Level
          (- (* Price Stock-Level) Balance))
      (+ (CMP Stock-Level Price) Price))
   2)
```

Note: CMP returns 1 if the value of its first argument is greater than that of its second, 0 if the arguments are equal, or −1 if the first argument is less than the second.

---

crossover between two programs by chopping off a randomly chosen branch from one tree and attaching it to the other at a random location. A tree can be mutated by randomly selecting an operator or variable and exchanging it for another. Further details can be found in Koza (1992). Chattoe and Gilbert (1997) show that using genetic programming it is possible to evolve agents which are able to budget effectively even in the face of low income and irregular demands and commitments.

LEARNING CLASSIFIER SYSTEMS

Agents that incorporated production systems – sets of condition-action rules and a rule interpreter – were introduced in Chapter 8. Although the internal states of such agents (retained in working memory) change as they act on and react to their environment, the rules themselves remain unchanged. In learning classifier systems (Holland *et al.* 1986), the agent is able to improve its rule set by learning from feedback about its actions. Learning takes two forms which interact: the relative priorities of rules are modified, so that the conditions of high priority rules are examined before low priority ones, and the rules themselves evolve using a form of genetic algorithm.

In a classifier system, the working memory is implemented using 'messages', which are bit strings representing the state of the agent. The condition parts of rules are also formed of strings of ones and zeroes (and a special symbol called the 'don't care' symbol, meaning that either one or zero can match in this position). The rule interpreter works by matching the rules against each of the messages.

The relative priority of the rules is adjusted using what is called the *bucket brigade* algorithm. All rules are rated according to their specificity, that is, how few 'don't care' symbols there are in their condition parts. Rules also have a strength, a value which is adjusted by the interpreter, but which is initially set at random. The priority of a rule is then proportional to the product of its strength and its specificity (meaning that strong specific rules are have higher priority than weak general ones).

At each step, a message is selected from working memory and all rules which match it are located by the rule interpreter. One of these will have the greatest priority and this one is chosen to fire. The action part of this rule will generate a new message, and may also cause the agent to perform some task in the environment. The rule which did fire pays a 'tax' equal to its priority and this tax is distributed to the rules which created the message that matched the selected rule. Eventually a rule fires which causes an action to be performed and instead of getting its reward from successor rule firings, it gets its reward from the environment, according to the fitness of the action performed. This algorithm therefore rewards both the rules that are ultimately effective in performing actions and the rules which generated the preconditions for those rules – hence the name 'bucket brigade', as rewards are passed back from one rule to its predecessors.

For a learning classifier system, the initial rules can be generated randomly, an easy process since they consist only of sets of ones, zeroes and don't care symbols. Then, at infrequent intervals (perhaps once every thousand time steps), the rules are treated as a population of genes, with fitness proportional to the rule strength, and new rules are bred from the old using crossover and mutation. The new set of rules replaces the old and the bucket brigade algorithm continues.

THE EVOLUTIONARY PROCESS

What we have called the classical GA was first devised by John Holland (1975) and was inspired by the processes underlying biological evolution. At around the same time, or even earlier, other researchers were independently developing evolutionary algorithms based on biological metaphors, and these alternative approaches are still used and have their advocates. They are worth considering for social simulation if one is creating an explicitly evolutionary model, rather than using the algorithm as a 'black box' optimizer. In the latter case, the classical GA is to be preferred because it is convenient and better understood and documented than its rivals.

Evolution strategies (ESs) were developed in Berlin in the 1960s to optimize the aerodynamic shapes of solid bodies, a problem requiring the tuning of several real-valued parameters (Michalewicz 1996: Chapter 8). They differ from the classical genetic algorithm in not using a crossover operator and breeding new populations somewhat differently. In a GA, crossover and mutation operations are applied to randomly selected individuals from the 'old' population (see Figure 10.7), while in ESs, the whole of the old population is subjected to mutation and then the new population is selected from this pool of individuals. A consequence is that, while it is possible for an individual to be selected twice in a GA, this is not possible using ESs. A second difference between the two approaches is that, in an ES, the probability of and amount of mutation (that is, the size of the increment randomly added to a small number of the genes) vary during the evolution, while the evolutionary operators do not change in most GAs.

As can be seen from this contrast between ESs and GAs, the two approaches differ mainly in details. The same is true of the third approach, evolutionary programming (EP), which follows the general design of an ES, but uses the chromosome to represent a finite-state machine (FSM). An FSM is a device that, given a sequence of input symbols, produces one or more output symbols. For example, FSMs have been used as compilers (the program to compile is the sequence of input symbols and the output is the machine code used to drive the computer) and to control machines such as the automatic teller machines that provide cash from your bank account. An FSM can be thought of as a set of nodes (each representing one of the states in which the machine can be) linked by arrows representing the transition from one state to another. Each transition is associated with an input symbol and possibly an output symbol. For instance, when one has entered the amount of money to withdraw on a teller machine's keyboard (the 'input symbol'), the machine will change from the state of 'requesting the amount to be withdrawn' to the state of 'preparing to dispense cash', and the screen might show a message asking the user to wait (the 'output symbol').

FSMs can also be useful as representations of agents: Axelrod's agents are FSMs, and the shopping agent used in the example of multi-agent systems at the end of Chapter 8 is also an FSM, although a complex one. In the original EP approach (Fogel *et al.* 1966, see also Fogel 1995), each parent produces a single offspring by subjecting its own FSM design to random mutations involving changing the output symbol, changing a state transition, adding or deleting a state and changing the state at which the machine is initialized. Then the best individuals are selected from the combined populations of parents and offspring.

This brief discussion of ESs and EP has shown that the design of the classical GA is not cast in stone: substantial variations in the algorithm and the genetic representation can be made in order to provide a better model or a more efficient method of encoding and yet the algorithm still has a good chance of converging or exhibiting interesting behaviour. The literature includes many more variations, such as GAs used evolve the parameters of artificial neural networks (Beltratti *et al.* 1996; Klüver 1998) and an evolutionary algorithm known as a cultural algorithm which implements the simultaneous evolution of both individual traits and group beliefs (Reynolds 1994). Nowadays, all these are included as variations of evolutionary computation.

Further reading

The standard reference on artificial neural networks, although now becoming rather out of date, is

- Rumelhart, D. and McClelland, G. (1986) *Parallel Distributed Processing*, vols. I and II. MIT Press, Cambridge, MA.

A useful text that considers in more detail the practical issues of building and using neural networks is

- Swingler, K. (1996) *Applying Neural Networks: A Practical Guide.* Academic Press, London

and

- Gurney, K. (1997) *Introduction to Neural Networks.* Routledge, London explains the technicalities clearly.

A text on using neural networks for social simulation is

- Garson, David G. (1998) *Neural Networks: an Introductory Guide for Social Scientists*. Sage Publications, London

and

- Beltratti, A. *et al.* (1996) *Neural Networks for Economic and Financial Modelling*. International Thomson Computer Press, London

offers a brief introduction to both artificial neural networks and genetic algorithms and shows how the two can be used together to create models of economic markets.

Implementations of neural networks for tasks such as pattern recognition, data mining and optimization are available commercially, for example from Mathworks as an add-on to MATLAB (Neural Network Toolbox, see http://www.mathworks.com/products/neuralnet/) and from NeuralWare (http://www.neuralware.com/products.jsp). These suppliers also provide practically oriented user manuals for their products. However, they are orientated towards the prediction and classification tasks found in business and are of limited value for social simulation.

Recent textbooks on evolutionary computation are

- Eiben, A. E. and Smith, J. E. (2003) *Introduction to Evolutionary Computing*. Springer-Verlag, Berlin.

- Michalewicz, Z. and Fogel, D. (2000) *How to Solve It: Modern Heuristics*. Springer-Verlag, Berlin.

- Mitchell, Melanie (1998) *An Introduction to Genetic Algorithms*. MIT Press, Cambridge, MA.

- Michalewicz, Z. (1996) *Genetic Algorithms + Data Structures = Evolution Programs*, 3rd edn. Springer-Verlag, Berlin.

An article that reviews the value of GAs for social simulation is

- Chattoe, E. (1998) Just How (Un)realistic are Evolutionary Algorithms as Representations of Social Processes? *Journal of Artificial Societies and Social Simulation*, 1(3): http://www.soc.surrey.ac.uk/JASSS/1/3/2.html

The original source for the genetic algorithm is

- Holland, J. H. (1975) *Adaptation in Natural and Artificial Systems.* University of Michigan Press, Ann Arbor, MI.

A second edition was published in 1992.
A useful textbook on genetic programming is

- Banzhaf, W. *et al.* (1998) *Genetic Programming: an Introduction.* Morgan Kaufmann, San Francisco, CA

which provides a wide-ranging introduction and descriptions of implementations.
The original reference for genetic programming is

- Koza, J. R. (1992) *Genetic Programming.* MIT Press, Cambridge, MA

and three further volumes with the same title.

Appendix A

Web sites

This appendix lists some of the Web sites[1] that provide information about social simulation and related topics. The Web is constantly changing and so some of the addresses shown below may have gone and others come. Nevertheless, this list provides a good starting point for exploration.

General

Copies of most of the program code included in this book can be found at `http://cress.soc.surrey.ac.uk/s4ss/`
There is an e-mail distribution list for simulation in the social sciences. To subscribe, fill in your details at the subscription page, `http://www.jiscmail.ac.uk/lists/simsoc.html`

Programs, packages and languages

MIMOSE
`http://www.uni-koblenz.de/~moeh/projekte/mimose.html`
MIMOSE consists of a model description language and an experimental framework for the simulation of models. The main purpose of the MIMOSE project has been the development of a modelling language that considers the

---

[1] The longer Web addresses (URLs) below have been broken into two lines to fit them on the page. When typing them into a browser, do not leave any space between the two parts.

special demands of modelling in social science, especially the description of nonlinear quantitative and qualitative relations, stochastic influences, birth and death processes, and micro and multilevel models. The aim is that describing models in MIMOSE should not burden the modeller with a lot of programming and implementation details.

MIMOSE was created by Michael Möhring of Computer Science Applications in the Social Sciences, Department of Computer Science, University of Koblenz-Landau, Rheinau 1, D-56075 Koblenz, Germany.

Release 2.0 requires Sun Sparc (SunOS, Solaris, X11R5/6 or LINUX. A Java interface is under development and the next release will be usable with Java-enabled browsers. The current release is usable with Java-enabled browsers, given that the server process runs on a SunOS or LINUX machine.

NETLOGO

http://ccl.northwestern.edu/netlogo/
NetLogo is a programmable modelling environment for simulating natural and social phenomena. It is particularly well suited for modelling complex systems developing over time. Modellers can give instructions to hundreds or thousands of independent 'agents' all operating concurrently. This makes it possible to explore the connection between the micro-level behaviour of individuals and the macro-level patterns that emerge from the interaction of many individuals.

NetLogo lets students open simulations and 'play' with them, exploring their behaviour under various conditions. It is also an authoring environment that enables students, teachers and curriculum developers to create their own models. NetLogo is simple enough that students and teachers can easily run simulations or even build their own. It is advanced enough to serve as a powerful tool for researchers in many fields.

NetLogo has extensive documentation and tutorials. It also comes with a models library, which is a large collection of pre-written simulations that can be used and modified. These simulations address many content areas in the natural and social sciences, including biology and medicine, physics and chemistry, mathematics and computer science, and economics and social psychology. Several model-based inquiry curricula using NetLogo are currently under development.

SWARM

http://wiki.swarm.org/
Swarm is a software package for multi-agent simulation of complex systems developed at the Santa Fe Institute. It is intended to be a useful tool for

researchers in a variety of disciplines, especially artificial life. The basic architecture of Swarm is the simulation of collections of concurrently interacting agents: with this architecture, a large variety of agent-based models can be implemented. It runs on UNIX machines with GNU Objective C and X-windows: the source code is freely available under GNU licensing terms; more recent versions use Java and also run on Windows machines.

Swarm is available for download in both source and binary versions.

RePast

http://repast.sourceforge.net/
RePast is a free software framework for creating agent-based simulations using the Java language (requires version Java 1.4 or greater). It provides a library of classes for creating, running, displaying and collecting data from an agent-based simulation. In addition, RePast can take snapshots of running simulations, and create quicktime movies of simulations. RePast borrows much from the Swarm simulation toolkit and can properly be termed 'Swarm-like'. In addition, RePast includes such features as run-time model manipulation via graphical user interface widgets.

MASON

http://cs.gmu.edu/~eclab/projects/mason/
MASON is a free, fast discrete-event multi-agent simulation library core in Java, designed to be the foundation for large custom-purpose Java simulations, and also to provide functionality for many lightweight simulation needs. MASON contains both a model library and an optional suite of visualization tools in 2D and 3D.

SDML

http://sdml.cfpm.org/
SDML is a strictly declarative modelling language with object-oriented features specifically designed for modelling tasks in the social sciences. It enables the building of sophisticated simulations involving agents, compound agents, multiple time levels, complex organizations and so on. Its declarative logic-based style of programming allows for complete rigour as well as for the capturing of a mixture of qualitative as well as quantitative aspects. Although it has a sharp learning curve, once learnt, sophisticated models of interacting organizations and cognitive agents can be swiftly developed. For further information contact the Centre for Policy Modelling, Manchester Metropolitan University. Written by Steve Wallis, original version by Scott

Moss.

SDML is available for UNIX, PC (Windows 3.11 or 95) or Macintosh, and requires 32 Mb of RAM. Commercial users also require Digitalk/Parcplace Visual Works, but academic researchers can obtain a version free from the Centre for Policy Modelling.

SIMPACK

`http://www.cise.ufl.edu/~fishwick/simpack.html`
Although Simpack is not specifically oriented towards social simulation, it supports a wide variety of event scheduling and continuous-time simulation models.

MAGSY

`http://www.dfki.uni-sb.de/~kuf/magsy.html`
MAGSY is a development platform for multi-agent applications. Each agent in MAGSY has a forward chaining rule interpreter in its kernel. This rule interpreter is a complete re-implementation of an OPS5 system, further enhanced to make it more suitable for the development of multi-agent system applications.

MAGSY runs on UNIX, LINUX, SunOS and Solaris systems.

CORMAS

`http://cormas.cirad.fr/en/outil/outil.htm`
Cormas is a programming environment dedicated to the creation of multi-agent systems, specifically for the domain of natural-resources management. It provides a framework for developing simulation models of coordination modes between individuals and groups that jointly exploit common resources. It is written in the programming language Smalltalk.

MADKIT

`http://www.madkit.org/`
MadKit is a Java multi-agent platform built upon an organizational model. It provides general agent facilities, such as lifecycle management, message passing and distribution, and allows high heterogeneity in agent architectures and communication languages, and various customizations. MadKit communication is based on a peer-to-peer mechanism which allows developers to develop distributed applications quickly using agent principles. MadKit is free and licensed under the GPL/LGPL licence.

Electronic journals

There are several electronic journals which publish papers relating to computer simulation available on the Web. The most relevant of these is the *Journal of Artificial Societies and Social Simulation*, at http://jasss.soc.surrey.ac.uk/JASSS.html
    Others worthy of mention are:

- *Complexity International* (http://journal-ci.csse.monash.edu.au/ci/info-journal.html), an electronic refereed journal including a wide range of papers on complexity theory;
- *Complexity Digest* (http://www.comdig.org/), a weekly newsletter about complexity in the natural and social sciences, which includes links to relevant reviews, notices of articles, conference announcements and so forth;
- *Artificial Life Online* (http://www.alife.org/), the online companion to the (paper) journal *Artificial Life*, published by the Santa Fe Institute (http://www.santafe.edu/).

System dynamics

STELLA

http://www.iseesystems.com/
This is the site for the Stella simulation package, one of the best-known packages for scientists, and for ithink, a version aimed at business use.

DESERT ISLAND DYNAMICS: AN ANNOTATED SURVEY OF THE ESSENTIAL SYSTEM DYNAMICS LITERATURE

http://web.mit.edu/jsterman/www/DID.html
This 1992 survey of the English-language system dynamics literature by M. Anjali Sastry and John D. Sterman identifies and summarizes some of the papers, books, games and software programs that have most influenced the development of the field.

THE SYSTEM DYNAMICS SOCIETY

http://www.albany.edu/cpr/sds/ or http://www.systemdynamics.org
The System Dynamics Society is an international, non-profit organization devoted to encouraging the development and use of system dynamics around

the world.

GENE BELLINGER'S SYSTEMS PAGE

http://systems-thinking.org
This site has information on a variety of systems-based topics.

POWERSIM

http://www.powersim.com/
This is the home of the Powersim package; it has an example of system dynamics applied to the UK Newbury Bypass traffic scheme.

INSTITUTE OF ROBOTICS AND SYSTEM DYNAMICS

http://www.op.dlr.de/FF-DR/ff_dr_homepage_engl.html
The Institute of Robotics and System Dynamics is part of the German Aerospace Research Establishment.

LONDON BUSINESS SCHOOL SYSTEM DYNAMICS GROUP

http://www.lbs.ac.uk/sysdyn/
This group works on topics involving system dynamics, systems thinking and strategic modelling.

'VIOLATING AN OCCUPATIONAL SEX-STEREOTYPE: ISRAELI WOMEN EARNING ENGINEERING DEGREES'

http://www.socresonline.org.uk/socresonline/1/4/3.html
This is a paper in *Sociological Research Online* by Chanoch Jacobsen and Tamar Vanki on applying system dynamics to a sociological issue.

Microsimulation

CAMBRIDGE MICROSIMULATION UNIT

http://www.econ.cam.ac.uk/dae/mu/microsim.htm
The Cambridge Microsimulation Unit is part of the Department of Applied Economics at the University of Cambridge and carries out a range of social and economic policy work using microsimulation.

CORNELL MICROSIMULATION

http://www.strategicforecasting.com/corsim/

This is the home of CORSIM, a dynamic microsimulation model based at Cornell University.

THE NATIONAL CENTRE FOR SOCIAL AND ECONOMIC MODELLING, CANBERRA, AUSTRALIA

http://www.natsem.canberra.edu.au/index.html
NATSEM maintains an extensive microsimulation site.

EUROMOD

http://www.econ.cam.ac.uk/dae/mu/emod.htm
EUROMOD is a 15-country Europe-wide benefit-tax model. It involves a team of researchers from all of the 15 states that formed the European Union until May 2004.
    EUROMOD provides estimates of the distributional impact of changes to personal tax and transfer policy, with (a) the specification of policy changes, (b) the application of revenue constraints and (c) the evaluation of results each taking place at either the national or the European level. Thus EURO-MOD is of value both in assessing the consequences of consolidated social policies and in understanding how different policies in different countries may contribute to common objectives.

MICROSIMULATION AND ECONOMETRICS AT THE INSTITUTE OF FISCAL STUDIES

http://www.ifs.org.uk/
The Institute of Fiscal Studies in London uses microsimulation for some of its policy research.

STATISTICS CANADA MICROSIMULATION MODELS

http://www.statcan.ca/english/spsd/
For over a decade Canada's national statistical agency has developed static models (SPSD/M), dynamic models (LifePaths) and a general simulation language (ModGen) for social policy, tax policy and other applications.

DYNAMIC MICROSIMULATION OF ELDERS' HEALTH AND WELL-BEING

http://www-cpr.maxwell.syr.edu/microsim/microlst.htm
From the Center for Demography and Economics of Aging at Syracuse University.

ASPEN: MP MICROSIMULATION MODEL OF THE UNITED STATES ECONOMY

http://www.cs.sandia.gov/tech_reports/rjpryor/Aspen.html
ASPEN was a project to develop an agent-based microsimulation model of the United States economy on the massively parallel Intel Paragon computer.

TRANSIMS

http://transims.tsasa.lanl.gov/home.html
This page is about the US TRansportation ANalysis SIMulation System.

PROGRAM FOR IMPROVED VEHICLE DEMAND FORECASTING MODELS

http://128.200.36.2/its/research/fuel.html
The aim of this project is to develop a microsimulation model system for traffic loads.

Queuing models

Details of a number of discrete event simulation modelling packages are available on the Web. In some cases, the Web sites also offer demonstrations and tutorials about the packages.

STELLA

http://www.iseesystems.com/
This is the site for the Stella simulation package, one of the best-known packages for scientists, and for ithink, a version aimed at business use.

SIMSCRIPT

http://www.caciasl.com/
A description of the SimScript II simulation programming language and development environment can be found here. This site also describes Sim-process, which is a related simulation tool with a graphical user interface.

SIMPLEX 3

http://www.or.uni-passau.de/english/3/simplex.php3
This is the home page for Simplex3, an object-oriented modelling tool for discrete event simulation. Simplex3 is available free from this site.

EMPLANT

http://www.emPlant.de/simulation.html
emPlant, successor to SIMPLE++, is designed for the planning of manufacturing plants and production processes by means of simulation. It includes a scalable factory model and features for the construction of a graphical user interface.

EXTEND

http://www.imaginethatinc.com/
This is an extensible simulator with a sophisticated user interface.

Cellular automata

OPEN DIRECTORY

http://search.dmoz.org/cgi-bin/search?search=cellular+automata
A good starting place for further information on cellular automata is the Open Directory, a voluntary effort to create a directory of the Web.

MODERN CELLULAR AUTOMATA

http://www.collidoscope.com/modernca/welcome.html
This page has many examples of CAs and offers a Java applet that can be embedded in a Web page to produce many more variations.

DDLAB

http://www.ddlab.com/
DDLab is an interactive graphics program for researching discrete dynamical networks, relevant to the study of complexity, emergent phenomena, neural networks, and aspects of theoretical biology such as gene regulatory networks. A network can be set up with any architecture from cellular autamata (CA) to 'random Boolean networks' (RBN, networks with arbitrary connections and heterogeneous rules). Network dimensions may be 1d, 2d or 3d. The network may also have heterogeneous neighbourhood sizes.

STEPHEN WOLFRAM'S COLLECTED PAPERS ON CELLULAR AUTOMATA AND COMPLEXITY

http://www.stephenwolfram.com/publications/

Wolfram has provided an extensive set of pages on cellular automata and their uses.

Multi-agent systems

AGENT-BASED COMPUTATIONAL ECONOMICS: GROWING ECONOMIES FROM THE BOTTOM UP

http://www.econ.iastate.edu/tesfatsi/ace.htm
This site has a comprehensive bibliography and links to everything to do with computational economics and social simulation, and is especially good on links to multi-agent simulations. It also includes a tutorial on agent-based computational economics.

INTELLIGENT SOFTWARE AGENTS

http://www.sics.se/isl/abc/survey.html
Sverker Janson has a page on the Swedish Institute of Computer Science site with a huge number of agent-based links.

MULTI-AGENT SYSTEMS

fhttp://www.multiagent.com/
This site contains pointers to information about multi-agent systems, including both research and industrial references.

Neural networks

NEURAL NETWORKS WAREHOUSE

http://neuralnetworks.ai-depot.com/
A comprehensive site with links to books, tutorials, software and descriptions of applications.

ARTIFICIAL NEURAL NETWORKS TUTORIAL

http://www.gc.ssr.upm.es/inves/neural/ann1/anntutorial.html
A tutorial with a short bibliography.

NEURAL JAVA

http://diwww.epfl.ch/mantra/tutorial/english/

Neural Java is a series of exercises and demonstrations. Each exercise consists of a short introduction, a small demonstration program written in Java as an Applet, and a series of questions which are intended as an invitation to play with the programs and explore the possibilities of different algorithms.

Evolutionary computation

EVOWEB

http://evonet.lri.fr

The website of EvoNet, the European Network of Excellence in Evolutionary Computing. It includes many tutorial resources.

THE GENETIC ALGORITHMS ARCHIVE

http://www.aic.nrl.navy.mil/galist/

This site provides a good set of genetic algorithm resources, including archives of the GA discussion list and source code.

GENETIC PROGRAMMING

http://www.geneticprogramming.org/

This is a guide to genetic algorithms and genetic programming, with many links.

INTRODUCTION TO GENETIC ALGORITHMS

http://cs.felk.cvut.cz/~xobitko/ga/

These pages introduce some of the fundamentals of genetics algorithms. Several interactive Java applets have been included to demonstrate basic concepts of genetic algorithms.

EMAIL LISTS

There are several mailing lists for news about conferences, books and events related to evolutionary computing. Sign up at:

http://ec-digest.research.ucf.edu

http://www.jiscmail.ac.uk/lists/evolutionary-computing.html

http://www.genetic-programming.org/gpmailinglist.html

Appendix B

Linear stability analysis of the dove–hawk–law-abider model

For the purpose of linear stability analysis, we approximate a system of nonlinear differential equations with its first-order Taylor expansion. In the case of the dove–hawk–law-abider model this means approximating

$$
\dot{\boldsymbol{p}} = \begin{pmatrix} \dot{p}_D \\ \dot{p}_H \end{pmatrix} = \boldsymbol{f}(\boldsymbol{p}) \tag{B.1}
$$

$$
\dot{p}_D = -\frac{p_D^2 p_H}{2}(2c_D + c_H) + \frac{p_D p_H}{4}(2c_D + 2c_H - u) +
$$
$$
+\frac{p_D^2}{4}(2c_D + u) - \frac{p_D}{4}(2c_D + u)
$$

$$
\dot{p}_H = -\frac{p_D p_H^2}{2}(2c_D + c_H) + \frac{p_H^2}{4}(c_H - u) +
$$
$$
+\frac{p_D p_H}{4}(4c_D + c_H + u) - \frac{p_H}{4}(c_H - u)
$$

with the linear system

$$
\boldsymbol{f}^*(\boldsymbol{p}) = \boldsymbol{f}(\boldsymbol{p}_0) + \boldsymbol{J}(\boldsymbol{p}_0)(\boldsymbol{p} - \boldsymbol{p}_0) \tag{B.2}
$$

where $\boldsymbol{J}(\boldsymbol{p}_0)$ is the Jacobian matrix of the system at the stationary state $\boldsymbol{p}_0$, that is, the matrix

$$
\begin{pmatrix} \frac{\partial f_D}{\partial p_D}(\boldsymbol{p}_0) & \frac{\partial f_D}{\partial p_H}(\boldsymbol{p}_0) \\ \frac{\partial f_H}{\partial p_D}(\boldsymbol{p}_0) & \frac{\partial f_H}{\partial p_H}(\boldsymbol{p}_0) \end{pmatrix} \tag{B.3}
$$

where $\frac{\partial f_i}{\partial p_j}(\boldsymbol{p}_0)$ is the partial derivative of f_i with respect to p_j at $\boldsymbol{p}_0$. The partial derivatives evaluate as

$$\frac{\partial f_D}{\partial p_D} = -p_D p_H (2c_D + c_H) + \frac{p_H}{4}(2c_D + 2c_H - u) +$$
$$+\frac{p_D}{2}(2c_D + u) - \frac{2c_D + u}{4} \tag{B.4}$$

$$\frac{\partial f_D}{\partial p_H} = -\frac{p_D^2}{2}(2c_D + c_H) + \frac{p_D}{4}(2c_D + 2c_H - u) \tag{B.5}$$

$$\frac{\partial f_H}{\partial p_D} = \frac{p_H}{4}(4c_D + c_H + u) - \frac{p_H^2}{2}(2c_D + c_H) \tag{B.6}$$

$$\frac{\partial f_H}{\partial p_H} = -p_D p_H (2c_D + c_H) + \frac{p_H}{2}(c_H - u) +$$
$$+\frac{p_D}{4}(4c_D + c_H + u) - \frac{c_H - u}{4} \tag{B.7}$$

A comparison of $\frac{\partial f_D}{\partial p_H}$ and $\frac{\partial f_H}{\partial p_D}$ shows that a global stability analysis will be most cumbersome. Their inequality makes clear that f_D and f_H are not derivatives of a so-called potential function V with respect to p_D and p_H, respectively. If there existed such a potential function, then we could plot it; its graph would look like a mountain range. The deepest points in valleys would then correspond to stable stationary states (which in this context are also called sinks), summits would correspond to stationary states unstable in all directions (sources), and saddles (ridges, cols) would correspond to stationary states that are unstable only with respect to certain directions. Trajectories – the paths the model describes in its state space – would correspond to rivers and creeks. This type of global stability analysis can yield quite perspicuous results, but it is restricted to cases where a potential function (or, alternatively, a so-called Lyapunov function, which is usually hard to find) exists.

The function $\boldsymbol{f}^*$ is a close approximation to the function $\boldsymbol{f}$ – but only in an infinitesimal neighbourhood of the stationary state $\boldsymbol{p}_0$. It can be converted into a linear combination of two exponential functions whose exponents are $\lambda_i t$, with λ_i the eigenvalues of the Jacobian matrix:

$$\boldsymbol{f}^*(\boldsymbol{p}) = \boldsymbol{f}(\boldsymbol{p}_0) + \boldsymbol{v}_1 \exp(\lambda_1 t) + \boldsymbol{v}_2 \exp(\lambda_2 t)$$

in which $\boldsymbol{v}_i$ are the eigenvectors of the Jacobian. This is why we need only these eigenvalues: positive eigenvalues lead to an ever increasing value of $\boldsymbol{f}^*$, which means that over time the system leaves the neighbourhood of the stationary state. If all eigenvalues of a Jacobian in a stationary state are negative, the linearized system approaches the stationary state, since for $t \to \infty$ the exponential functions vanish.

Here we return to triplets: $(1,0,0)$ means: all doves, no hawks, no law-abiders. For the four stationary states $(1,0,0)$, $(0,1,0)$, $(0,0,1)$, and $(\frac{c_H-u}{2c_D+c_H}, \frac{2c_D+u}{2c_D+c_H}, 0)$ the Jacobian evaluates to

$$(1,0,0): \quad \begin{pmatrix} \frac{2c_D+u}{4} & -\frac{2c_D+u}{4} \\ 0 & \frac{2c_D+u}{2} \end{pmatrix}$$

$$(0,1,0): \quad \begin{pmatrix} \frac{c_H-u}{2} & 0 \\ -\frac{c_H-u}{4} & \frac{c_H-u}{4} \end{pmatrix}$$

$$(0,0,1): \quad \begin{pmatrix} -\frac{2c_D+u}{4} & 0 \\ 0 & -\frac{c_H-u}{4} \end{pmatrix}$$

$$(\frac{c_H-u}{2c_D+c_H}, \frac{2c_D+u}{2c_D+c_H}, 0): \quad \begin{pmatrix} -\frac{(c_H-u)(2c_D+u)}{4(2c_D+c_H)} & \frac{(c_H-u)(2c_D+u)}{4(2c_D+c_H)} \\ \frac{(c_H-u)(2c_D+u)}{4(2c_D+c_H)} & -\frac{(c_H-u)(2c_D+u)}{4(2c_D+c_H)} \end{pmatrix}$$

The eigenvalues of the Jacobian are the following

$(1,0,0)$	$(0,1,0)$	$(0,0,1)$	$(\frac{c_H-u}{2c_D+c_H}, \frac{2c_D+u}{2c_D+c_H}, 0)$
$\lambda_1 = \frac{2c_D+u}{2}$	$\lambda_1 = \frac{c_H-u}{4}$	$\lambda_1 = -\frac{c_H-u}{4}$	$\lambda_1 = -\frac{(c_H-u)(u+2c_D)}{4(2c_D+c_H)}$
$\lambda_2 = \frac{2c_D+u}{2}$	$\lambda_2 = \frac{c_H-u}{2}$	$\lambda_2 = -\frac{2c_D+u}{4}$	$\lambda_2 = 0$

(note that $c_D < u < c_H$, and that all expressions in parentheses, denominators and numerators are written so that they are positive).

There is one stationary state with only negative eigenvalues, namely the third, which is when only the law-abiders survive. This is the only stable state the system can assume – the system behaves like a ball that always returns to the deepest point in a basin. The other stationary states are not attractors and so the system will escape their neighbourhood. States 1 and 2 are so-called sources,[1] in which the system is unstable with respect to all directions and behaves like a ball at the summit of a hill: the least fluctuation will drive it away in some direction. State 4 is a so-called saddle point, which means that there is one direction in which the system approaches this point (the direction from the summit to a saddle), while in all other directions the system is removed from the neighbourhood of the saddle (note that at a saddle we normally have some negative and some positive eigenvalues, while here we have one negative and one vanishing eigenvalue, but as we saw, it is in fact a saddle).

---

[1]Note that in linear stability analysis 'source' has a different meaning than in system dynamics.

Although statements about the stability of the system hold only for an infinitesimal neighbourhood when they are derived from a linear stability analysis, in this case they are sufficient to describe the behaviour of our model. Since the stationary states lie at the corners and on one edge of the region of interest (all p_i positive and summing to 1), the overall behaviour of the system is clear. From every point in the phase space, the system will end up with only law-abiders, perhaps after it has more-or-less approached the saddle point (without law-abiders) first.

A global stability analysis – which is not detailed here – reveals the same, and a graph derived from the results of this global analysis shows at the same time why the most interesting state of this model (this system of differential equations) is called a saddle. Global stability analysis tries to find a scalar function of the variables of the system (called the potential function) whose derivatives with respect to these variables are exactly the right-hand sides of the original system of differential equations. Such a function does not exist for our system, but a close relative, the so-called Lyapunov function (named after its inventor, the Russian mathematician Aleksandr Lyapunov) V_L exists. Its shape is shown in Figure B.1.

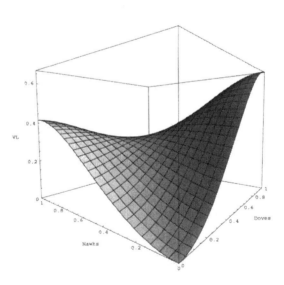

Figure B.1: Lyapunov function of the dove–hawk–law-abider model

The representative point of our system would always move downhill on the landscape drawn in Figure B.1 (although, in the case of Lyapunov functions the representative point will not take the steepest descent, as it does in the case of ordinary potentials). If the representative point of the system is started somewhere on the ridge of the landscape, it will stop at the saddle point, *viz.* the deepest point of the ridge, and only if it starts slightly beside the ridge will it approach the deepest point of the ridge, and shortly before it arrives there, it will turn down to the deepest point of the basin (representing the system state without any hawks and doves).

Appendix C

Random number generators

Random events are usually modelled and simulated using pseudo-random number generators. If an event has to occur with probability p, then a continuous random variable which is uniformly distributed between 0 and 1 is sampled and if its realization is less than p the event occurs, otherwise the event does not occur. So the problem reduces to the problem of realizing uniformly distributed random numbers. Another related problem is the production of random variables with other distributions, such as an exponentially distributed arrival time. A continuous random variable X is exponentially distributed with parameter λ (mean $\frac{1}{\lambda}$) if its probability density function is

$$f_X(x) = \begin{cases} \lambda e^{-\lambda x} & \text{for } x \geq 0 \\ 0 & \text{for } x < 0 \end{cases} \tag{C.1}$$

Its distribution function $F_X(x)$ (which yields the probability that $X \leq x$) is

$$F_X(x) = \begin{cases} 1 - e^{-\lambda x} & \text{for } x \geq 0 \\ 0 & \text{for } x < 0 \end{cases} \tag{C.2}$$

This function (which is strictly increasing) has an inverse function (which is also strictly increasing):

$$y = F_X(x) \quad \text{if and only if} \quad x = F_X^{-1}(y) \tag{C.3}$$

A random quantity X with the distribution function $F_X(x)$ can now be computed by setting

$$X = F_X^{-1}(U) \tag{C.4}$$

which in the case of the exponential distribution is

$$X = -\frac{\ln(1 - U)}{\lambda} \tag{C.5}$$

where ln is the natural logarithm and U is a uniformly distributed random variable between 0 and 1. This is because the probability that $X \leq x$ is the probability that $F_X^{-1}(U) \leq x$, and this is in turn the probability that $U \leq F_X(x)$, and this probability is $F_X(x)$ (because the distribution function $F_U(x)$ of a uniform random variable between 0 and 1 is $F_U(x) = x$; note that for the generation of exponentially distributed random numbers, the formula $X = -\ln(U)/\lambda$ can also be used, because if U is uniformly distributed between 0 and 1, the same holds for $1 - U$). So, this problem, too, reduces to the problem of generating uniform random numbers between 0 and 1. The same applies to a number of other distributions whose distribution functions have inverse functions that can easily be calculated. Normally distributed random variables cannot be generated by this method; there are other methods to sample normal random numbers, the most important ones deriving from the so-called polar method (see, for example, Knuth 1981: 117–118; Ahrens and Dieter 1988).

Thus, the main problem in modelling and simulating stochastic processes in a digital computer is calculating a stream of pseudo-random, uniformly distributed numbers.[1] The most popular random number generators used today (and integrated into most programming libraries) are linear congruential generators. A sequence of pseudo-random numbers is generated by the formula (Knuth 1981: 9)

$$X_{n+1} = (aX_n + c) \bmod m \tag{C.6}$$

where mod is the modulo operation, which yields the remainder after division by m, the modulus. The numbers a and c, $0 \leq a, c < m$, are called the *multiplier* and the *increment*, X_0 is called the starting value or *seed* (which a user should be able to select so that a particular simulation run can be replicated). Pseudo-random numbers generated this way always come in cycles. The longest possible cycle has length m. After this all possible values of X_n must have occurred, and a new cycle starts. The period can be shorter, depending on the values of m, a and c. A recommended combination of values is

$$m = 2^{31} - 1 \qquad a = 7^5 \qquad c = 0 \tag{C.7}$$

---

[1] An alternative to this calculation would be a radioactive source whose fissions would be counted. The time between two fission events is exponentially distributed, so uniform random numbers could be generated using the inverse of the operation described above.

Here, the modulus is prime (and quite convenient, considering that on most machines the word length is 32), the generator has the full period, that is, all 2,147,483,647 different numbers occur, and the algorithm can be implemented in any high-level programming language (Park and Miller 1988).

A new generation of pseudo-random number generators was invented by Matsumoto and Nishimura (1998). Their *Mersenne Twister*, which is also used by NetLogo, has a period of $2^{19937} - 1$ (as compared to the period length of $2^{32} - 1$ in the classical, linear congruential pseudo-random number generators) and was shown to produce uniformly distributed random numbers in 623 dimensions (as compared to five dimensions for linear congruential generators), thus the danger of serial correlation between successive random numbers is drastically reduced.

So far we have generated only integer numbers; their conversion into real numbers in the interval between 0 and 1 is straightforward: the value returned by the algorithm is divided by m. In many simulation systems, more than one stream of random numbers can be generated (as for instance in SimScript, in which the last argument of all random functions indicates the number of such a stream). All streams are normally produced by the same generator, each stream starting at a different place in the period. It still seems to be an open question whether this is a real advantage (cf. Bratley *et al.* 1987: 226).

References

Abelson, R. P. and Bernstein, A. (1963) A computer simulation of community referendum controversies. *Public Opinion Quarterly*, 27: 93–122.

Agre, P. E. and Chapman, D. (1987) Pengi: an implementation of a theory of activity. In *Proceedings of AAAI-87*, pp. 268–272. Morgan Kaufmann, Los Angeles, CA.

Ahrens, J. H. and Dieter, U. (1988) Efficient table-free sampling methods for the exponential, Cauchy, and normal distributions. *Communications of the ACM*, 31: 1330–1337.

Alvin, P. and Foley, D. (1992) Decentralized, dispersed exchange without an auctioneer. *Journal of Economic Behaviour and Organization*, 18: 27–51.

an der Heiden, U. (1992) Chaos in health and disease. In W. Tschacher, G. Schiepek and J. Brunner (eds), *Self-Organization and Clinical Psychology*, Springer Series in Synergetics, Vol. 58, pp. 55–87. Springer-Verlag, Berlin.

Anderson, J. R. and Lebiere, C. (1998) *The Atomic Components of Thought*. Erlbaum, Mahwah, NJ.

Antcliff, S. (1993) An introduction to DYNAMOD: A dynamic microsimulation model. Technical Report 1, National Centre for Social and Economic Modelling (NATSEM), University of Canberra, Canberra.

Archer, M. (1995) *Realist Social Theory: The Morphogenetic Approach*. Cambridge University Press, Cambridge.

Arnold, K. and Gosling, J. (1998) *The Java Programming Language*. 2nd edn. Addison-Wesley, Reading, MA.

Axelrod, R. (1987) The evolution of strategies in the iterated prisoner's dilemma. In L. Davis (ed.), *Genetic Algorithms and Simulated Annealing*. Pitman, London.

Axelrod, R. (1995) A model of the emergence of new political actors. In N. Gilbert and R. Conte (eds), *Artificial Societies: The Computer Simulation of Social Life*. UCL Press, London.

Axelrod, R. (1997a) Advancing the art of simulation in the social sciences. In R. Conte, R. Hegselmann and P. Terna (eds), *Simulating Social Phenomena*, pp. 21–40. Springer-Verlag, Berlin.

Axelrod, R. (1997b) Advancing the art of simulation in the social sciences. *Complexity*, 3: 16–22.

Babloyantz, A. (1980) Self-organization phenomena in multiple unit systems. In H. Haken (ed.), *Dynamics of Synergetic Systems*, Springer Series in Synergetics, Vol. 6, pp. 180–190. Springer-Verlag, Berlin.

Bak, P. (1996) *How Nature Works: The Science of Self-Organized Criticality*. Springer-Verlag, New York, NY.

Balci, O. (1994) Validation, verification, and testing techniques throughout the life cycle of a simulation study. *Annals of Operations Research*, 53: 121–173.

Banks, J. (ed.) (1998) *Handbook of Simulation: Principles, Methodology, Advances, Applications, and Practice*. Wiley, New York, NY.

Banzhaf, W., Nordin, P., Keller, R. E. and Francone, F. D. (1998) *Genetic Programming: an Introduction*. Morgan Kaufmann, San Francisco, CA.

Beck, K. (1999) *Extreme Programming Explained*. Addison-Wesley, Boston, MA.

Beltratti, A., Margarita, S. and Terna, P. (1996) *Neural Networks for Economic and Financial Modelling*. International Thomson Computer Press, London.

Berlekamp, E., Conway, J. and Guy, R. (1982) *Winning Ways for Your Mathematical Plays, Vol. 2: Games in Particular*. Academic Press, London.

Bond, A. H. and Gasser, L. (1988) *Readings in Distributed Artificial Intelligence*. Morgan Kaufmann, Los Altos, CA.

Booch, G., Rumbaugh, J. and Jacobson, I. (2000) *The Unified Modeling Language User Guide*. 6th print edn. Addison-Wesley, Reading, MA.

Box, G., Hunter, W. and Hunter, J. (1978) *Statistics for Experimenters*. Wiley, New York, NY.

Brajnik, G. and Lines, M. (1998) Qualitative modeling and simulation of socio-economic phenomena. *Journal of Artificial Societies and Social Simulation*, 1. http://www.soc.surrey.ac.uk/JASSS/1/1/2.html.

Bratley, P., Fox, B. L. and Schrage, L. E. (1987) *A Guide to Simulation*. 2nd edn. Springer-Verlag, New York, NY.

Bremer, S. A. (ed.) (1987) *The GLOBUS Model. Computer Simulation of Worldwide Political and Economic Development*. Campus/Westview, Frankfurt.

Brooks, R. (1990) Elephants don't play chess. *Robotics and Autonomous Systems*, 6: 3–15.

Brown, L. and Harding, A. (2002) Social modelling and public policy: Application of microsimulation modelling in Australia. *Journal of Artificial Societies and Social Simulation*, 5/4/6. http://jasss.soc.surrey.ac.uk/5/4/6.html.

Bunge, M. (1977) *Ontology I: The Furniture of the World. Treatise on Basic Philosophy, Vol. 3*. Reidel, Dordrecht.

Bunge, M. (1979) *Ontology II: A World of Systems. Treatise on Basic Philosophy, Vol. 4*. Reidel, Dordrecht.

CACI Products Company (2003) *SIMPROCESS Release 4 User's Manual*. CACI, Arlington, VA.

Caldwell, S. B. (1993) CORSIM 2.0: A dynamic microanalytic model of persons and families in the United States. *Forefronts*, 8. http://www.tc.cornell.edu/Forefronts/forefronts.html.

Cangelosi, A. and Parisi, D. (eds) (2001) *Simulating the Evolution of Language*. Springer Verlag, London.

Chaib-draa, B., Moulin, B., Mandiau, R. and Millot, P. (1992) Trends in distributed artificial intelligence. *Artificial Intelligence Review*, 6: 35–66.

Chattoe, E. (1998) Just how (un)realistic are evolutionary algorithms as representations of social processes? *Journal of Artificial Societies and Social Simulation*. http://www.soc.surrey.ac.uk/JASSS/1/3/2.html.

Chattoe, E. and Gilbert, N. (1996) The simulation of budgetary decision-making and mechanisms of social evolution. Technical report, University of Surrey.

Chattoe, E. and Gilbert, N. (1997) A simulation of adaptation mechanisms in budgetary decision making. In R. Conte, R. Hegselmann and P. Terna (eds), *Simulating Social Phenomena*, pp. 401–418. Springer-Verlag, Berlin.

Chen, P. P. (1976) The entity-relationship model – toward a unified view of data. *ACM Transactions on Database Systems*, 1: 9–36.

Christiansen, M. and Kirby, S. (eds) (2003) *Language Evolution: The States of the Art*. Oxford University Press, Oxford.

Chung, C. A. (2003) *Simulation Modeling Handbook: A Practical Approach*. CRC Press, Boca Raton. FL.

Citro, C. F. and Hanushek, E. A. (eds) (1991) *The Uses of Microsimulation Modelling. Vol. 1: Review and Recommendations*. National Academy Press, Washington, DC.

Conte, R. and Castelfranchi, C. (1995) Understanding the functions of norms in social groups. In N. Gilbert and R. Conte (eds), *Artificial Societies: The Computer Simulation of Social Life*, pp. 252–267. UCL Press, London.

Conte, R. and Gilbert, N. (1995) Introduction. In N. Gilbert and R. Conte (eds), *Artificial Societies: The Computer Simulation of Social Life*, pp. 1–15. UCL Press, London.

Conte, R., Hegselmann, R. and Terna, P. (1997) *Simulating Social Phenomena*. Springer-Verlag, Berlin.

Creedy, J. and Duncan, A. S. (2002) *Microsimulation Modelling of Taxation and the Labour Market: The Melbourne Institute Tax and Transfer Simulation*. Edward Elgar, Cheltenham.

Deffuant, G., Amblard, F., Weisbuch, G. and Faure, T. (2002) How can extremism prevail? a study based on the relative agreement interaction model. *Journal of Artificial Societies and Social Simulation*. http://www.soc.surrey.ac.uk/JASSS/5/4/1.html.

Deffuant, G., Amblard, F., Weisbuch, G. and Faure, T. (2003) Simple is beautiful and necessary. *Journal of Artificial Societies and Social Simulation*. http://www.soc.surrey.ac.uk/JASSS/6/1/6.html.

Deutsch, K. W. (1987) GLOBUS – the rise of a new field of political science. In S. A. Bremer (ed.), *The GLOBUS Model. Computer Simulation of Worldwide Political and Economic Development*, pp. vii–xxiii. Campus, Frankfurt.

Doran, J. E. (1997a) Foreknowledge in artificial societies. In R. Conte, R. Hegselmann and P. Terna (eds), *Simulating Social Phenomena*, pp. 457–470. Springer-Verlag, Berlin.

Doran, J. E. (1997b) From computer simulation to artificial societies. *Transactions of the Society for Computer Simulation International*, 14: 69–78.

Doran, J. E. (1998) Simulating collective misbelief. *Journal of Artificial Societies and Social Simulation*, 1. http://www.soc.surrey.ac.uk/JASSS/1/1/3.html.

Doran, J. E. and Gilbert, N. (1994) Simulating societies: an introduction. In N. Gilbert and J. E. Doran (eds), *Simulating Societies: The Computer Simulation of Social Phenomena*, pp. 1–18. UCL Press, London.

Doran, J. E. and Palmer, M. (1995) The EOS project: integrating two models of Palaeolithic social change. In N. Gilbert and R. Conte (eds), *Artificial Societies: The Computer Simulation of Social Life*, pp. 103–125. UCL Press, London.

Doran, J. E., Palmer, M., Gilbert, N. and Mellars, P. (1994) The EOS project: modelling Upper Paleolithic social change. In N. Gilbert and J. E. Doran (eds), *Simulating Societies: The Computer Simulation of Social Phenomena*, pp. 195–222. UCL Press, London.

Drogoul, A., Corbara, B. and Lalande, S. (1995) Manta: new experimental results on the emergence of (artificial) ant societies. In N. Gilbert and R. Conte (eds), *Artificial Societies: The Computer Simulation of Social Life*. UCL Press, London.

Drogoul, A. and Ferber, J. (1994) Multi-agent simulation as a tool for studying emergent processes in societies. In J. E. Doran and N. Gilbert (eds), *Simulating Societies: The Computer Simulation of Social Phenomena*, pp. 127–142. UCL Press, London.

Durkheim, E. (1895) *The Rules of Sociological Method. Readings from Emile Durkheim*, edited by Kenneth Thompson. Ellis Horwood, Chichester.

Eason, R. J. (1996) Microsimulation of direct taxes and fiscal policy in the United Kingdom. In A. Harding (ed.), *Microsimulation and Public Policy*, Contributions to Economic Analysis, Vol. 3, pp. 23–45. North-Holland, Amsterdam.

Eiben, A. E. and Smith, J. E. (2003) *Introduction to Evolutionary Computing*. Springer-Verlag, Berlin.

Eigen, M. and Schuster, P. (1979) *The Hypercycle. A Principle of Natural Self-Organization*. Springer-Verlag, Berlin.

Elster, J. (1986) *Rational Choice*. Basil Blackwell, Oxford.

Elster, J. (1989) *Nuts and Bolts for the Social Sciences*. Cambridge University Press, Cambridge.

Epstein, J. M. and Axtell, R. (1996) *Growing Artificial Societies – Social Science from the Bottom Up*. MIT Press, Cambridge, MA.

Etienne, M., Page, C. L. and Cohen, M. (2003) A step-by-step approach to building land management scenarios based on multiple viewpoints on multi-agent system simulations. *Journal of Artificial Societies and Social Simulation*, 6. http://www.soc.surrey.ac.uk/JASSS/6/2/2.html.

Ferber, J. (1998) *Multi-agent systems*. Addison-Wesley, Reading, MA.

Fisher, M. and Wooldridge, M. (1995) A logical approach to simulating societies. In N. Gilbert and R. Conte (eds), *Artificial Societies: The Computer Simulation of Social Life*. UCL Press, London.

Fogel, D. (1995) *Evolutionary Computation: Towards a New Philosophy of Machine Intelligence*. IEEE Press, Piscataway, NJ.

Fogel, L., Owens, A. and Walsh, M. (1966) *Artificial Intelligence through Simulated Evolution*. Wiley, Chichester.

Forrester, J. W. (1971) *World Dynamics*. MIT Press, Cambridge, MA.

Forrester, J. W. (1980) *Principles of Systems*. 2nd preliminary edn. MIT Press, Cambridge, MA. First published in 1968.

Fowler, M. and Scott, K. (1999) *UML Distilled*. 2nd edn. Addison Wesley, Reading, MA.

Frey, B. S. and Eichenberger, R. (1996) Marriage paradoxes. *Rationality and Society*, 8: 187–206.

Galler, H. P. (1990) Verwandtschaftsnetzwerke im demographischen Modell – Ergebnisse einer Modellrechnung. *Acta Demographica*, 1: 63–84.

Galler, H. P. (1997) Discrete-time and continuous-time approaches to dynamic microsimulation reconsidered. Technical Report 13, National Centre for Social and Economic Modelling (NATSEM), University of Canberra, Canberra.

Gamble, C. (1991) The social context for European Palaeolithic art. *Proceedings of the Prehistoric Society*, 57: 3–15.

Garson, G. D. (1998) *Neural Networks: An Introductory Guide for Social Scientists*. Sage Publications, London.

Gazdar, G. and Mellish, C. (1989) *Natural Language Processing in Prolog*. Addison-Wesley, London.

Gilbert, N. (1993) *Analyzing Tabular Data: Loglinear and Logistic Models for Social Researchers*. UCL Press, London.

Gilbert, N. (1995) Emergence in social simulation. In N. Gilbert and R. Conte (eds), *Artificial Societies: The Computer Simulation of Social Life*, pp. 144–156. UCL Press, London.

Gilbert, N. (1996) Simulation as a research strategy. In K. G. Troitzsch, U. Mueller, N. Gilbert and J. E. Doran (eds), *Social Science Microsimulation*, pp. 448–454. Springer-Verlag, Berlin.

Gilbert, N. and Conte, R. (1995) *Artificial Societies: The Computer Simulation of Social Life*. UCL Press, London.

Gilbert, N. and Doran, J. E. (1994) *Simulating Societies: The Computer Simulation of Social Phenomena*. UCL Press, London.

Gilbert, N., Maltby, S. and Asakawa, T. (2002) Participatory simulations for developing scenarios in environmental resource management. In C. Urban (ed.), *Third Workshop on Agent-Based Simulation*, pp. 67–72. SCS-Europe, Passau, Germany.

Gilbert, N. and Terna, P. (2000) How to build and use agent-based models in social science. *Mind and Society*, 1: 57–72.

Goldberg, A. (1989) *Smalltalk-80: The Language*. Addison-Wesley, London.

Goldberg, D. and Deb, K. (1991) A comparative analysis of selection schemes used in genetic algorithms. In G. J. E. Rawlins (ed.), *Foundations of Genetic Algorithms*, pp. 69–93. Morgan Kaufmann, San Mateo, CA.

Goldspink, C. (2002) Methodological implications of complex systems approaches to sociality: Simulation as a foundation for knowledge. *Journal of Artificial Societies and Social Simulation*, 5. http://www.soc.surrey.ac.uk/JASSS/5/1/3.html.

Graham, P. (1996) *ANSI Common Lisp*. Prentice Hall, Englewood Cliffs, NJ.

Grünbaum, A. (1962) Temporally-asymmetric principles, parity between explanation and prediction, and mechanism and teleology. *Philosophy of Science*, 29: 162–170.

Gurney, K. (1997) *Introduction to Neural Networks*. Routledge, London.

Haken, H. (1978) *Synergetics. An Introduction. Nonequilibrium Phase Transitions and Self-Organization in Physics, Chemistry and Biology*. Springer Series in Synergetics, Vol. 1. 2nd enlarged edn. Springer-Verlag, Berlin.

Haken, H. (1996) Synergetik und Sozialwissenschaften. *Ethik und Sozialwissenschaften. Streitforum für Erwägungskultur*, 7: 587–594.

Hales, D., Rouchier, J. and Edmonds, B. (2003) Model-to-model analysis. *Journal of Artificial Societies and Social Simulation*, 6. http://www.soc.surrey.ac.uk/JASSS/6/4/5.html.

Hamilton, W. (1964) The evolution of social behavior. *Journal of Theoretical Biology*, 7: 1–52.

Hanneman, R. A. (1988) *Computer-Assisted Theory Building. Modeling Dynamic Social Systems*. Sage, Newbury Park, CA.

Harding, A. (1990) Dynamic microsimulation models: problems and prospects. Discussion Paper 48, Welfare State Programme, London School of Economics.

Harding, A. (ed.) (1996) *Microsimulation and Public Policy*, Contributions to Economic Analysis, Vol. 232. Elsevier North Holland, Amsterdam.

Hare, M., Gilbert, N., Maltby, S. and Pahl-Wostl, C. (2002) An Internet-based role playing game for developing stakeholders' strategies for sustainable water management: experiences and comparisons with face-to-face gaming. In *ISEE 2002*. Sousee, Tunisia.

Hare, M., Letcher, R. and Jakeman, A. (2003) Participatory modelling in natural resource management: A comparison of four case studies. *Integrated Assessment*, 4: 62–72.

Hauser, R., Hochmuth, U. and Schwarze, J. (1994a) *Mikroanalytische Grundlagen der Gesellschaftspolitik. Band 1: Ausgewählte Probleme und Lösungsansätze. Ergebnisse aus dem gleichnamigen Sonderforschungsbereich an den Universitäten Frankfurt und Mannheim.* Akademie-Verlag, Berlin.

Hauser, R., Ott, N. and Wagner, G. (1994b) *Mikroanalytische Grundlagen der Gesellschaftspolitik. Band 2: Erhebungsverfahren, Analysemethoden und Mikrosimulation. Ergebnisse aus dem gleichnamigen Sonderforschungsbereich an den Universitäten Frankfurt und Mannheim.* Akademie-Verlag, Berlin.

Hayes-Roth, F., Waterman, D. and Lenat, D. (1983) *Building Expert Systems.* Addison-Wesley, Reading, MA.

Hegselmann, R. (1996) Understanding social dynamics: The cellular automata approach. In K. G. Troitzsch, U. Mueller, N. Gilbert and J. E. Doran (eds), *Social Science Microsimulation*, pp. 282–306. Springer-Verlag, Berlin.

Heike, H.-D., Beckmann, K., Kaufmann, A., Ritz, H. and Sauerbier, T. (1996) A comparison of a 4GL and an object-oriented approach in micro macro simulation. In K. G. Troitzsch, U. Mueller, N. Gilbert and J. E. Doran (eds), *Social Science Microsimulation*, pp. 3–32. Springer-Verlag, Berlin.

Helbing, D. (1994a) A mathematical model for the behavior of individuals in a social field. *Journal of Mathematical Sociology*, 19: 189–219.

Helbing, D. (1994b) *Quantitative Sociodynamics. Stochastic Methods and Models of Social Interaction Processes.* Kluwer, Dordrecht.

Henize, J. (1984) Critical issues in evaluating socio-economic models. In T. I. Oren, B. P. Zeigler and M. S. Elzas (eds), *Simulation and Model-Based Methodologies: An Integrative View*, NATO Advanced Science Institutes Series, Vol. 10, pp. 557–590. Springer-Verlag, Berlin.

Hochschild, A. (1983) *The Managed Heart: The Commercialisation of Human Feeling.* University of California Press, Berkeley, CA.

Holland, J. H. (1975) *Adaptation in Natural and Artificial Systems.* University of Michigan Press, Ann Arbor, MI.

Holland, J. H., Holyoak, K. J., Nisbett, R. E. and Thagard, P. R. (1986) *Induction: Processes of Inference, Learning, and Discovery.* Bradford, Cambridge, MA.

Hughes, B. B. (1999) *International Futures: Choices in the Face of Uncertainty.* Westview, Boulder, CO.

Huhns, M. and Singh, M. P. (1998) *Readings in Agents.* Morgan Kaufmann, San Mateo, CA.

Hurford, J. R., Studdert-Kennedy, M. and Knight, C. (1998a) *Approaches to the Evolution of Language.* Cambridge University Press, Cambridge.

Hurford, J. R., Studdert-Kennedy, M. and Knight, C. (eds) (1998b) *Approaches to the Evolution of Language.* Cambridge University Press, Cambridge.

Hutchins, E. and Hazlehurst, B. (1995) How to invent a lexicon: the development of shared symbols in interaction. In N. Gilbert and R. Conte (eds), *Artificial Societies: The Computer Simulation of Social Life*, pp. 157–189. UCL Press, London.

Ilachinski, A. (2001) *Cellular Automata. A Discrete Universe.* World Scientific, Singapore, New Jersey, London, Hong Kong.

Jager, W., Popping, R. and Sande, H. v. d. (2001) Clustering and fighting in two-party crowds: Simulating the approach-avoidance conflict. *Journal of Artificial Societies and Social Simulation*, 4. http://www.soc.surrey.ac.uk/JASSS/4/3/7.html.

Jurafsky, D. and Martin, J. H. (2000) *Speech and Language Processing: An Introduction to Natural Language Processing, Computational Linguistics and Speech Recognition.* Prentice Hall, Englewood Cliffs, NJ.

Karlin, S. and Taylor, H. M. (1975) *A First Course in Stochastic Processes.* 2nd edn. Academic Press, Orlando, FL.

Kauffman, S. (1995) *At Home in the Universe.* Oxford University Press, Oxford.

Kheir, N. A. (1988) *Systems Modeling and Computer Simulation,* Electrical Engineering and Electronics, Vol. 1. Marcel Dekker, New York, NY.

Klee, A. and Troitzsch, K. G. (1993) Chaotic behaviour in social systems: Modelling with GEMM. In K. G. Troitzsch (ed.), *Catastrophe, Chaos, and Self-Organization in Social Systems. Invited Papers of a Seminar Series on Catastrophic Phenomena in Soviet Society and Self-Organized Behaviour of Social Systems Held at the Institute of Sociology of the Academy of Sciences of the Ukrainian Republic, Kiev, September 4 to 11, 1992,* pp. 81–104. Universität Koblenz–Landau, Koblenz.

Klösgen, W. (1986) Software implementation of microanalytic simulation models – state of the art and outlook. In G. H. Orcutt, J. Merz and H. Quinke (eds), *Microanalytic Simulation Models to Support Social and Financial Policy,* Information Research and Resource Reports, Vol. 7, pp. 475–491. North-Holland, Amsterdam.

Klüver, J. (1998) The simulation of scientific theories. In P. Ahrweiler and N. Gilbert (eds), *Computer Simulations in Science and Technology Studies.* Springer-Verlag, Berlin.

Knuth, D. E. (1981) *The Art of Computer Programming. Vol. 2: Seminumerical Algorithms.* 2nd edn. Addison-Wesley, Reading, MA.

Kohler, T. A., Van West, C. R., Carr, E. P. and Langton, C. G. (1996) Agent-based modelling of prehistoric settlement systems in the northern American South-west. In *Third International Conference Integrating GIS and Environmental Modelling.* Santa Barbara: National Center for Geographic Information and Analysis, Santa Fe, NM. http://www.ncgia.ucsb.edu/conf/SANTA_FE_CD_ROM/sf_papers/kohler_tim/kohler.html.

Kolesar, P. and Walker, W. (1975) A simulation model of police patrol operations. Technical report, Rand Corporation, Santa Monica, CA.

Kontopoulos, K. M. (1993) *The Logics of Social Structure.* Cambridge University Press, Cambridge.

Koza, J. (1992) *Genetic Programming.* MIT Press, Cambridge, MA.

Koza, J. (1994) *Genetic Programming 2.* MIT Press, Cambridge, MA.

Kraul, M., Troitzsch, K. G. and Wirrer, R. (1995) Lehrerinnen und Lehrer an Gymnasien: Empirische Ergebnisse aus Rheinland-Pfalz und Resultate einer Simulationsstudie. In H. Sahner and S. Schwendtner (eds), *Kongreß der Deutschen Soziologie Halle an der Saale 1995. Kongreßband II: Berichte aus den Sektionen und Arbeitsgruppen,* pp. 334–340. Westdeutscher Verlag, Opladen.

Kreutzer, W. (1986) *System Simulation. Programming Styles and Languages.* Addison-Wesley, Sydney.

Kuipers, B. (1994) *Qualitative Reasoning. Modeling and Simulation with Incomplete Knowledge.* MIT Press, Cambridge, MA.

Laird, J. E., Newell, A. and Rosenbloom, P. S. (1987) Soar: An architecture for general intelligence. *Artificial Intelligence,* 33: 1–64.

Lambert, S., Percival, R., Schofield, D. and Paul, S. (1994) An introduction to STINMOD: A static microsimulation model. Technical Report 1, National Centre for Social and Economic Modelling (NATSEM), University of Canberra, Canberra.

Lansing, J. S. (1991) *Priests and Programmmers: Technologies of Power in the Engineered Landscape of Bali*. Princeton University Press, Princeton, NJ.

Latané, B. (1981) The psychology of social impact. *American Psychologist*, 36: 343–356.

Latané, B. (1996) Dynamic social impact. Robust predictions from simple theory. In R. Hegselmann, U. Mueller and K. G. Troitzsch (eds), *Modelling and Simulation in the Social Sciences from a Philosophy of Science Point of View*, Theory and Decision Library, Series A: Philosophy and Methodology of the Social Sciences, pp. 287–310. Kluwer, Dordrecht.

Lave, C. A. and March, J. G. (1993) *An introduction to models in the social sciences*. University Press of America, Lanham, MD, London. Originally published by Harper & Row, New York 1975.

Lewis, G. H. and Michel, R. C. (eds) (1989) *Microsimulation Techniques for Tax and Transfer Analysis*. Urban Institute Press, Washington, DC.

Lomborg, B. (1996) Nucleus and shield: the evolution of social structure in the iterated prisoner's dilemma. *American Sociological Review*, 61: 278–307.

Lumsden, C. J. and Wilson, E. O. (1981) *Genes, Mind, and Culture. The Coevolutionary Process*. Harvard University Press, Cambridge, MA.

Maes, P. (1994) Agents that reduce work and information overload. *Communications of the ACM*, 37: 31–40.

Malerba, F., Nelson, R., Orsenigo, L. and Winter, S. (1999) History friendly models of industry evolution: the computer industry. *Industrial and Corporate Change*, 1: 3–40.

Martinez Coll, J. C. (1986) A bioeconomic model of Hobbes' 'state of nature'. *Social Science Information*, 25: 493–505.

Matsumoto, M. and Nishimura, T. (1998) Mersenne twister: A 623-dimensionally equidistributed uniform pseudorandom number generator. *ACM Transactioons on Modeling and Computer Simulations*, 8: 3–30.

Maturana, H. and Varela, F. J. (1992) *The Tree of Knowledge: The Biological Roots of Human Understanding*. Revised edn. Shambhala/New Science Press, Boston, MA.

Mayfield, J., Labrou, Y. and Finin, T. (1996) Evaluation of KQML as an agent communication language. In M. Wooldridge, J. P. Müller and M. Tambe (eds), *Intelligent Agents II – Agent Theories, Architectures and Languages*, Lecture Notes in Artificial Intelligence. Springer-Verlag, Berlin.

Maynard Smith, J. (1982) *Evolution and the Theory of Games*. Cambridge University Press, Cambridge.

Meadows, D. H., Meadows, D. L. and Randers, J. (1992) *Beyond the Limits*. Chelsea Green, Post Mills, VT.

Meadows, D. L., Behrens III, W. W., Meadows, D. H., Naill, R. F., Randers, J. and Zahn, E. K. (1974) *The Dynamics of Growth in a Finite World*. MIT Press, Cambridge, MA.

Mellars, P. (1985) The ecological basis of social complexity in the Upper Palaeolithic of southwestern France. In T. Douglas-Price and J. A. Brown (eds), *Prehistoric Hunter-Gatherers: The Emergence of Cultural Complexity*, pp. 271–297. Academic Press, New York, NY.

Merz, J. (1996) MICSIM: Concept, developments, and applications of a PC microsimulation model for research and teaching. In K. G. Troitzsch, U. Mueller, N. Gilbert and J. E. Doran (eds), *Social Science Microsimulation*, pp. 33–65. Springer-Verlag, Berlin.

Michalewicz, Z. (1996) *Genetic Algorithms + Data Structures = Evolution Programs*. 3rd edn. Springer-Verlag, Berlin.

Michalewicz, Z. and Fogel, D. (2000) *How to Solve It: Modern Heuristics*. Springer-Verlag,

Berlin.

Michalski, R., Carbonell, J. and Mitchell, T. M. (1983) *Machine Learning: An Artificial Intelligence Approach*. Tioga, Palo Alto, CA.

Mitchell, M. (1998) *An Introduction to Genetic Algorithms*. MIT Press, Cambridge, MA.

Mitton, L., Sutherland, H. and Weeks, M. (eds) (2000) *Microsimulation Modelling for Policy Analysis: Challenges and Innovations*. Cambridge University Press, Cambridge.

Möhring, M. (1990) *MIMOSE. Eine funktionale Sprache zur Beschreibung und Simulation individuellen Verhaltens in interagierenden Populationen*. Doctoral thesis, Universität Koblenz.

Molnár, P. (1996) A microsimulation tool for social forces. In K. G. Troitzsch, U. Mueller, G. N. Gilbert and J. E. Doran (eds), *Social Science Microsimulation*. Springer-Verlag, Berlin.

Newell, A. and Simon, H. A. (1976) Computer science as empirical enquiry. *Communications of the ACM*, 19: 113–126.

NeXT Corporation (1993) *Object Oriented Programming and the Objective C Language*. Addison-Wesley, London.

Nilsson, N. J. (1998) *Artificial Intelligence: a new synthesis*. Morgan Kaufmann, San Franscisco, CA.

Oatley, K. (1992) *Best Laid Schemes: The Psychology of Emotions*. Cambridge University Press, Cambridge.

Olson, M. (1965) *The Logic of Collective Action: Public Goods and the Theory of Groups*. Harvard University Press, Cambridge, MA.

Orcutt, G. H. (1986) Views on microanalytic simulation modeling. In G. H. Orcutt, J. Merz and H. Quinke (eds), *Microanalytic Simulation Models to Support Social and Financial Policy*, Information Research and Resource Reports, vol. 7, pp. 9–26. North-Holland, Amsterdam.

Orcutt, G. H., Merz, J. and Quinke, H. (eds) (1986) *Microanalytic Simulation Models to Support Social and Financial Policy*. Information Research and Resource Reports, Vol. 7. North-Holland, Amsterdam.

Ortony, A., Clore, K. and Collins, A. (1988) *The Cognitive Structure of Emotions*. Cambridge University Press, Cambridge.

Papert, S. (1980) *Mindstorms*. Basic Books, New York, NY.

Parisi, D., Cecconi, F. and Cerini, A. (1995) Kin-directed altruism and attachment behaviour in an evolving population of neural networks. In N. Gilbert and R. Conte (eds), *Artificial Societies: The Computer Simulation of Social Life*, pp. 238–251. UCL Press, London.

Park, S. K. and Miller, K. W. (1988) Random number generators: Good ones are hard to find. *Communications of the ACM*, 31: 1192–1201.

Pidd, M. (1984) *Computer Simulation in Management Science*. Wiley, Chichester.

Pugh III, A. L. (1976) *DYNAMO User's Manual*. MIT Press, Cambridge, MA.

Punch, K. F. (2000) *Developing Effective Research Proposals*. Sage, London.

Ramanath, A. M. and Gilbert, N. (2004) Techniques for the construction and evaluation of participatory simulations. *Journal of Artificial Societies and Social Simulation*, 7. http://www.soc.surrey.ac.uk/JASSS/7/4/1.html.

Redmond, G., Sutherland, H. and Wilson, M. (1998) *The Arithmetic of Tax and Social Security Reform: A User's Guide to Microsimulation Methods and Analysis*. Cambridge University Press, Cambridge.

Reeves, C. R. (1993) Using genetic algorithms with small populations. In S. Forrest (ed.), *Proceedings of the Fifth International Conference on Genetic Algorithms, University of*

Illinois at Urbana-Champaign, pp. 92–99. Morgan Kaufmann, San Mateo, CA.

Resnick, M. (1994) *Turtles, Termites and Traffic Jams: Explorations in Massively Parallel Microworlds*. MIT Press, Boston, MA.

Reynolds, R. (1994) Learning to cooperate using cultural algorithms. In N. Gilbert and J. E. Doran (eds), *Simulating Societies: The Computer Simulation of Social Phenomena*, pp. 223–244. UCL Press, London.

Rockloff, M. J. and Latané, B. (1996) Simulating the social context of human choice. In K. G. Troitzsch, U. Mueller, N. Gilbert and J. E. Doran (eds), *Social Science Microsimulation*. Springer-Verlag, Berlin.

Rosenbloom, P. S., Laird, J. E. and Newell, A. (eds) (1993) *The Soar Papers: Research on Integrated Intelligence*. MIT Press, Cambridge, MA.

Rubinstein, R. Y. and Melamed, B. (1998) *Modern Simulation and Modeling*. Wiley Interscience, New York, NY.

Rumelhart, D. and McClelland, G. (1986) *Parallel Distributed Processing*. MIT Press, Cambridge, MA.

Sauerbier, T. (2002) UMDBS — a new tool for dynamic microsimulation. *Journal of Artificial Societies and Social Simulation*, 5/2/5. http://jasss.soc.surrey.ac.uk/5/2/5.html.

Sawyer, R. K. (2001) Emergence in sociology: Contemporary philosophy of mind and some implications for sociological theory. *American Journal of Sociology*, 107: 551–585.

Sawyer, R. K. (forthcoming) *Social emergence: Societies as complex systems*. Cambridge University Press, New York, NY.

Schelling, T. C. (1971) Dynamic models of segregation. *Journal of Mathematical Sociology*, 1: 143–186.

Schmidt, B. (1987) *Model Construction with GPSS-FORTRAN Version 3*. Springer-Verlag, New York, NY.

Scriven, M. (1969) Explanation and prediction as non-symmetrical. Explanation and prediction in evolutionary theory. In L. I. Krimerman (ed.), *The Nature and Scope of Social Science. A Critical Anthology*, pp. 117–125. Appleton-Century-Crofts, New York, NY. First published in 1959 in *Science* 130: 477–482.

Shoham, Y. (1990) Agent-oriented programming. *Artificial Intelligence*, 60: 51–92.

Simon, H. A. (1996) *The sciences of the artificial*. MIT Press, Cambridge, MA, London.

Smith, R. G. and Davis, R. (1981) Frameworks for cooperation in distributed problem solving. *IEEE Transactions on Systems Man Cybernetics*, SMC-11: 61–70.

Sola Pool, I. d. and Abelson, R. P. (1962) The simulmatics project. In H. Guetzkow (ed.), *Simulation in Social Science: Readings*, pp. 70–81. Prentice Hall, Englewood Cliffs, NJ. Originally in Public Opinion Quarterly 25, 1961, 167-183.

Sole, R. and Goodwin, B. (2002) *Signs of Life: How Complexity Pervades Biology*. Basic Books, New York, NY.

Statistisches Bundesamt (ed.) (2001) *Statistisches Jahrbuch der Bundesrepublik Deutschland*. Metzler, Wiesbaden.

Steels, L. and Brooks, R. (1995) *The Artificial Life Route to Artificial Intelligence*. Lawrence Erlbaum, Hillsdale, NJ.

Sterman, J. D. (2000) *Business Dynamics: Systems Thinking and Modeling for a Complex World. With CD-ROM*. McGraw-Hill, New York, NY.

Stroustrup, B. (1993) *The C++ Programming Language*. 2nd edn. Addison-Wesley, London.

Suchman, L. A. (1987) *Plans and Situated Action*. Cambridge University Press, Cambridge.

Sun, R. (ed.) (2005) *Cognition and Multi-Agent Interaction: From Cognitive Modeling to*

Social Simulation. Cambridge University Press, Cambridge.

Sutherland, H. (2001) Euromod: An integrated european benefit-tax model. Technical report, EUROMOD. http://www.econ.cam.ac.uk/dae/mu/publications/em901_cov.pdf.

Swingler, K. (1996) *Applying Neural Networks: a Practical Guide.* Academic Press, London.

Taber, C. S. and Timpone, R. J. (1996) *Computational modeling.* Quantitative applications in the social sciences 113. Sage, Thousand Oaks ; London.

Todd, P. M. (1997) Searching for the next best mate. In R. Conte, R. Hegselmann and P. Terna (eds), *Simulating Social Phenomena.* Springer-Verlag, Berlin.

Toffoli, T. and Margolus, N. (1987) *Cellular Automata Machines.* MIT Press, Cambridge, MA.

Troitzsch, K. G. (1994) The evolution of technologies. In J. E. Doran and N. Gilbert (eds), *Simulating Societies: The Computer Simulation of Social Phenomena*, pp. 41–62. UCL Press, London.

Troitzsch, K. G. (1996) Chaotic behaviour in social systems. In R. Hegselmann and H.-O. Peitgen (eds), *Modelle sozialer Dynamiken. Ordnung, Chaos und Komplexität*, pp. 162–186. Hölder-Pichler-Tempsky, Wien.

Troitzsch, K. G. (1997) Social simulation – origins, prospects, purposes. In R. Conte, R. Hegselmann and P. Terna (eds), *Simulating Social Phenomena*, Lecture Notes in Economics and Mathematical Systems, Vol. 456, pp. 41–54. Springer-Verlag, Berlin.

Troitzsch, K. G. (2004a) A multi-agent model of bilingualism in a small population. In H. Coelho, B. Espinasse and M.-M. Seidel (eds), *5th Workshop on Agent-Based Simulation*, pp. 38–43. SCS Publishing House, Erlangen, San Diego, CA.

Troitzsch, K. G. (2004b) Validating simulation models. In G. Horton (ed.), *18th European Simulation Multiconference: Networked Simulation and Simulated Networks*, pp. 265–270. SCS Publishing House, Erlangen, San Diego, CA.

Troitzsch, K. G., Mueller, U., Gilbert, N. and Doran, J. E. (eds) (1996) *Social Science Microsimulation.* Springer-Verlag, Berlin.

Van West, C. R. (1994) *Modeling Prehistoric Agricultural Productivity in Southwestern Colorado: a GIS Approach.* Doctoral thesis, Washington State University, Pullman.

Varela, F. J., Thompson, E. and Rosch, E. (1991) *The Embodied Mind: Cognitive Science and Human Experience.* MIT Press, Cambridge, MA.

Waldrop, M. (1992) *Complexity: The Emerging Science at the Edge of Chaos.* Simon & Schuster, New York, NY.

Watkins, J. W. (1955) Methodological individualism: a reply. *Philosophy of Science*, 22: 58–62.

Weidlich, W. (1972) The use of statistical models in sociology. *Collective Phenomena*, 1: 51–59.

Weidlich, W. (1991) Physics and social science – the approach of synergetics. *Physics Reports*, 204: 1–163.

Weidlich, W. and Haag, G. (1983) *Concepts and Models of a Quantitative Sociology. The Dynamics of Interacting Populations.* Springer Series in Synergetics, Vol. 14. Springer-Verlag, Berlin.

Weisbuch, G., Kirman, A. and Herreiner, D. (1997) Market organisation. In R. Conte, R. Hegselmann and P. Terna (eds), *Simulating Social Phenomena*, pp. 221–240. Springer-Verlag, Berlin.

Werner, G. M. and Davis, J. N. (1997) Cooperation without memory. In R. Conte, R. Hegselmann and P. Terna (eds), *Simulating Social Phenomena*, pp. 179–185. Springer-Verlag, Berlin.

Wilensky, U. (1998) Netlogo rumor mill model. Center for Connected Learning and Computer-Based Modeling, Northwestern University, Evanston, IL. http://ccl.northwestern.edu/netlogo/models/RumorMill.

Winograd, T. and Flores, F. (1986) *Understanding Computers and Cognition*. Ablex, Norwood, NJ.

Winston, P. H. (1992) *Artificial Intelligence*. Addison Wesley, Reading, MA.

Wirrer, R. (1997) *Koedukation im Rückblick. Die Entwicklung der rheinland-pfälzischen Gymnasien vor dem Hintergrund pädagogischer und bildungspolitischer Kontroversen*. Blaue Eule, Essen.

Wolfram, S. (1986) *Theory and Applications of Cellular Automata*. World Scientific, Singapore.

Wolfram, S. (2002) *A new kind of science*. Wolfram Media, Champaign, IL.

Wooldridge, M. and Jennings, N. R. (1995) Intelligent agents: theory and practice. *Knowledge Engineering Review*, 10: 115–152.

Wray, R. E. and Jones, R. M. (2005) An introduction to soar as an agent architecture. In R. Sun (ed.), *Cognition and Multi-Agent Interaction: From Cognitive Modeling to Social Simulation*. Cambridge Univerity Press, Cambridge.

Wright, I. (1996) Reinforcement learning and animat emotions. Technical Report CSRP-96-4, University of Birmingham School of Computer Science.

Zeigler, B. P. (1985) *Theory of Modelling and Simulation*. Krieger, Malabar. Reprint, first published in 1976, Wiley, New York, NY.

Zwicker, E. (1981) *Simulation und Analyse dynamischer Systeme in den Wirtschafts- und Sozialwissenschaften*. De Gruyter, Berlin.

Author index

Subject index

SOCIAL RESEARCH
Issues, Methods and Process

Tim May

> "The third edition of this tried and tested book works very well and should be extremely successful ... its strength is that it covers all the principal areas of research in an accessible and lively style, treating each approach in relation to the philosophical and methodological debates that underpin them. It is logically organized and each chapter is well-structured...complex topics are clearly explained for the inexperienced reader, at the same time it contains enough of substance and food for thought for more advanced students."

John Scott, University of Essex

Praise for the previous edition:

> "This is the finest introduction to social research I have ever read ... Methods are meticulously worked through from official statistics to comparative research via surveys, interviews, observation and documentary analysis ... The writing is clear, concise and scholarly with the bibliography a delightful A to Z compendium of the best in sociology."

British Sociological Association Network

The fully revised and updated third edition of this hugely popular text incorporates the latest developments in the interdisciplinary field of social research, while retaining the style and structure that appealed to so many in the first two editions. Tim May successfully bridges the gap between theory and methods in social research, clearly illuminating these essential components for understanding the dynamics of social relations.

The book is divided into two parts, with Part I examining the issues and perspectives in social research and Part II setting out the methods and processes. Revisions and additions have been made to Part I to take account of new ways of thinking about the relationship between theory and research, and values and ethics in the research process. These take on board advances in post-empiricist thinking, as well as the relations between values, objectivity and data collection. Where necessary, recommended readings and references to studies that form the bases of discussions throughout the book have been updated. In Part II, additions have been made to the chapter on questionnaires, and elsewhere, new discussions have been introduced, for example, on research on the Internet, narratives, case studies and new technologies. The reader will detect many other changes, the intention of which is to aid understanding by staying up-to-date with the latest innovations in social research. The chapters follow a common structure to enable a clear appreciation of the place, process and analysis of each method, and to allow the comparison of their strengths and weaknesses in the context of discussions in Part I.

The clear writing style, chapter summaries, questions for reflection and signposts to further readings continue to make this book the ideal companion to social research for students across the social sciences. In addition, it will be recognized as an invaluable source of reference for those practising and teaching social research who wish to keep abreast of key developments in the field.

Contents

Introduction – Part one: Issues in social research – Perspectives on social scientific research – Social theory and social research – Values and ethics in the research process – Part two: Methods of social research – Official statistics: topic and resource – Social surveys: design to analysis – Interviewing: methods and process – Participant observation: perspectives and practice – Documentary research: excavations and evidence – Comparative research: potential and problems – Bibliography – Author index – Subject index.

272pp   0 335 20612 3   (Paperback)   0 335 20613 1   (Hardback)

ADVANCED QUANTITATIVE DATA ANALYSIS

Duncan Cramer

- What do advanced statistical techniques do?
- When is it appropriate to use them?
- How are they carried out and reported?

There are a variety of statistical techniques used to analyse quantitative data that masters students, advanced undergraduates and researchers in the social sciences are expected to be able to understand and undertake. This book explains these techniques, when it is appropriate to use them, how to carry them out and how to write up the results. Most books that describe these techniques do so at too advanced or technical a level to be readily understood by many students who need to use them. In contrast the following features characterize this book:

- Concise and accessible introduction to calculating and interpreting advanced statistical techniques
- Use of a small data set of simple numbers specifically designed to illustrate the nature and manual calculation of the most important statistics in each technique
- Succinct illustration of writing up the results of these analyses
- Minimum of mathematical, statistical and technical notation
- Annotated bibliography and glossary of key concepts

Commonly used software is introduced, and instructions are presented for carrying out analyses and interpreting the output using the computer programs of SPSS Release 11 for Windows and a version of LISREL 8.51, which is freely available online.

Designed as a textbook for postgraduate and advanced undergraduate courses across the socio-behavioural sciences, this book will also serve as a personal reference for researchers in disciplines such as sociology and psychology.

Contents
Series editor's foreword – Preface – Introduction – PART 1: Grouping quantitative variables together – Exploratory factor analysis – Confirmatory factor analysis – Cluster analysis – PART 2: Explaining the variance of a quantitative variable – Stepwise multiple regression – Hierarchical multiple regression – PART 3: Sequencing the relationships between three or more quantitative variables – Path analysis assuming no measurement error – Path analysis accounting for measurement error – PART 4: Explaining the probability of a dichotomous variable – Binary logistic regression – PART 5: Testing differences between group means – An introduction to analysis of variance and covariance – Unrelated one-way analysis of covariance – Unrelated two-way analysis of variance – PART 6: Discriminating between groups – Discriminant analysis – PART 7: Analysing frequency tables with three or more qualitative variables – Log-linear analysis – Glossary – References – Index.

288pp   0 335 20059 1 (Paperback)   0 335 20062 1 (Hardback)

QUALITATIVE DATA ANALYSIS
Explorations with NVivo

Graham R. Gibbs

"...*a very detailed, clearly expressed and structured text which will be of immense help to anyone wanting to use NVivo for a research project.*"
Professor Colin Robson, author of Real World Research

- How can qualitative analysis of textual data be undertaken?
- How can the core procedures of qualitative analysis be followed using computer software such as NVivo?
- How can the extra tools NVivo offers the analyst be used to support and improve qualitative analysis?

Qualitative Data Analysis introduces readers to key approaches in qualitative analysis, demonstrating in each case how to carry then out using NVivo. NVivo is a new, powerful computer package from QSR, the developers of NUD*IST. It provides the researcher with an extensive range of tools and the book shows clearly how each can be used to support standard qualitative analysis techniques such as coding, theory building, theory testing, cross-sectional analysis, modelling and writing. The book demonstrates how different styles of analysis, such as grounded theory and narrative, rhetorical and structured approaches, can be undertaken using NVivo. In most cases, the analysis is illustrated using documents from a single data set. There are copious figures, tables, guides and hints for good practice. The result is an invaluable text for undergraduates and an essential reference for postgraduates and researchers needing to learn both qualitative analysis techniques and the use of software such as NVivo.

Contents

Introduction – What is qualitative analysis? – Getting started with NVivo – Data Preparation – Coding – Memos and attributes – Searching for text – Developing an analytic scheme – Three analytic styles – Visualizing the data – Communicating – Glossary – References – Index.

224pp   0 335 20084 2 (Paperback)   0 335 20085 0 (Hardback)